Comics, Comix & Graphic Novels

Acknowledgments
It is my pleasure to record my thanks
to the following:
The Phaidon team: David Jenkins,
for commissioning the book, for his
patience and for not shouting at me
when things went a bit wobbly; Polly
Clayden, for her hard work, extra time
and visual sense; and especially,
Helen Castle, who deserves some kind
of Royal award for Services to Editing.
Honourable mention also should go
to Victoria Routledge, who helped so
much in the final stages.
The design team: Stephen Coates for
such a terrific job on the pictures, and
for making me welcome in his studio.
Also, his assistants Jason Beard, Siân
Cook and Marc Shillum.
Individuals who have lent comics and
magazines or gone out of their way
to be helpful: Chrys Mordin, Dick Jude
and Rob Pontefract at Forbidden
Planet; Jo Ellen Wisnosky at The
Vintage Magazine Company; Steve
Edgell; and Stephen Calloway. Finally,
for encouragement and ideas, the
Montgolfier Society, students and
colleagues at St Martin's and the
LCPDT, family and friends.

Additional picture acknowledgements
(t= top; l= left; r= right; c= centre;
b= bottom). Courtesy BFI p 118 t.
Courtesy Christie's pp 37 tl; 47 bl; 57 tl,
bl; 60 tl, tc, br; 61 tl. Courtesy Hulton
Deutsch p 117 bc. Courtesy the Kobal
Collection p 61 bl, br. Courtesy the
Master and Fellows of Magdalene
College, Cambridge p 11 tl. Courtesy
the Stapleton Collection pp 10; 11 tr, cl,
br; 12; 13 t, br; 14. Courtesy the Vintage
Magazine Company pp 15; 16; 17; 18;
19 t; 20 tl; 24 b; 28 l; 32 t, bc; 33; 36; 42
bl bc; 44 c; 46; 47 tl, tr, br; 48; 49; 51;
52; 63 bl, br; 64–5; 68 cr; 75; 80 bl; 82
tr; 83; 84; 85, 87. Courtesy Paramount
p 43. Courtesy Picture Post Archive/
Hulton Deutsch p 26. Courtesy Rex
Features pp 74; 157 tl.

Contents

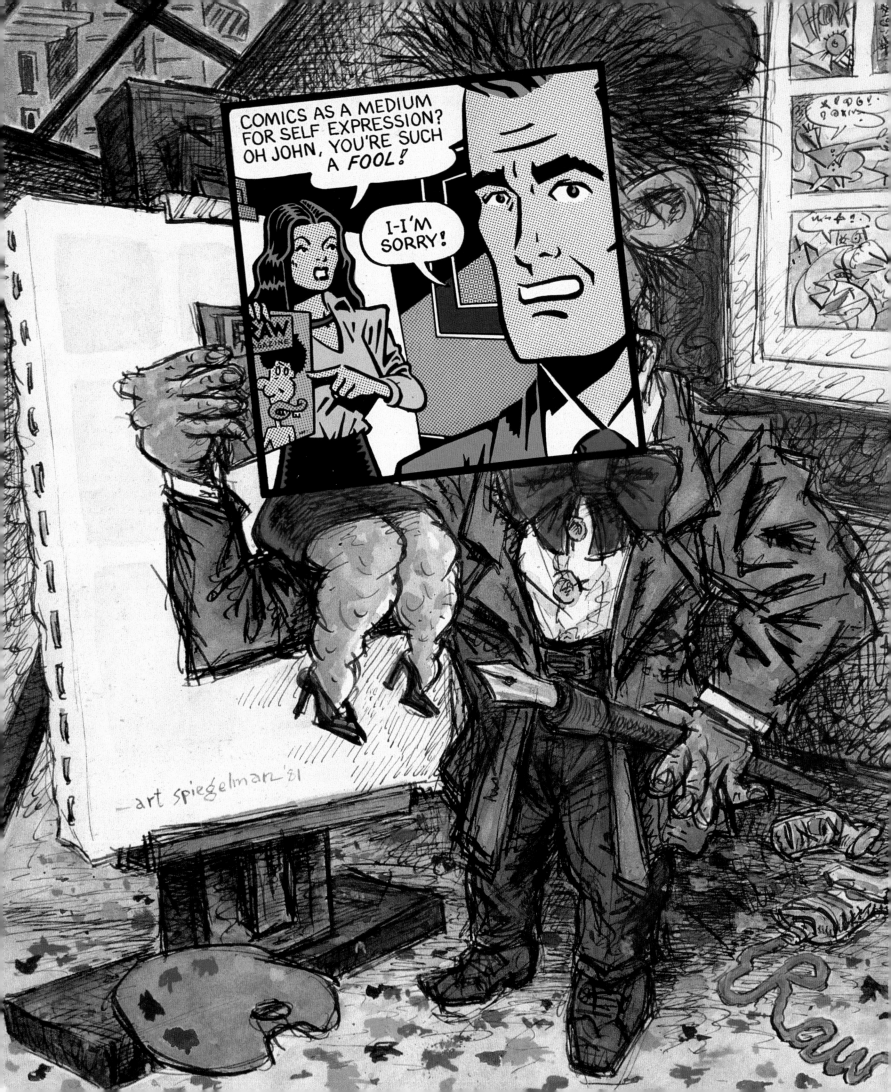

Not quite art

Comics have smuggled their way into art books before. Invariably they have been there, however, as an aside, a digression, to demonstrate the inspiration for the 'proper' art that constitutes the bulk of the book. Just take a look at any of the numerous tomes available about Pop, Graffiti and Outsider artists, and there they are – present, but unacknowledged as anything other than a convenient pop culture prop.

So it was maybe time for a book that took a different tack. *Comics, Comix and Graphic Novels* includes no canvases by Roy Lichtenstein or Philip Guston. Instead, the intention here is to celebrate comics in their own right, to explore their richness and diversity since the end of the nineteenth century to the present day. Hopefully, the illustrations will tell their own story, showing where comics have been, where they are going, and above all what they can do. In the end, it's surprising how well 'disposable' pop culture can last.

There were, however, other reasons why such a book was appropriate at this point in time. For in the last decade and a half, comics have been through something of a revolution. Enormous improvements in printing technology coupled with the emergence of a 'direct sales' system of marketing to specialist comics shops, have heralded a radical transformation in the way comics are produced. This in turn has opened up new spaces for more complex and imaginative stories and artwork than ever before. Whereas previously, the common image of a comic was of a throwaway, cheaply produced, poorly drawn slice of entertainment for children, today photographic-quality paper and fully painted artwork are commonplace, and there is a huge array of subject matter for adults – everything from splatter horror and sexual fantasy, to satire and political documentary.

Historically speaking, these changes have meant the revival of the entire industry, which many were predicting would die by the end of the 1970s. Our story, then, is one of the rise, fall and resurrection of the medium, and as such will include not just the star creators of the 'first wave', but also those of the second. Thus, where the first half takes in such familiar material as the manic clowning of Leo Baxendale *(The Beano)*, the observational adventure of Frank Hampson *(The Eagle)*, the bombastic power-plays of Jack Kirby *(The Incredible

Hulk)* the 'clear line' mysteries of Hergé *(Tintin)* and the underground scatology of Robert Crumb *(Zap)*, the second concentrates on less well-known themes and names: for examples, the post-punk satire of Dan Clowes *(Eightball)*, the gothic superheroics of Frank Miller *(The Dark Knight Returns)*, the inspired lunacy of Chris Donald *(Viz)*, the anthropomorphic dramas of Art Spiegelman *(Maus)* and the breakneck cyberpunk of Katsuhiro Otomo *(Akira)*. These are the creators, among many more, who are currently providing comics with a new lease of life.

The changing industrial contexts in which these comics were produced will be explored. This includes: how the traditional children's comics were subverted in the 1960s and 1970s by the underground 'comix' movement (as in X-rated), which turned the medium

Above: Page from Will Eisner's *Comics and Sequential Art* (Poorhouse Press, 1985), demonstrating the flexibility of facial expressions. Eisner's book was the first in English to take a close look at the mechanics of comics storytelling.

on its head by adding sex, drugs and radical politics; and how, in turn, these gave way to a fan-based production system that privileged superhero stories, and which spawned a multiplicity of styles and formats, including the controversial 'graphic novel'.

We need to be clear. The book is not about making a statement that comics are 'Art'. Why comics have not been invited to enter the cosy world conjured up by that term is not difficult to explain. Throughout their history they have been perceived as intrinsically 'commercial', mass-produced for a lowest-common-denominator audience, and therefore automatically outside notions of artistic credibility. (By the same token, the most successful comics commercially have been those least likely to appeal to a 'sophisticated' palette.) This is why comics have been relegated by the hip art world to the status of 'found objects' and 'trash icons'. It is also why comics creators have never been respected as 'artists', and have historically been left open to exploitation: not uncommonly, they remain anonymous while the characters they have created go on to become household names (everybody knows who Superman is, but how many people can name his creators?).

Excluding comics from cultural legitimacy in this way raises other questions, like: exactly who decides which mediums qualify and which do not? Is commercialism per se any less valid than 'self-expression'? How much of this prejudice has to do with the tastes of different social classes? And so on. Indeed, many comics creators themselves are suspicious of respectability. To quote one of Robert Crumb's typically foaming strips: '"ART" is just a racket! A HOAX perpetrated on the public by so-called "Artists" who set themselves up on a pedestal, and promoted by pantywaste (sic) ivory-tower intellectuals and sob-sister "critics" who think the world owes them a living!'[1]

It would be futile to get bogged down in such a debate here. The essential idea implicit in the history told in these pages is that comics may or may not be 'art', but they are indisputably an artform. There is a difference, of course, but the distinction may be unusual to some readers. After all, if one has grown up with the old-fashioned notion of comics as nothing but mindless pap, then there is no great incentive to think about their subtleties as a medium of communication.

In fact, there has been a lot of 'thinking' recently about these very properties. With the emergence of the new, sophisticated titles in the 1980s and 1990s there has appeared an accompanying literature analysing the mechanics of how the medium works. These studies have shown that comics are a language: they combine to constitute a weave of writing and art which has its own syntax, grammar and conventions, and which can communicate ideas in a totally unique fashion. They point, for example, to the way in which words and images can be juxtaposed to generate a mood; to how the amount of time that is allowed to elapse between images can be used for dramatic effect; to the way that cinematic cutting can be used for extra movement; and to the fact that, ultimately, there is no limit to what a comic can do other than that imposed by a creator's imagination.

In other words, everything in a comic has to work – words, pictures and timing – or else it fails. Sometimes, when it succeeds, it is capable of generating a thrill that is impossible in any other medium. As Frank Miller once explained: 'The illustrations are not really illustrations of what's going on. The narration isn't really describing what's going on, either. There's a gap there, and somewhere in that gap is reality.'[2]

The first notable attempt in English to assess these properties was Will Eisner's *Comics and Sequential Art*, 1985 (though in Europe there had been a tradition of semiotic analysis dating back to the 1960s). Eisner himself was (and is) a greatly respected comics creator, and the book gave an insider's view of the creative process (see p 8). It was followed by a flurry of articles, both in the comics press and academia, and finally by Scott McCloud's superb *Understanding Comics* (1993), which drew many of the threads together; it was a book so confident in its claim that comics are capable of expressing anything that it was itself produced as a graphic novel. McCloud's book may not be definitive (could any such study claim to be?), but it is highly recommended to readers wishing to find out more about the nuts and bolts of the medium.

In this way, once it had been confirmed beyond any doubt that the comic book was an artform, the question of whether or not it was a 'good artform' became irrelevant. Clearly, it is as good or bad as any other. For example, critics are fond of pointing out that ninety per cent of comics are rubbish. That may be true; but then, undoubtedly the same figure holds true for any other medium (how many of the films that are released every week does one really want to see?). Needless to say, it is the ten per cent of comics that make things interesting, and we will be concentrating on the ten per cent here.

Finally, this line of argument also makes clear, in an oblique fashion, why comics are such a vibrant medium at this particular moment in history. For if they are not able to become respectable in a way that only 'Art' can be, then at least they can remain unfettered by the critical machinery that this status implies. In other words, comics do not merit official cultural analysis: for instance, there is virtually no space given to reviews of comics in newspapers compared to reviews of books or movies, and no airtime at all allocated to the subject on TV and radio. It is difficult not to agree with Art Spiegelman that, 'comics fly below critical radar'.[3]

This all goes some way towards explaining why comics have become a place, par excellence, for writers and artists to 'play'. There is a real sense in which they are a site where 'nobody is looking', and where it is possible to experiment and flex creative muscles. The results are often astonishing – as the illustrations to the final few chapters of the book prove. In the end, if the official arbiters of taste will not acknowledge comics' cultural value, then at least this means that the form remains a 'free medium' – and there are not many of those left.

Right: Page from *Miracleman* (Harper Collins, 1993), making satirical comment on the passage from comics to art, and back to comics. Warhol had been one of the main 'borrowers' of comics imagery during the Pop Art boom, and here finds himself in strip-limbo. Art: Mark Buckingham. Script: Neil Gaiman. Below: Cover and interior page from Scott McCloud's *Understanding Comics* (Harper Collins, 1994). McCloud's superb book updated Eisner, and became a kind of Baedeker Guide to 'the invisible art'.

76

1 Robert Crumb, *Despair* (1969).
2 Frank Miller, quoted in *Amazing Heroes* magazine, July 1986, pp 37–8.
3 Art Spiegelman, interviewed on 'The Late Show', BBC2, 12 October 1993.

One

The Pioneers

Opposite: Detail from an English Civil War pamphlet depicting 'the resolution of London women in sending their husbands to war', c 1644. Far right: Broadsheet showing the arrival of His Majesty, Prince Charles, at the Spanish Court in 1623. Right: 'Execution broadsheet' depicting the beheading of Lord William Russell for high treason in London in 1683. Below: Broadsheet to demonstrate the drawing of the Great Standing Lottery for Virginia, 1615. Below right: Broadsheet showing Londoners fleeing to the country because of the plague, 1630. Anonymous woodcuts such as these were the earliest form of illustrated mass communication, and flourished in the seventeenth century.

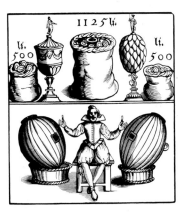

Where to begin? Although the comic itself is an invention of the nineteenth century, its antecedents date back to the Middle Ages. It was only with the origins of printing in Europe that images were produced for a mass audience. It is true that before this there had been illustrations, paintings and other artworks designed for public view; there had even been narratives in sequential pictures, such as Trajan's Column in Rome (dedicated AD 113) and the Bayeux Tapestry in Normandy (c 1100). But, in order to see these, people had to travel to them. After the advent of the printing press, images could travel to the people. In other words, the simple fact of accessibility ushered in the era of the 'mass medium'.[1]

This book seeks to explore the history of comics in Britain and the United States. As such, the convention will be to always deal with Britain first. Thus, in England, the first real evidence of this revolution came in the form of 'broadsheets', anonymously produced woodcuts, on a single side of paper or parchment, typically involving subjects like religion and current affairs. These were hawked by sellers in the street, and usually they included words as well as pictures, although the audience would have been assumed to be illiterate. On the whole, the drawings tended to be bold and simple, with thick linework, primarily because wood did not allow for much subtlety. The blocks did not last long because they were easily damaged, and reproduction was not guaranteeable from one sheet to the next: of the woodcuts that survive, many have parts of the image missing.

Indeed, because so few early woodcuts have survived,

there is controversy among historians about when the conventions we associate with modern comics originated. Certainly, these sheets show evidence of word-balloons and speed-lines, as well as a certain level of dexterity in juxtaposing words and images. Also, panelled borders were not uncommon (the first religious sheets were sometimes subdivided like altarpieces). Thus the idea that the 'language of comics' was solely the invention of the modern era is manifestly mistaken.[2]

Arguably the next key step in the development of mass-circulation broadsheets was the industry that grew up around public executions, where artists' impressions of the grisly events were sold as souvenirs. The main centre for executions in Britain was Tyburn, in London (near what is now Marble Arch) where between 1300 and 1783 roughly 10,000 people were put to death by various means (hanging and burning being the most common). The gibbet was surrounded by open galleries for the public – crowds of 100,000 were not unusual – where the sheet-sellers would ply their trade.

The sheets themselves were woodcuts in the traditional manner, and again usually of very poor quality. The main aim of the publishers was to make as much money on the day for as little outlay as possible – a spiv-like attitude that set the tone for the illustrated publication industry thereafter. So far as the accuracy of the sheets was concerned, they physically could not provide a record of the event for the simple reason that they were produced several days before, and therefore it would have been virtually impossible for the artist to know what the accused, or the execution scene, would look like. It was even true that sometimes the same broadsheet was sold at different events.

From these grim beginnings, gradually publishers began to realize that there might be a market for sheets involving humour. Thus, broadsheets began to appear involving caricatures of famous people and funny illustrations. The first examples tended to be expensive, and designed for a middle-class, monied audience with some knowledge of politics. Later, a working-class market thrived based on more slapstick themes. In both cases, the language of pictorial joke-telling was refined to the point where the use of captions and panelled borders became commonplace, with some gags being told in the form of strips. Indeed, there is evidence that these broadsheets were known as 'the comicals', sometimes abbreviated to 'the comics'.[3]

One important aspect of this shift towards humour was that the subversive power of pictorial satire was felt for the first time. Occasionally, things could get dangerous, as artists used the sheets to say things about royalty and politicians that they knew they could not get away with in the written word. As a result, the history of this period is peppered with stories of cartoonists being imprisoned, attacked or even assassinated for going too far.[4]

One of the reasons that satire and caricature worked so effectively was that their subjects could be reproduced with unprecedented verisimilitude. Gone were the days of blurry woodcuts: printing was now moving into the era of copperplate engraving. This meant that once a picture was drawn it had to be redrawn with an etching needle on the surface of the metal plate, which then went through a process involving immersion in acid (to eat away certain areas), and the application of ink. It was a laborious process, often carried out by several people, but the detailed linework that resulted was certainly worth the effort.

Thus, in time, a network of print shops emerged, where the sheets could be produced and sold. By the 1820s, we can speak of a 'satire industry', based in London, but with branches in every major city in the country. As an industry, it had its Dickensian aspects: despite the new technology, most of the funny sheets were predicated on cost-cutting. Thus for most artists there was nothing very funny about the industry at all: they worked for very little pay in cramped conditions, and were usually not even allowed to sign their work.

Nevertheless, there were a few artists who rose above the pack, and managed to foster a reputation. Famous names, who either worked in plate engraving or had their work translated into sheets, included: William Hogarth (1697–1764), James Gillray (1757–1815), George Cruickshank (1792–1878) and Thomas Rowlandson (1757–1827). Much has been written about these figures elsewhere, suffice to say that they were responsible for raising pictorial satire to new levels: their skill for exaggeration and ironic juxtaposition of words and pictures set an aesthetic template that has endured to this day. It is also interesting to note that three of the four artists considered strips and prints produced in sequence to be an integral part of their repertoire: see for example, Hogarth's *Rake's Progress*, Rowlandson's *The Tours of Dr Syntax* and Gillray's *John Bull's Progress*.[5]

In the mid-1800s, there came a significant technological breakthrough. Improvements in photo-processing made possible, for the first time, facsimile reproduction straight from the drawing. Artists no longer had to copy every single line of their picture or be subject to the engraver's personal interpretation. Now their drawings could be faithfully reproduced. For the publisher, this reduced the price of printing, opening the way for cheaper publications.

This coincided with improvements in the technology of binding, and increasingly the idea of selling 'magazines' of broadsheets bound together became more financially viable. (This was the point, then, when the basic look of today's magazines and comics was established.) The emergent Victorian industry then took a variety of directions. The result was that hundreds of different magazine titles were published on both a weekly and monthly basis.

In brief, the most mainstream of the new magazines

Right: Detail from *A Rake's Progress*, 1755, by William Hogarth. This savage satirical print, engraved from a painting, was part of a story in sequential pictures – one of the first of its kind. Below: Print by the great James Gillray entitled *John Bull's Progress*, 1793, a remarkably contemporary-looking commentary on the fate of the common soldier (compare, for example, the anti-Vietnam cartoon reproduced on p 92). Below right: 'A Pair of Broad Bottoms', depicting 'the presentation of a Hotentot at the Court of King George IV'. (Probably an early George Cruickshank.) In the eighteenth century, etchings such as these were sometimes known as 'the comicals'.

O, Vanity of youthfull Blood, / So by Misuse to poison Good! / Woman, form'd for Social Love, / Fairest Gift of Powers above, / Source of every Houshold Blessing, / All Charm in Innocence possessing, / But turn'd to Vice, all Plagues above, / Foe to thy Being, Foe to Love; / Guest Divine to outward Viewing, / Abler Minister of Ruen! / Dost Thou thy friendly Host betray, / Sweet Poison of Misused Wine! / With Freedom led to every Part, / And secret Chamber of y.e Heart; / Dost Thou thy riotous Gang if may, / To enter in with covert Treason, / O'erthrow the drowsy Guard of Reason, / To ransack the abandon'd Place, / And revel there with wild Excess? Plate 3.

Invented, Painted, Engrav'd, & Publish'd by W.m Hogarth June y.e 25. 1735. According to Act of Parliament.

JOHN BULL *Happy.*

JOHN BULL, *going to the* WARS.

JOHN BULL'S *Property in danger.*

JOHN BULL'S *glorious Return.*

JOHN BULL'S *PROGRESS.*

A PAIR of BROAD BOTTOMS

were 'documentary' in style, and concerned with the affairs of the day. They consisted of prose articles accompanied by illustrations, and were in some ways an echo of the serious broadsheets of the Middle Ages. The most famous examples were the *Illustrated London News* (1842), which built up a reputation on the basis of its eyewitness artists' impressions of home news stories and foreign wars, and the *Illustrated Police News* (1864), a much sleazier enterprise which traded in sensational reports and illustrations of murders and hangings (the direct descendant, in fact, of the execution broadsheets).

The second main genre was that of the fictional story papers. These 'penny dreadfuls' (so called for their lurid subject matter) were serialized prose stories, again with accompanying pictures, commonly involving tales that glorified criminals, but also anti-aristocratic romances, and sensational derivatives of popular gothic novels. The most popular dreadfuls included *Black Bess* (1863), *Black Rollo, the Pirate* (1864), *Wild Boys* (1865) and *Sweeney Todd, the Demon Barber of Fleet Street* (1878). Designed for a working-class readership, they were read primarily by young men, and at one point were feared to be so politically subversive that a censorship campaign was initiated to ban them. Officially, the reason for the clampdown was given to be their violent nature: in fact,

anti-establishment story lines were considered much more of a threat.[6]

In time, the dreadfuls gave way to another kind of story paper, in many ways a reaction against them. These were designed to offer boys a 'wholesome' alternative, which usually meant an emphasis on the ideals of 'muscular Christianity' popular at the time. 'Adventure' in this context denoted stories about proving one's 'moral fibre' on the sports field and also the battlefield: yarns about the moral rectitude of 'killing natives' for one's country were especially popular. The tone was set by *Boys of England* (1866), which in its regular editorial explained that: 'true manliness [is] the cause of England's moral as well as physical supremacy over the other nations of the earth'. It was followed by *The Boy's Own Paper* (1879), published by the Religious Tract Society, which followed a similar patriotic/Christian/conservative line.

The third kind of magazine, much more relevant to our investigation of the origins of comics, was humorous. These publications were once again a mix of text and illustrations, but generally much more visual than the other two genres. The boom was begun by *Punch* (1841), a satirical monthly following the tradition of the middle-class broadsheet. Political caricature was its stock in trade, though its reputation was also based on the quality of

Below: *Kissing Hands* by H Heath, demonstrating some oleaginous behaviour at the Court of Queen Caroline, 1827. By the 1820s, it is possible to speak of a 'satire industry' existing in the big cities. This is a typical print designed for a middle-class audience, making extensive use of word-balloons.

KISSING HANDS.

LONDON CHARLES FOX, 4, SHOE LANE, FLEET STREET, E.C.

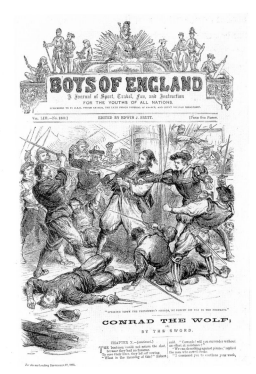

its ink drawings. Although most contributors saw little return for their association with the title, a few artists were simply too outstanding to remain anonymous – the most famous examples being John Leech and John Tenniel.[7]

Punch (R Bryant, 1841) was followed by a clutch of middle-class imitators, and also by a larger number of titles aimed primarily at a working-class readership. *Judy* (Gilbert Dalziel, 1867), *Funny Folks* (James Henderson, 1874), *Scraps* (James Henderson, 1883) and others, stuck to the basic formula pioneered by *Punch*, but added more slapstick and reduced the amount of text. In the circulation war that developed between them, costs were minimized, and pay for contributors was pegged at unprecedentedly low levels. It was even true that some titles stole strips and cartoons from contemporaneous foreign publications – especially the American magazines *Judge* (Judge Publishing, 1881), *Life* (Life Publishing, 1883), and *Puck* (Keppler and Schwarzmann, 1876). The readership may have benefited by being introduced to the work of cartoonists like American Fred Opper and German Wilhelm Busch

Above left: Cover, *Sweeney Todd, Demon Barber of Fleet Street* (Charles Fox, 1878). Art: Anon. This 'penny dreadful' was one of the most notorious of the Victorian shockers. Above right: Cover, *Boys of England* (E J Brett, 1892). Art: Anon. The 'story papers' were a 'wholesome' response to the dreadfuls, dealing in ripping yarns from the Empire. Below right: Cartoon from the satirical monthly *Punch* (R Bryant, 1879). Art/script: John Tenniel. Here, a grim-faced Prime Minister Disraeli ponders his foreign policy problems. By the late nineteenth century, picture magazines such as these were enormously popular among all social classes.

(whose '*Max and Moritz*', a strip about a couple of tearaways, became a firm favourite), but for native creators it was yet more bad news.

These cartoon magazines were very nearly comics as we know them – and indeed, some historians have chosen to classify them as such. The practice of privileging pictures over text, the addition of more strips and the emphasis on slapstick were all steps on the road to becoming comics. However, there was still something missing. For in order for a title to merit being called the first of this new kind of publication, there had to be an extra element: a central continuing character.

So we come at last to the first comic agreed to be worthy of the name: the curiously titled *Ally Sloper's Half Holiday* (Gilbert Dalziel, 1884).[8] This was a cheap (one penny), black-and-white tabloid weekly that mixed strips, cartoons and prose stories, and which boasted a regular starring character: the eponymous Alexander Sloper. Although very few people have heard of the title today, it is undoubtedly one of the most important comics in the history of the medium, not just because it was first, but because it set standards in so many areas, both commercial and artistic.

For the sake of a ready reference, *Ally Sloper* is perhaps best thought of as a Victorian *Viz* (House of Viz, 1979). It shared many of the same characteristics: it was meant for an adult readership; it was based on identifiable working-class characters; it drew on music hall traditions in the same way that *Viz* would later draw on alternative comedy; it spawned a huge quantity of merchandising; and finally, and most importantly, like *Viz* it somehow managed to capture the zeitgeist, and to become a publishing sensation.

Alexander Sloper himself was a working-class wastrel: when the rent collector calls he 'slopes off' down the alley. In the early days of his existence, what money he did manage to accrue (always by dubious means), he spent on drink: his nose was red and swollen, he had a permanent hangover, and on at least one occasion he was arrested for being drunk and disorderly. Later, the character changed in subtle ways, and became more fleshed-out. He remained working class, but was mock-gentrified and was placed in middle-class and upper-class settings. The laughs came both from the pleasure of seeing a working man enjoying the good life, and from his social faux pas – both verbal and sartorial.[9]

Sloper was a vehicle through which cartoonists could comment upon Victorian leisure. When he was on 'half holiday', he visited the local pub, the races, and, above all, the seaside. Often he did this alone, but sometimes he was accompanied by his daughter, Tootsie (the first female character to be successful in a comic), and his Jewish friend Ikey Mo. Together, they enjoyed to the full what spare time industrial capitalism allowed them, and in this sense, the comic was about 'letting go', and forgetting the travails of urban, working life. By the same token, political point-scoring was never the aim. There was no implication of class war, or even of a questioning of the power of one's social superiors. The comic was thus not in the tradition of the radical broadsheets.[10]

This page and opposite: Covers and interior strips from *Ally Sloper's Half Holiday* (Gilbert Dalziel, 1888, 1889 and 1892). Art: Main cover cartoons by WF Thomas. Generally agreed to be the first comic ever produced, *Ally Sloper* was a kind of Victorian *Viz*, and starred the working-class anti-hero Alexander Sloper, seen above getting his ear tweaked for ogling the nudes at a Royal Academy show, and opposite receiving a watery come-uppance. By demonstrating the huge appeal of music hall-style slapstick, the title opened up a whole new market.

Ally Sloper's Half Holiday

FOUNDED AND CONDUCTED BY GILBERT DALZIEL.

Vol. IX.—No. 418.]   SATURDAY, APRIL 30, 1892.   [ONE PENNY.

THE MAY QUEEN.

"*The idea of holding a May Day gathering in our back yard can certainly lay claim to originality, and Poor Pa deserves commendation on this account. May Day falling upon a Sunday made things a bit awkward; but Papa cleverly overcame this difficulty by ordaining that the celebration should take place last Tuesday. Out of compliment to Alexandry, Evelina was elected May Queen, and would doubtless have filled that position with becoming dignity but for the unseemly conduct of our neighbours. As it was, the whole affair ended miserably, and a general feeling of dampness prevailed.*"—TOOTSIE.

FAITH, HOPE, BUT NOT CHARITY.

Hungry! Yes, Billy was very hungry, so, spotting an individual looming in the distance, he tries on the old dodge of standing before an attractive looking eating-house, and glancing wistfully in the—

Window. As our hero had hoped, the individual drew up, and after gazing at the attractive plum-duff, turned to Billy, causing that youth's heart to bubble spasmodically in his bosom. Would the stranger—

stand treat? It appeared so, for, turning to Billy, he inquired whether he would like some plum-duff. Receiving an affirmative answer, he murmured, mournfully, "So should I," and walked dejectedly away.

THE PHAETON AND PAIR.

WILLIAM PAGE was the son of a Hampton farmer, and was sent to London to a relation, who was a haberdasher, to learn the business; but the young man neglected his work and spent an allowance he received from his father in riotous living. "He was such a consummate coxcomb," says his biographer, "that he was perpetually employing tailors to alter his clothes to the newest fashion, till his kinsman desired the tailors in the neighbourhood to refuse his orders, on which he procured a dark lantern, hid it under the bed, and when all the family were asleep, altered the clothes himself."

Having no other means of getting pocket-money, Page began to rob the till, his first offence being committed to discharge a supposed debt, contracted by his sweetheart, of over fifteen pounds. The haberdasher then planted some marked money, and Page, falling into the snare, some of it was found in his pocket, and he was turned out of the house.

He went at once to his sweetheart; but she, being told what had happened, turned him out of her house, also saying it was no place for thieves. He wandered down to Gravesend, and, when almost starving, wrote to the haberdasher, who sent him a guinea, and said as a P.S. that if he ever asked for more he would be prosecuted for the theft. By the next day Page and his sweetheart had spent the money. He then tramped home to his father, who ordered

The changes that the character went through make it difficult to pin his success down to any one cartoonist. He was created by Charles Ross and drawn by a number of artists over time, among them Marie Duval (Ross's wife, and the first woman comics artist), WF Thomas and William G Baxter (arguably the most talented of them all). However, there is little evidence that they, or any of the other writers and artists on the comic, reaped the benefits of his fame. In time-honoured fashion, the publishers managed to exploit the staff, in this case by keeping pay rates down by reprinting old material, and by inviting contributions from readers and amateur cartoonists (a ploy, incidentally, which was also used by *Viz* in the 1990s).

Though there was more to the comic than Sloper, it was his presence every week that guaranteed a massive readership. The artwork was in the tradition of other humour magazines, with lots of detailed, heavily shaded drawings, invariably with text underneath. Similarly, there were huge chunks of densely set prose, including stories, and bogus 'reports' (it should be remembered that the working class was fairly literate by this point in history due to the various education acts). The new attraction, however, was the fact that readers could develop a relationship with the lead character over time – something which would be imitated by nearly every comic that followed.

Marketing was the final part of the comic's success story. For the publishers were able to open up new avenues. From the start, *Ally Sloper's Half Holiday* was sold through newsagents, like other magazines, then it was found to be popular reading for train journeys, and was promoted especially hard through railway kiosks.[11]

Passengers would pick up a copy at the beginning of their journey, read it between stops, and throw it away at the end. The comic thus became known as 'railway literature', and played up to this by offering a 'free gift' of an accident insurance policy (see, for example, the top of the cover reproduced on p 17). This was so that anybody found dead in a railway accident with a copy of the comic on their person would have their life insurance policy paid off by the publishers. It was undoubtedly a macabre, if wacky, gimmick, but it should be remembered that Victorian railways were far from safe, and as our illustration bears testimony, 'three claims' had already been paid by 1892.

In this way, the comic became, in its own words 'the biggest selling penny paper in the world'. As we have seen, this was mainly among working-class readers, though also with significant middle-class patronage (William Morris was a fan). Sloper himself was a national institution, and by the 1890s, merchandising based on the character was in full swing, with a range of mugs, posters and dolls for sale. More pertinently, the comic's format, quality and marketing created a template for the future.

After *Sloper*, other British titles began to enter the field, only cautiously at first, because its domination was so strong. Indeed, publishers reasoned that the only way they could compete was by copying the basic formula (rather in the same way that the 1990s *Viz* imitators stepped into the market opened by that title). Examples of other penny papers in the immediate post-Sloper period included *Illustrated Bits* (1885) and CH Ross's *Variety Paper* (1887), set up by the creator of Sloper after the character had been taken away from him.

The real flood did not come until 1890, heralded by the so-called 'halfpenny revolution'. One publisher, the

Above: Cover, *Comic Cuts* (Amalgamated Press, 1912). Art/script: 'Tom, the Ticket-of-Leave Man' by Percy Cocking. The first title to use the word 'comic' in its name.
Below left: A popular *Comic Cuts* strip from 1923, starring the 'Colony Nigs' (political correctness was never the title's strong point). Art/script: Anon.
Below right: Cover, *Illustrated Chips* (Amalgamated Press, 1913). Art/script:

'Weary Willie and Tired Tim' by Tom Browne. Today Tom Browne is recognized as one of the all-time great artists. These two titles, both dating to 1890, established the 'halfpenny revolution' in comics, and shifted the balance of power in publishing firmly into the hands of the Amalgamated Press, owned by Alfred Harmsworth, later Lord Northcliffe.

Top: Cover, *The Wonder* (Amalgamated Press, 1901). Art/script: Anon. Above: Cover, *Funny Cuts* (Amalgamated Press, 1917). Art/script: Anon. Suddenly, halfpenny titles were everywhere, and most of them were very poor indeed.

twenty-five-year-old Alfred Harmsworth, proprietor of the Amalgamated Press, decided to launch a line of comics predicated on the idea that success was possible if the price could be cut by half. This was a huge gamble at the time, and depended on the twin imperatives of keeping costs down and circulations up (indeed, many newsagents responded hostilely to the prospect, because they could not envisage making a profit with prices so low). Harmsworth also had a personal dislike of the penny dreadfuls, and intended his new comics to be 'wholesome entertainment', in order to attract readers away from them (a campaign he would later consolidate by publishing a series of story papers).[12]

His and the Amalgamated Press's flagship title was *Comic Cuts*, launched in 1890 (the first of the new publications to use the word 'comic' in its name), closely followed by *Illustrated Chips* (1890).[13] These were based on knockabout humour in the established fashion, and followed the pattern set by Sloper quite closely. *Chips* was exceptional for the fact that it boasted one of the all-time great comics artists, Tom Browne. His continuing characters Weary Willie and Tired Tim became almost as famous as Sloper, and marked him out as a master of slapstick rendering.

Other publishers joined in with their own halfpenny titles, similarly based on paring back costs to the minimum. Harmsworth was not to be outdone. He responded with scores of others. His ruthlessness made him a fortune, on which he established a newspaper empire, becoming Lord Northcliffe in the process. Pre-1914 comics included *Funny Cuts, Snap Shots, The Joker, The World's Comic, Larks!* and *The Funny Wonder* (later *The Wonder*).

The trouble was that this glut in the halfpenny titles led to an overall crash in quality (the writer AA Milne later commented that Harmsworth's comics and story papers had 'killed the penny dreadful with the ha'penny dreadfuller'). Superficially, they continued to imitate Sloper: they were nearly always tabloids; they mixed strips, cartoons and prose. They also tended to star their own misfits, tramps and petty criminals: the aforementioned Weary Willie and Tired Tim (*Chips*), Nobbler and Jerry (*Funny Cuts*) and The Three Lodgers (*Larks!*). Their politics were also the same: satirical to a point, but no further. The publishers were out to make a financial killing, after all, and not to end up in jail.

The panache of their progenitor was missing. In contrast with most of the new titles, *Sloper* looked almost classy. Corners were cut in a number of ways: the paper quality was terrible, the printing cut-price, the ink cheap and the page-sizes reduced. Inevitably, the writers and artists also suffered, to the point where *The World's Comic* felt it was necessary to reassure readers that: 'We are no "sweaters". Everybody who draws and writes [for us] ... is well paid for his work.' Nobody involved in the industry would have believed this for a minute.[14]

An additional price saving device was to pirate material from America. At first, the British comics stole from publications like *Life* and *Judge* (in the same way that the satirical magazines had before them); later, they did the

same from Sunday newspaper strips. *Snap Shots* was the most famous culprit, and was composed entirely of American material. Whatever the morality of this policy, it did allow British audiences to get to know American characters like the Katzenjammer Kids (see below) – themselves direct descendants of the aforementioned Max and Moritz. It also opened the doors to greater artistic influence from America, though the significance of this pre-1914 is open to debate.[15]

Inevitably, perhaps, the new comics attracted criticism. They were increasingly seen not just as harmless railway literature, but as something more sinister. Middle-class paternalists now attacked this new form of working-class entertainment with as much vigour as they had previously reserved for the penny dreadfuls (despite Harmsworth's desire that they should be viewed in a different light). They were said to be a 'threat to literacy' on two, contradictory, levels. First, any publication based on pictures was deemed to be automatically inferior to prose material: reading was associated with an 'improving' ethic, whereas strips and cartoons had the opposite effect. Secondly, it was argued that the close print in the new comics was bad for the eyesight. Comics, it seems, could not win either way.

More than this, conservatives began to complain more generally about cultural debasement. The fact that comics were so popular meant they became symbols of declining standards in the nation; and of course, this popularity was with the working class, which implied a whole range of additional prejudices. Snobbery was thus at the heart of much of the counter reaction, with words like 'vulgar' and 'gauche' becoming common descriptions of the craze.

It was too late! By the time the backlash took hold, British comics were already selling in their hundreds of thousands. Whatever the arbiters of taste might say, there was not a newsagent in the country who would take any notice. The tinny clang of Edwardian cash registers was always going to be louder than complaining voices, and commercially, it had been proved beyond any doubt that even with rock-bottom prices, it was still possible to make huge profits. Harmsworth's gamble had paid off. Comics were here to stay.

In the United States, comics followed a quite different evolutionary path. Here, the main precursors to the form were newspaper strips rather than satirical magazines. This is not to say that there were not some similarities to the British experience: as we have seen, America had her own *Punch*-like publications, such as *Puck, Life* and *Judge*, and there were also equivalents to the *Illustrated London News* and its ilk, such as the remarkable *Frank Leslie's Illustrated Newspaper*, which carried battlefield sketches of the Civil War plus drawings of murders and disasters. Additionally, although in Britain the tradition of book illustration was certainly an influence on comics, in the States the impact was profound: in particular, Mark Twain was a believer in the power of pictures, and selected various artists to illustrate his novels, which in turn became extremely popular.[16]

If pictures pushed up the sales of books in the United States, they could certainly do the same for newspapers. Single-image cartoons became a feature first of all, and

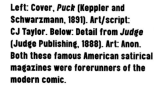

Left: Cover, *Puck* (Keppler and Schwarzmann, 1891). Art/script: CJ Taylor. Below: Detail from *Judge* (Judge Publishing, 1888). Art: Anon. Both these famous American satirical magazines were forerunners of the modern comic.

Below: The newspaper cartoon-cum-strip, 'The Yellow Kid' (*New York World*, 1896). Art/script: Richard Outcault. The strip was about a slum urchin dressed in a yellow smock. Outcault had previously worked for *Judge*, but blazed a new trail with 'The Kid': its use of the colour yellow made full-colour reproduction possible in newspaper illustrations, and led to the widespread introduction of strips in the American popular press.

then proper strips: these were modest affairs at first – a few, black-and-white, limited-panel gags at the bottom of a page – but soon grew into full-colour supplements, usually between four and eight pages in length. Almost always these supplements appeared on a Sunday, and over time they became known as 'the Sunday Funnies': the term 'the comics' was similarly used in the United States to mean an integral part of a newspaper. By the turn of the century, they were a thriving genre, a situation that was reinforced by the emergence of 'strip syndicates', which could provide different newspapers all over the country with the same strips.

The main commercial reason for introducing such an innovation into papers was to reach the immigrant populations in the big cities. The two great press barons of the era, Joseph Pulitzer and William Randolph Hearst, were not slow to capitalize on the idea, but had slightly different aims in doing so (both were hard-headed businessmen, but Pulitzer dreamed of eventually reproducing great European paintings in colour to bring high culture to the masses). Hearst was the first to have a major hit with Richard Outcault's 'The Yellow Kid', which ran in *The New York Journal* from 1896. Outcault had previously contributed to the middle-class *Life* and *Judge*, but here went downmarket with a satire on urban slum life, peppered with ethnic slurs: the eponymous 'kid' was a Chinese-looking urchin, and a kind of manic idiot savant.[17] What was remarkable about the strip was that it used the colour yellow, which made full-colour reproduction possible in newspapers for the first time.

After 'The Yellow Kid', a fierce circulation war was initiated that used strips as a weapon. Hundreds of strips made their appearance in papers all over the country, on a variety of humorous subjects, ranging from highbrow satire to dumb slapstick. Suddenly, cartoonists were in demand, and the press barons fought hard to retain them. Artistically speaking, historians usually identify three names as being particularly outstanding: Winsor McCay, Lyonel Feininger and George Herriman. All were widely syndicated.

McCay's 'Little Nemo in Slumberland' (1905) was intended in some ways as a middle-class reponse to 'The Yellow Kid': it used a more sophisticated rendering style, influenced by Art Nouveau, to tell the story of a child from a well-to-do family, and the wild dreams he has when the lights go out at bedtime. Its use of perspective and colour were astounding, as was the way in which panels were structured in a cinematic fashion (McCay was also a pioneer of early animated cartoons): stories would typically involve surreal characters and animals dressed in bright costumes, with panels expanded and stretched for extra dramatic impact, ending with a smaller closing panel in which Nemo wakes up with a start.

For all their technical brilliance, the 'Nemo' stories were often emotionally cold. McCay was obviously more interested in his drawing than in his writing, and this was a flaw he never really overcame. The same was also true of his more adult strip, 'The Dreams of a Rarebit Fiend' (1905), which was similarly about a character who has trouble sleeping, but which took the dream/nightmare

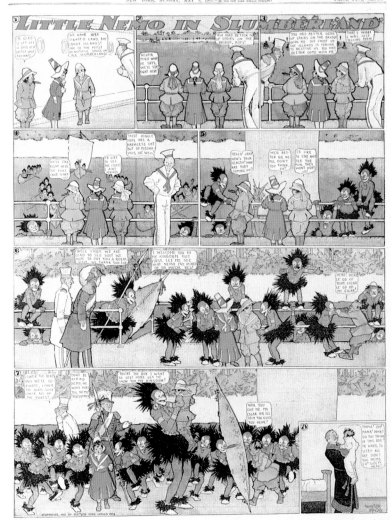

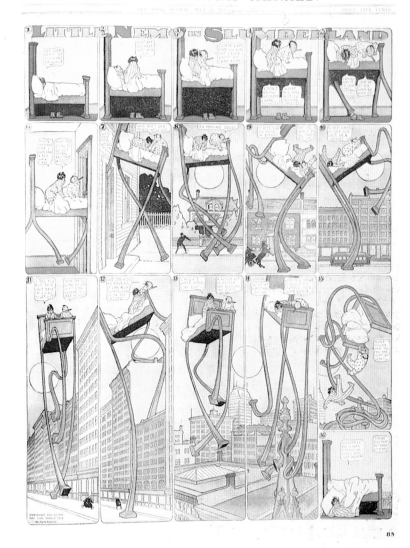

Above left and right: 'Little Nemo in Slumberland'(*New York Herald*, 1907 and 1908). Art/script: Winsor McCay. McCay's use of surreal imagery, colour and innovative panel compositions secured Nemo's place as an early classic of the strip form; interestingly, though perhaps not surprisingly, McCay was also a pioneer of film animation. Below left and right: 'The Kin-der-Kids' (*Chicago Sunday Tribune*, 1906). Art/script: Lyonel Feininger. The 'Famous German artist' was also known for his cubist and Bauhaus paintings. By 1910, the 'Sunday Funnies', the pull-out newspaper comics supplements exemplified by these strips, were a way of life in America.

Opposite and near right: 'Krazy Kat'
(King Features Syndicate, 1926 and 1918).
Art/script: George Herriman. The strip
was much more than cat-and-mouse slapstick, and could be read on a number of
political and metaphorical levels. For this
reason, it was a favourite with America's
intellectual elite. Right: 'Dreams of the
Rarebit Fiend' (*New York Herald*, 1905).
Art/script: Winsor McCay. McCay also
made a play for an adult readership with
this often nightmarish offering. Below:
'The Katzenjammer Kids' (*San Francisco
Examiner*, 1912). Art/script: Rudolph Dirks.
A far simpler strip trading in knockabout
burlesque, the 'Katzenjammers' was
more indicative of what the mass of the
American public were really interested in.

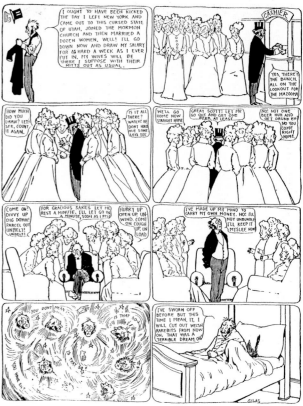

sequences into often quite horrific territory.

Lyonel Feininger was a rival to McCay, and was similarly experimental with panel layouts and strip design, though his strip career lasted less than a year. Feininger was also known for his cubist and Bauhaus paintings, and this was clearly a big influence on his work. His two masterpieces, 'The Kin-der-Kids' (1906) and 'Wee Willie Winkie's World' (1906), were ostensibly for children, but were enjoyed by adults for their playful expressionism. Buildings yawn, the sun flexes its ray-like hands and trees dance; all are rendered in a beautifully sombre palettes.

George Herriman was the last of the 'big three', but probably the most talented (the 'comics laureate', as he has been dubbed). His first successful strip was 'The Dingbat Family' (1910), a situation comedy about warring neighbours in an apartment block. But it was two supporting characters in that strip – a cat and a mouse – that would form the basis for his enduring masterwork, 'Krazy Kat' (1913). This strip elaborated on the love-hate relationship between the two animals, but set it against a background of abstract and ever-changing landscapes. The deceptively simple plot, which was repeated with minor variations for over thirty years, went as follows: Krazy is in love with Ignatz the mouse, whose sole passion is to throw bricks at Krazy. Though it is intended as an act of aggression, the bricks are interpreted by Krazy as an act of love. However the friendly policeman, Offissa Pupp (who also has designs on Krazy) is having none of it, and locks Ignatz up in a prison made of – what else? – bricks.

This bizarre love triangle was interpreted by some as a meditation on anarchism and democracy; by others as a satire on heaven and hell. Others still linked Herriman

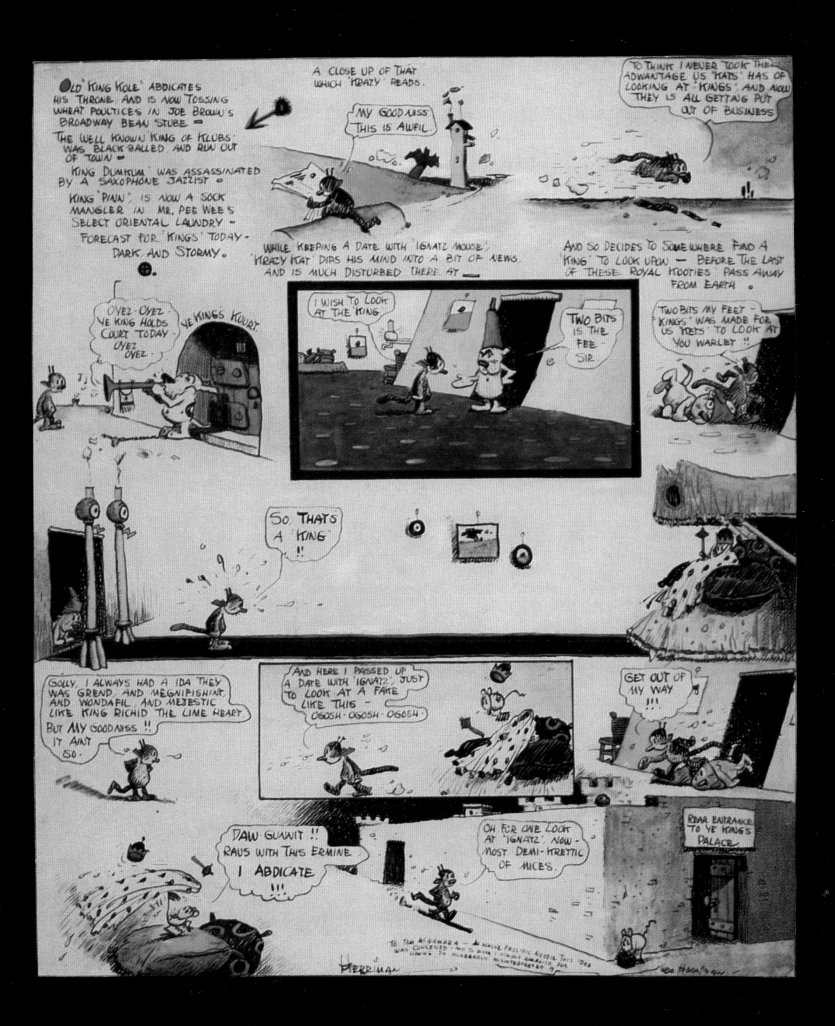

early strips. Examples that placed them centre stage included Jimmy Swinnerton's 'Mr Jack' (1903), about a tiger who had an office job, a wife, and several admiring lady friends; Fred Opper's 'And Her Name was Maud!' (1904), about a taciturn mule who packed a mighty kick; and Billy DeBeck's 'Barney Google', which co-starred a racehorse called 'Spark Plug'.

Yet, by far the most popular of the early strip genres was the domestic comedy. Commonly, these stories had political undercurrents, and articulated the class tensions of the day – especially when it came to immigrant or minority communities. Most famously, George McManus's 'Bringing up Father' (1913) focused on the marital conflicts that ensued when an Irish couple win a fortune on the horses: the wife adapts to a nouveau riche existence, but her husband slides back into his low-class origins and the comforts of Dinty Moore's Saloon. Similarly class-conscious, though in a gentler vein, were Fred Opper's 'Happy Hooligan' (1900), about an Irish tramp (an eternal loser with a heart of gold); and Abie Hershfield's 'Abie the Agent' (1914), which depicted the milieu of a Jewish middle-class businessman.

Other notable domestic soaps included: Bud Fisher's 'Mutt and Jeff' (1907), a vaudevillian double-act about two continually warring friends (Mutt being a depressed cynic, Jeff a wise fool); Cliff Sterett's 'Polly and her Pals' (1912), about a 'new woman', her suitors, and her father's reaction to them; Harry Tuthill's 'Bungle Family' (1918), about a bunch of (quite likeable) misanthropes; Frank King's 'Gasoline Alley' (1918), about a neighbourhood and the effects of (among other things) the automobile craze; and Sidney Smith's 'The Gumps' (1917), concerning the problems faced by a family during a period of rapid industrial change. Again, these strips often had serious subtexts, as one historian explains: 'Both The Gumps and Gasoline Alley showed that narratives about the problems of middle-class families of the Midwest trying to get ahead and hoping to achieve the American Dream of financial security struck a responsive chord in Americans facing the same difficulties.'[19]

The first decade of the twentieth century saw an assortment of books published, which collected together the most popular of the newspaper strips, and can be regarded as early precursors of the 'comic books' we know today. These were irregularly published affairs, often in hardback, and subject matter tended towards the most commercial fare. To give some idea of the split between 'highbrow' and 'lowbrow' strip-republications:

with the Dada movement: however, according to one historian, 'During his lifetime, Herriman probably remained unaware of his acceptance by the Dadaists ... and was likely only vaguely aware of their existence. He had achieved the unconventional art and humour he practiced independently and without the philosophic posturing of the Dadists.'[18] Whatever the case, 'Krazy Kat' remains one of the most remarkable strips in the history of the medium.

Though McCay, Feininger and Herriman may have been pioneering in the artistic sense, their strips did not necessarily do the best commercially. The really popular, and extensively syndicated, stories tended to be more lightweight, with an emphasis on slapstick. One example was the dumber kind of 'kid' strip. The archetype here was undoubtedly Rudolph Dirks's 'Katzenjammer Kids', about the antics of two German immigrant urchins, Hans and Fritz: an exercise in raucous vulgarity which became the longest-running strip in American history. (Feininger's 'Kin-der-Kids' had been intended as a direct competitor.) Others included Carl Schultze's 'Foxy Grandpa' (1900), about an old man who outfoxes his nephews; and Richard Outcault's 'Buster Brown' (1902), a follow-up to 'The Yellow Kid', about a middle-class brat dressed like Little Lord Fauntleroy, who constantly breaks his promises to be good.

Animals, too, were a popular feature of many of these

1. Although most histories still trace the genesis of printing to Gutenberg in the fifteenth century, the process had existed in China since the eleventh century (though some historians argue that the essential difference lies in the application of movable type to a phonetic alphabet). For the purposes of this book, however, we are concerned primarily with the Western world.

2. Indeed, some conventions have roots that are much earlier than the broadsheets. Word-balloons, for example, can be seen in friezes from ancient Mayan temples.

3. See the two excellent histories by David Kunzle, *History of the Comic Strip: The Early Comic Strips*, vol 1, *The Nineteenth Century*, vol 2 (Berkley, California, University of California Press, 1973 and 1989).

4. This is not just a historical phenomenon. For example, cartoonist Naji Salim Al-Ali was shot in London in 1987 after producing a cartoon satirizing Yasser Arafat's girlfriend.

5. Broadsheet 'stories' are sometimes problematic because individual images were often created with the aim of being reproduced both singly and in conjunction with others. For example, Hogarth's prints were often sold individually as self-contained satires, but were also intended to be read in sequence as a story (though they were physically too big to be reproduced on a page in the form of a comic strip).

6. On the clampdown on the dreadfuls, see Martin Barker, *Comics: Ideology, Power and the Critics* (Manchester University Press, 1989), pp 99–105. For an overview of the genre, three histories are especially useful: Louis James, *Fiction for the Working Man* (Harmondsworth, Penguin, 1974); Michael Anglo, *Penny Dreadfuls* (London, Jupiter Books, 1977); and Kevin Carpenter (ed) *Penny Dreadfuls and Comics* (London, Victoria and Albert Museum, 1983).

7. Many of the *Punch* cartoonists also worked in the burgeoning world of book illustration. For example, John Leech contributed to the novels of Charles Dickens.

8. The question of which publication was the 'first' comic is hotly debated by historians. The two other main contenders are a volume of 'Dr Syntax' and *Funny Folks*. In America, the first comic strip is usually held to be 'The Yellow Kid' (1895), and the first comic book *Famous Funnies* (1934).

9. Sloper had previously appeared in a magazine called *Judy* – a companion to *Punch* – and was well known from there (to the extent that a collection of cartoons and strips had been published in 1873, entitled *Ally Sloper: A Moral Lesson*).

10. A good discussion of the politics of Sloper can be found in: Peter Bailey 'Ally Sloper's Half Holiday: Comic Art in the 1880s' in *Historical Journal* (1971), pp 349–58.

11. The WH Smith chain began as a railway newsagent business.

12. Perhaps the most famous of these story papers was *The Boy's Friend* (1895). See Carpenter, *Penny Dreadfuls and Comics*, p 51.

13. The word 'cut' was publishing trade slang for a printing block, deriving from 'wood cuts'.

14. It would appear that one of the very few exceptions to this cycle of exploitation was Tom Browne, who managed to make a reasonable living from his comics.

15. The early American newspaper strips that are today considered 'classics' – for example, 'Krazy Kat' and 'Little Nemo in Slumberland' (see below, pp 20–2) – remained virtually unknown in Britain. Only much later, during the rise of comics fandom in the 1970s and 1980s, were these strips given the attention and acclaim they deserved.

16. Artists famous for their book illustrations included NC Wyeth, WW Denslow and Howard Pyle.

17. In fact, the character who would later become the Yellow Kid first made his appearance in a cartoon-cum-strip called 'Hogan's Alley' in a Pulitzer newspaper (*New York World*). But in the scramble for comics artists, Outcault was poached by Hearst, along with a number of other Pulitzer creators. This tussle over 'The Yellow Kid' eventually gave rise to the term 'yellow journalism'.

18. M Thomas Inge, 'Krazy Kat as American Dada Art', *Comics as Culture* (University of Mississippi Press, 1990), p 41.

19. M Thomas Inge, 'The Comics', *Great American Comics: 100 Years of Cartoon Art* (Exhibition guide, Smithsonian Institute, 1990), p 19.

Foxy Grandpa and Buster Brown featured in dozens of books; Little Nemo appeared in only two; while Feininger and Herriman do not seem to have been collected at all until much later. Usually the publishers of such books were the newspapers in which they had first appeared (notably, the *New York Journal*), but some independent companies, such as Cupples and Leon, also did well.

In spite of the growing interest in both newspaper strips and reprint-books, there was a backlash from certain sectors of American society. This shared much in common with the British attack on comics: the mix of words and pictures was similarly said to be intrinsically lowbrow, trashy and detrimental to 'proper' reading. However, what was different about the American experience was that the inherent class prejudice took on religious and racial overtones. Most importantly, some extreme Christians resented the fact that the comics were published on a Sunday: the fact that the comics were reaching immigrant populations in the cities, who were not necessarily Christian themselves, added an extra dimension to their objections.

Nevertheless, the backlash was not well organized, and amounted to little more than a few church meetings and a drizzle of complaining letters to newspapers. As in Britain, the strip form was already too well established: events had passed the point of no return, and too many dollars had been spent. The newspaper strip boom and the fledgling reprint book publishing industry were laying the foundations for a major comics explosion, and nobody was going to stop it. How the American 'comic book' came into existence as a publication of a particular size and design, and consisting of original strip material, is one of the themes of our next chapter.

Comical comics

The great age for comedy comics was *c* 1935–65. During this period, a flood of titles emerged from Britain and the United States, 'chock full of laughter' (in the words of one early example), and selling in numbers that were never matched before or since – in other words, millions rather than thousands.[1] Although the subject matter reflected formulas that had been developed previously, ranging from satire to slapstick, the audience was now predominantly children, and this naturally had an effect on how comics were perceived. Such was the cultural impact of this explosion that the definition of a comic, as given in the 1965 edition of the Oxford English Dictionary, became 'a publication for children designed to excite mirth'.

In the years leading up to the First World War, British comics went through a radical reorientation. Suddenly, they were being produced with bright colours, cleaner artwork and a much more vibrant sensibility. No longer were readers expected to squint at the detailed drawings and dense print of comics like *Ally Sloper's Half Holiday*: now, titles were designed to be speed-read in an instant. This was a recognition that for knockabout comedy to work, it had to flow, to move; and that for a comic to interest a child, it had to be as immediate as possible.

The historical origins of this change were to be found in the early Edwardian period (1901–11). Over a space of about ten years, the publishers of adult comics became aware that there might be a market among children, and so designed pull-out sections for them: these commonly featured strips about funny animals, clowns and so on,

and kept text to a minimum. The supplements proved so popular that the next logical step was to launch proper comics. After all, children now had some spending power: the concept of pocket money had become established in the late 1800s (as children no longer went out to work), and if a title could be kept within the range of the 'Saturday penny' then there was a chance it could do well.

In the process, comics' visual appeal was boosted: artwork became simpler, more attention was paid to making covers look eye-catching and more colour was introduced. Perhaps the best example of an adult comic that re-invented itself was *Puck* (Amalgamated Press, 1904). As one historian has written: '*Puck* no 1 was "the first number of the first coloured comic paper" ... [But] Clearly the comic was not finding a market. Adults, for whom it was intended, did not like the bright colours. But children did. In no 11, Puck began a section for children ... Ten weeks later, the juvenile interest had spread throughout the whole comic ... the children's comic had been born.'[2]

Other established titles followed *Puck*'s example by making themselves 'younger', including *Comic Cuts* and *Illustrated Chips*. So successful were the revamps that by 1914 almost the entire industry had reorientated its production towards readers of between eight and twelve: the age range it concentrated on until the 1980s. Almost overnight, it seemed, the adult comic had become a thing of the past.

What happened as a result was that the sociology of comics reading was transformed. No longer were comics supposed to be for workers to read during breaks or on trains during half holidays. Now, they were being bought by kids with their own pocket money, without adult supervision, and were being read as part of children's leisure time: their's to swap, discard or keep as they wished. The sense of ownership, so empowering for a child, was total.

More than this, comics became a private reading space for children, a place where they could negotiate adult power and authority, and where juvenile fantasies could be played out: a world of naughtiness, make believe violence and what primary school teachers used to call 'messy play'. For this reason above all, comics formed a strong bond between children: playground chat was commonly about the week's new releases, and if a child did not know the names of characters, then he or she might be excluded from the group. Indeed, the characters themselves became 'friends' in many instances: a relationship re-established and fortified every week.

The Amalgamated Press were the first to cash in. They built on the success of their (now passé) adult comics empire with a flood of children's titles. The inter-war years saw 'penny blacks' like *Jingles* (1934) and *Jolly* (1935) joined by 'tuppenny coloureds', including *My Favourite* (1928), *Crackers* (1929) and, most spectacular of all, *Happy Days* (1938), which was produced in stunning photogravure (a process involving photographically produced printing plates). All of them featured a mix of stories about funny animals and gormless families.[3]

More ambitiously, the Amalgamated Press supplemented these with a movie tie-in designed for children, but starring adults. *Film Fun* (1920) was a major success, and fed from the cinema in much the same way as the first adult comics had done from music hall. It tried to capture the look of silent films, with bold black and white drawings and an emphasis on sight gags, and was notable for its 'realistic' portrayals of stars such as Laurel and Hardy, Fatty Arbuckle and Harold Lloyd. It was later joined by the similarly styled *Radio Fun* (1938) (notable for some remarkable work by artist Roy Wilson) and *TV Fun* (1953).

Yet despite the commercial success of the Amalgamated Press comics, they had their weak points. In particular, they were old fashioned in the sense that they continued to run captions underneath the pictures. The company clung to this as an official policy, mainly as a sop to those critics who continued to complain that comics were a threat to literacy. Working conditions at the press also remained substantially the same since the nineteenth century. In fact, the need to keep costs down to appeal to youngsters and the extra expense of colour were used to justify continued exploitation.

Thus, it was not until the late 1930s that the boom in humour really began, when the Amalgamated Press were challenged by a newcomer to the comics field, DC Thomson. The company, based in Dundee, had previously published story papers, but now took a fresh approach to comics with a line that included *The Dandy* (1937) and *The Beano* (1938). These titles will be familiar to most Britons: they more than any others have defined modern perceptions of a comic in this country, and it is

a testimony to their phenomenal success that they are still being published in the 1990s.

What was so special about them? In one sense, they built on the legacy of the Amalgamated Press: they were likewise published on cheap paper with colour covers (and some colour internal pages), and they too featured funny animals ('Korky the Cat' was the cover star of *The Dandy* for forty-seven years). But in other respects, they were years ahead of their time: most strikingly, they dispensed with captions underneath the pictures and concentrated instead on keeping the dialogue within word-balloons. This style led to a much less static approach to rendering, and opened the way for more fluent joke-telling – the real secret of the comics' success.

The DC Thomson titles were unusual in other ways. For example, they had what can only be described as a 'Depression sensibility', insofar as the mood of the early comics reflected the place of their origin, Dundee, in the midst of the 1930s Great Depression. This was a world where social inequalities were pronounced, and where everybody was hungry: hence strips about relationships between 'toffs' and the working class, typically ending with a reward of a plate of 'grub' (such as a huge pile of mashed potato with bangers sticking out at odd angles). Curiously, this formula has remained little changed over the years.

The characters were unique. The early favourite was 'Desperate Dan', drawn for over thirty years by Dudley Watkins. Dan was a somewhat surreal creation: a cowboy who was so tough he shaved with a blowtorch, but who lived in a Western town (Cactusville) where there were English streetlamps and London buses. His female

Above: Cover, *Film Fun* (Amalgamated Press, 1924). Art/script for 'Harold Lloyd' by Bill Wakefield. Right: Cover, *The Dandy* (DC Thomson, 1938). Art/script for 'Korky the Cat' by James Crichton. These were two of the most popular inter-war titles: by the time of the latter, the old-fashioned notion of having captions underneath the picture (a sop to those who complained that comics led to illiteracy) had been dropped.

This page: A selection of favourite characters from *The Beano* and *The Dandy* (both DC Thomson). Above: 'Biffo the Bear' (*The Beano*, 1964). Art/script: Dudley Watkins. Right: 'Dennis the Menace' (*The Beano*, 1954). Art/script: David Law. Below: The first appearance of Desperate Dan (*The Dandy*, 1937). Below right: 'Roger the Dodger' (*The Beano*, 1954). Art/script: Ken Reid. Of all the comics on the racks, it was these two that set the definition of 'a comic' in most people's minds as a vehicle for juvenile, anarchic fun.

Over page: 'The Bash Street Kids' (*The Beano*, 1964). Art/script: Anon. from characters invented by Leo Baxendale. The grammar school from hell, populated by misfits with spots and jug-ears, and teachers with mortar boards and canes. The strip emphasized transgressions against authority and the adult world, and was vastly amusing for eight-year-olds at the time.

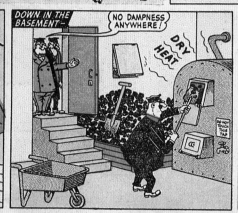

Above: 'Billy Bunter', *Knock-out* (Amalgamated Press, 1942). Art/script: Frank Richards. Below: 'Ginger', *The Beezer*, (DC Thomson, 1961). Art/script: Dudley Watkins. Below right: Cover, *The Topper* (DC Thomson, 1953). Art/script for 'Mickey the Monkey' by Dudley Watkins. Below far right: Cover, *The Beezer* (DC Thomson, 1962). Art/script for 'Pop, Dick and Harry' by Carmichael. As the circulation war hotted up in the humour market, so new titles and new characters were introduced. Not all were destined to catch on.

counterpart, 'Keyhole Kate', was a more conventional creation – a skinny, bespectacled troublemaker – designed to appeal to girls. Later, they would be joined by a string of other classic creations.

These elements endured through the 1940s and 1950s, and the two comics went from strength to strength (with *The Beano* having a slight edge over its rival in terms of sales). The old story structures were continued, but modified, and this was especially true when it came to transgressions against adults. In the 1950s, three creators, David Law, Ken Reid and Leo Baxendale, made juvenile naughtiness their trademark. Law was a barely average artist with a flair for creating memorable characters, most notably 'Dennis the Menace', a shock-haired urchin followed everywhere by his similarly shock-haired dog, Gnasher. Reid's strengths were expressive faces and comic horror, both used to good effect in his most famous strip,

'Roger the Dodger', about a scheming schoolboy ('trickier than a cageful of monkeys!'). Baxendale was more inclined to anarchy, and his 'Bash Street Kids', about a grammar school full of misfits ruled by sadistic teachers, is today recognized as a masterpiece of destructive slapstick.

These latter two, Reid and Baxendale, were superb draughtsmen, and together pushed the art of gag strips forward. They refined how much space to leave between panels for maximum comic effect, and, most importantly, when to throw the sucker punch. (Baxendale would later write: 'Comedy is a structure, a way of thinking; a way in particular of synthesising the unlikely, the unexpected. The most incongruous things that the mind may light on, can be joined in comedy in perfect congruence.'[4]) Their cartoony rendering was perfect for the new, wackier story lines, and together they set the next industry standard after Tom Browne: after them, every artist in comics was encouraged to draw in the same manner.

If the entry of DC Thomson into the industry improved comics, it did not improve staff conditions. Pay for creators continued to be calculated by the page, with no royalty and no control over characters. They were not allowed to sign work, ostensibly because then a child could see it was a drawing, but in practice because anonymity was in the publisher's interests and pre-empted notions of bargaining power. Moreover, DC Thomson had a non-union policy dating back to the General Strike of 1926. So, if anything, the company developed a reputation worse than Amalgamated Press.[5]

Nevertheless, DC Thomson's influence was far-reaching, and following the success of *The Beano* and *The Dandy*, a comics circulation war was initiated, the likes of which

Above: Covers, *Buster* (IPC/Fleetway, 1963) and *Whizzer and Chips* (IPC/Fleetway, 1983), two of the more imaginative later titles. Art/script for 'Buster's Diary' by Reg Smythe. Art/script for 'Sid's Snake' by Mike Lacey. Above right: Cover, *Mickey Mouse Weekly* (Willbank, 1937). Art/script: Anon. A rare example of a British comic with an American theme, and the first in full-colour photogravure.

had not been seen since Harmsworth first took on *Ally Sloper*. The Amalgamated Press struck first with *Knock-Out* (1939), starring Billy Bunter, 'the fattest schoolboy in the world'. However, DC Thomson soon hit back with *Topper* (1953) and *The Beezer* (1956), both of which featured superb work by Baxendale. All were big sellers.

It is important to note here that the British industry was fortunate in the 1940s and 1950s not to have any serious competition from abroad. This was especially true concerning American comics, which were not officially distributed until 1959, despite the fact that the United States had been the biggest comics producing nation in the world since the 1930s (see below). Partly this was because Britain had better things to import: during this postwar period, ships were mainly concerned with the delivery of munitions and essential supplies. It was also because of the British prejudice that existed against American culture, which was thought to be vulgar, over-commercial and and a threat to 'superior' European culture. (No doubt an underlying factor in this extraordinary hostility was the fact that the United States had just superseded Britain as the world's leading power.)

In fact, small numbers of American comics did find their way into the country, primarily through the ports, where ships would dock that used bundles of comics as ballast; and via American military bases, where comics were imported for servicemen's families. They eventually ended up, not in newsagents, but on market stalls and in dumpbins in stores like Woolworths. The comics, smaller and thicker than their British counterparts, were eagerly snapped up by schoolchildren, attracted by their full-colour production values and what could be considered as occasionally more adult content.

There were also British editions of American comics, typically in black-and-white, and published by small companies like Thorpe and Porter and L Miller and Son, plus indigenous titles based on American characters. Of these, none was more popular than the first, *Mickey Mouse Weekly* (Willbank, 1936), which lasted for an impressive 920 issues. It was a lively photogravure tabloid starring various Disney characters, well-known to young Britons from their cinema appearances; it mixed reprinted stories from American syndicated newspaper strips and new material by British artists. Other titles similarly used American cartoon characters as the basis for strips through the 1940s and 1950s.[6]

As the swinging 1960s dawned, there were further developments in the circulation war. In 1960, Amalgamated Press was bought up by the Mirror Group, publishers of the *Daily Mirror*, which then became the International Publishing Corporation (IPC). But the change of name did not mean a let-up in their publishing schedule. Their first move was to create a new imprint, Fleetway, and to publish *Buster* (1960), the eponymous hero of which was supposed to be the son of Andy Capp, the famous strip character created for the *Mirror*. *Buster* was a funnier-than-average title, and gave the Thomson comics a run for their money.

As other publishers joined the fray, competition was intensified still further. The running in the mid-1960s

was made by *Wham!* (Odhams, 1964), intended to be a 'super-*Beano*', and which featured new creations from Baxendale ('George's Germs') and Reid ('Frankie Stein'). It was followed by *Sparky* (DC Thomson, 1965), *Smash!* (Odhams/IPC 1966) *Pow!* (Odhams, 1967) and *Whizzer and Chips* (IPC/Fleetway 1969); and then in the 1970s by the inferior *Cor!!* (IPC, 1970), *Shiver and Shake* (IPC, 1973) and *Whoopee!* (IPC, 1974).

In the drive for readers during this period, subtle changes took place. For example, publishers turned increasingly to gimmicks and non-strip features. Letters pages became a major characteristic of many titles, and served to generate a sense of belonging for readers, and thus increase loyalty. Puzzles and competitions were similarly popular additions. Then there was the craze for free gifts: water pistols, masks, lollies and a plethora of other cheap novelties were given away in their thousands. These were often worth more than the comic itself, and usually given in the premier issue, such was the need to secure that vital first purchase.

Another change was that the quality of writing and art was driven down. The frantic need to meet deadlines, and the often unrealistic pressure on creators to imitate the work of people like Reid and Baxendale, meant that the vast majority of strips were derivative and dull. The jokes were often spread too thinly, and the artwork was typically second rate (unsurprising bearing in mind that creators were paid for quantity rather than quality). Today, it's enormously tempting for adults of a certain age to look back on these humour comics with nostalgia. Readers, however, should be warned against investigating them too closely, as we were all much less critical as children.

In the United States, comedy comics were equally as

This page: Examples of American newspaper strips from the 'golden age' of the funnies. Top: 'Alley Oop' (NEA Service Inc, 1946). Art/script: VT Hamlin. Centre: 'Li'l Abner' (United Features Syndicate, 1936). Art/script: Al Capp. Bottom: 'Blondie' (King Features Syndicate, 1931). Art/script: Chic Young.

successful over a similar period. As we have seen, their origin was in newspaper strips: in Chapter 1 we explored how the popular press became the home for strip supplements aimed at a mixed-age readership, which were then filleted by enterprising publishers to make collected book editions of individual stories. This process continued through the Depression era, with ever-greater popularity, as country-wide syndication became more organized. However, new strips rarely deviated from previously patented formulas: unarguably, the main genre remained domestic comedy.

To mention just a few favourites: Chic Young's 'Blondie' (1930) became one of the most widely syndicated strips in American history. Its star, Blondie Boopadoop was originally a flighty, dumb stereotype, but the gags became more domesticated when she married her beau, Dagwood Bumstead, and had a baby. VT Hamlin's 'Alley Oop' (1933) was a family strip with a difference in that it was set during the Neaderthal era (a sort of proto-Flintstones). The eponymous hero was a good-hearted caveman with a wife, female admirers, and a doting stegosaurus; later stories saw Alley and co time-travelling to various, more recent, historical eras, with predictably chucklesome results. Al Capp's 'Li'l Abner' (1934) was about a hick family and their sentimental, occasionally satirical, shenanigans in 'Dogpatch', a mythical mid-Western neighbourhood. Hal Fisher's

'Joe Palooka' (1930), about a dumb boxer, was a family strip in the sense that Joe had a sweetheart and devoted relatives, but was more about the surrogate family he collects as a result of his profession: notably, his manager, 'Knobby', and his black second, 'Smokey'.

Finally, but perhaps most famously, Elzie Crisler Segar's 'Thimble Theatre' was a soap which had been running since 1919, but which only really took off when the extended family of one 'Popeye the Sailor Man' was introduced in 1929: the constant perils threatening his wife Olive Oyl, and child Swee'pea, were warded off in a flurry of flying fists by the fearless seadog, fortified by his secret weapon: a can of spinach. (Legend has it that another character in the strip, J Wellington Wimpy, inspired the owners of a British fast-food chain to name their restaurants after him, due to his love of hamburgers.)

As the strip characters' fame grew, so the reprint book market went through a mini boom. In the 1920s, one publisher in particular became dominant: Cupples and Leon, famed for their books in a 10-by-10-inch format. In the early 1930s, they were superseded by Whitman Publishing, who produced square books in a smaller format, with single comics panels on the right-hand page and text on the left; these were skilfully marketed as 'The Big Little Book Series', and proved to be immensely popular.

The characters even became the focus for a series of

'bootleg' comics which parodied their antics by adding graphic sex. These remarkable items were the so-called 'Dirty Comics', or 'Tijuana Bibles', which flourished, albeit in a very marginalized sense, between the late 1920s and the late 1940s: eight-pages long, in black-and-white, they were sold 'under the counter'. Blondie, Popeye and many others were portrayed engaged in all manner of hardcore situations, typically accompanied by hilarious (in-character) dialogue.[7] The publishers were anonymous, as were the artists, thus pre-empting any chance of legal action. These comics' alternative nature has meant that they have been regarded by some historians as the forerunners of the 1960s underground comix movement (see Chapter 5).

The Dirty Comics aside, the transition to publications of original material was not a smooth one. There were a number of false starts, most notably the launch of *The Funnies* (Dell) in 1929, a tabloid comic of original strips based on the British model: it failed because people were reluctant to pay for something they considered should come free with their newspaper. The secret to success, it seemed, lay in the question of format: in 1934, a break-through was made in this respect with the launch of a reprint comic entitled *Famous Funnies* (Eastern Color). Masterminded by one Max C Gaines, this book was sized at a quarter the format of a Sunday page (roughly 10½ x 7 inches), with a high percentage of colour reproduction and a cover price of ten cents. It was as close to the modern American comic book as it was possible to get, and proved to be an unexpectedly healthy seller.

Having finally cracked the market, the final step was for publishers to produce comics in the same format, but with original material. *New Comics* (National Allied Publishing) filled that gap in 1935, boasting strips 'Never Printed Before Anywhere', and would be the first of many original humorous comic book anthologies.[8] These latest comics differed in length (sixty-four and eighty-four pages were common), but the content remained basically a variant on the newspaper strip tradition, give or take a few puzzles. In other words, the humour tended to be domestic comedy-based, and orientated towards a mixed-age readership. However, it soon became clear that a large market existed among younger readers, and thus comics were increasingly produced specifically for them.

The age range took a marked tumble with the rise of the funny animal genre in the 1940s. Of course, anthropomorphic characters had existed since the beginning of newspaper strips, but now one publisher, Dell, made the genre its own by arranging a licensing deal with the Disney studios.[9] Its main comic, *Walt Disney's Comics and Stories* (1940) ran for twenty-two years and featured original yarns starring Donald Duck, Mickey Mouse et al. It was immensely successful, partly because sales were boosted with every release of an animated film, and partly because it featured some of the best artwork in the business.

Two creators in particular were outstanding. The first was Carl Barks, who wrote and drew many of the duck stories between 1942 and the mid-1960s, and who created several new characters to boot, notably 'Uncle

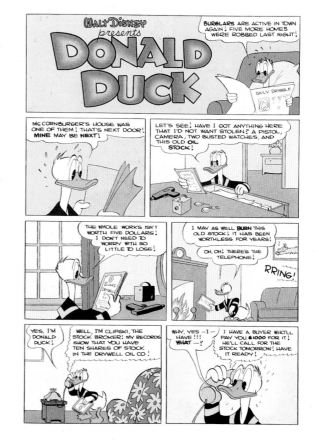

Scrooge', a 'fowl miser'. His stories were witty and well structured, while his rendering style was beautifully fluid and upbeat – perfect for its purpose.[10] Meanwhile, mouse duties were performed by the talented Floyd Gottfredson, who adapted his splendid Mickey Mouse newspaper strip for the comic. Both creators are today credited with producing the 'definitive' versions of their characters, though neither was given any recognition at the time (see below).

The Disney craze soon inspired comics starring other animated cartoon characters, notably those from the movie and TV shows produced by Warner Brothers, MGM, Walter Lantz and Hanna-Barbera. Again, Dell were in the forefront, hatching a particularly lucrative licensing deal with Warners, which resulted in *Looney Tunes and Merrie Melodies* in 1941 (complete with a regular final panel bearing the words 'That's All Folks!'). Titles devoted to individual characters in the comic followed, including *Bugs Bunny* (1942), *Porky Pig* (1942) and *Daffy Duck* (1953). Some strips were original stories, while others were adaptations of classic cartoons (commonly directed by the great Tex Avery).[11]

Despite these media crossovers, arguably the greatest funny animal creation was unique to comics: Pogo the Possum.[12] His creator, Walt Kelly, had been a Disney animator, and had also worked on the *Looney Tunes* comic. Pogo was first featured in *Animal Comics* (Dell, 1941) and then became the star of *Pogo Comics* (Dell) in 1946. He and his friends Albert the Alligator, Howland Owl, Churchy La Femme and all the other residents of Okefenokee Swamp had plenty of knockabout fun, but most interestingly, they behaved the way people would

Top left: Covers, *Looney Tunes and Merrie Melodies* (Dell, 1944 and 1946), featuring an exhortation by Bugs Bunny to 'Buy More War Bonds'. Art: Leon Schlesinger. Above right: Pages from *The Pogo Party* (Simon and Schuster, 1956). Art/script: Walt Kelly. Starring Pogo the Possum: a strip that grew in sophistication over the years, and made the unusual transition from comic to newspaper strip. Above: Cover, *Caspar the Friendly Ghost* (Harvey, 1953). Art: Anon. One of the better 'kid' comics. Below right: Panel from *I Love Lucy* (Dell, 1955). Art/script: Anon. One of the many TV show adaptations.

behave if guided more by nature and instinct than by man-made custom. The strip's fascination was in the characters' casual attitude to eating each other; to the way leadership developed among them; how they defined their moral ground; and generally, how they got along with each other. Finally, Pogo went on to become an internationally syndicated newspaper strip, when the characters took on a more overtly political aspect, becoming alternately defenders of civil rights and the environment, and opponents of censorship.

Another major genre that appealed to younger readers were the 'kid comics'. Again, these had a long line of predecessors in the newspapers, stretching back to the Katzenjammers (who themselves became the subject for a regular comic from 1945). The leading publisher in the field was unquestionably Harvey Comics, who had a string of hits including *Little Audrey* (1952), *Little Dot* (1955), *Little Lotta* (1955) and *Richie Rich* (1960). They also developed a variant on the kid theme with their comics about supernatural juveniles, including, most famously, *Caspar the Friendly Ghost* (1952), and his two main follow-ups, *Spooky the Tuff Little Ghost* (1955) and *Wendy the Good Little Witch* (1960). Other publishers too had their 'kid' successes. Dell, for example, had *Little Lulu* (1945), which wittily pictured a neighbourhood through a child's eyes; Standard had *Dennis the Menace* (1953) – no relation to the British character of the same name – about a blond-haired troublemaker who never gets punished; and, finally, DC Comics had *Sugar and Spike* (1956), about a boy and girl too young to talk, but old enough to get up to mischief.

Although it was true that these children's comics (the funny animal and kid titles) dominated the humour market in terms of numbers, the more adult readers of comics were never forgotten.[13] There was a parallel market aimed at a mixed-age readership, and this had two main expressions. Firstly, comics reprinted from newspaper strips continued to hold their own, while in

time the most popular characters had comics devoted to them consisting of original material. Hits included *Popeye* (Dell, 1941), *Joe Palooka* (Harvey, 1945), *Blondie* (1950) and *Dagwood* (1950). These were joined by newer characters that had debuted in newspapers. The most celebrated example was probably George Baker's *Sad Sack* (Harvey, 1949), which originally ran in the services newspaper *Yank*: it started out as a fairly acid commentary on army life (the title came from the phrase 'sad sack o' shit'), but was progressively toned down in its comic book form.

Secondly, for a more mixed-age readership, there were other kinds of media crossovers. For example, cartoon characters were not the only ones to make the switch from the screen to comics: real life American comedians were given the same treatment. TV shows like *Bilko, I Love Lucy, The Beverley Hillbillies* and *Bewitched* were also adapted, as were movies starring 'The Three Stooges' and 'Abbot and Costello'. These titles were instantly recognizable for their vivid photo-covers, but rarely captured the flavour of the screen originals.

American comics also catered specifically to teenagers. By far the most popular teen title was *Archie* (Archie

Comics, 1942), about a squeaky-clean, freckled, youth and his smalltown courtships. Its formula of rivalry within a teen gang, consisting of Archie, his side-kick Jughead, his competitor in love Reggie, and two sexy girls Betty and Veronica, set a template for a slew of other comics to follow, including *Andy* (Ace, 1948), *Ernie* (Ace, 1948) and *Dudley* (Standard, 1949). As one historian has written: 'Adolescents had only recently been discovered to be a separate tribe. Publishers, film producers, and other entrepreneurs looked at adolescents and saw a large segment of the population whose antics and rituals could be exploited for entertainment purposes, and who had money of their own to spend.'[14]

Teenagers were also the main target market for the satire genre, which really took off in the 1950s. The comic that revolutionized this particular field was *Mad* (1952), published by a company called Entertaining Comics (EC), which was run by William Gaines, son of Max, and which had already become notorious for its line of horror comics (see Chapter 3). *Mad*'s creator, and contributing editor for the first twenty-eight issues, was Harvey Kurtzman, one of the most influential figures in the history of humorous comics: 'The style I developed for *Mad*...', he wrote later, 'was necessarily thoughtful under the rowdy surface. Satire and parody work best when what you're talking about is accurately targeted; or, to put it another way, satire and parody work only when you reveal a fundamental flaw or untruth in your subject...the satirist/parodist tries not just to entertain his audience, but to remind it of what the real world is like.'[15]

Under Kurtzman's guidance, *Mad* started by sending up other comics: Starchie, Superduperman, Mickey Rodent and others made appearances, and were greeted with glee among readers. When targets from comics ran out, there were always movie stars, pop singers, politicians and even British royals.

This kind of iconoclasm was unusual enough, but *Mad* was also notable for the quality of its artwork. The EC stable included such luminaries as Wally Wood and Bill Elder, though perhaps the king of *Mad*-patented comedy was an occasional contributor, Basil Wolverton. His grotesque rendering of faces, every blemish highlighted in loving detail, was outstanding for its eccentricity, and much-imitated by up-and-coming cartoonists.

The *Mad* formula that developed in time included a self-mocking mix of strips, cartoons and fake adverts, all delighting in sending up the status quo. However, for some members of the establishment, it went too far. *Mad* was so cutting edge that it got caught up in the censorship campaign surrounding horror comics in the mid-1950s (see Chapter 3). This resulted in a Code being introduced in 1955 which imposed a suffocating set of standards designed to curtail adult themes. Most comedy comics survived unscathed (Dell did not even have to submit their titles for inspection), but *Mad* had to change its format. From 1954 onwards it was a black-and-white magazine.

Although the change from comic to magazine was a risky one in a commercial sense, *Mad* went from strength to strength in the 1960s. It added new creators to the team, most notably Don Martin ('*Mad*'s maddest artist'). There was also a monthly British version of the title from 1959, which anglicized some of the more obtuse American gags and increasingly added material by British creators. As a magazine, *Mad*'s satire in the 1960s and early 1970s became more focused, and occasionally more cynical, with many bitter references to the war in Vietnam. It is arguable whether it was ever politically subversive, but there is no question that its influence on the revolutionary 'underground' comics was profound (see Chapter 5).[16]

Mad was also responsible for spawning a variety of copyists – none of which garnered quite the same

Above left: Cover, *Life with Archie* (Archie Comics, 1961), starring the unfathomably attractive all-American teenager. Art: Anon, possibly Bill Vigoda. Far left and left: Examples from *Mad* (EC Comics, 1953 and 1964), a comic that marked a defining moment not just in the history of comedy comics, but of modern satire in general. Art/script for 'Superduperman': Wally Wood and Harvey Kurtzman. Fake soup advert by the *Mad* team. *Archie* and *Mad* were the opposite poles of the teenage market, one essentially conservative, the other an iconoclastic poke in the eye.

This page: Various examples from early *Mad*s (all EC Comics). Far right: Cover, *Mad* (1954). Art: Basil Wolverton. Below: 'Distinctive Picket Lines', *Mad* (1960). Art: George Woodbridge. Script: Frank Jacobs. Below right, in circle: Alfred E Neuman the *Mad* mascot. Art: Anon. Bottom left: Cover, *Mad* (1953). Art/script: Harvey Kurtzman. Bottom right: 'East Side Story', *Mad* (1963), which cast Kruschev and other Eastern bloc leaders as a street gang. Art: Mort Drucker. Script: Frank Jacobs. *Mad* took a magazine format in 1955 to avoid censorship, which meant black-and-white interiors. Nevertheless, the mix of art that was cartoony and 'realistic', sometimes including photographic backgrounds, kept things interesting visually.

BOOB AND CARNAL AND TAD AND ALAS

Opposite: Cover, *Mad* (1963). Art: Norman Mingo. Castro lights up. Top: 'Bob and Carnal and Tad and Alas', *Mad* (1970), a movie parody. Art: Mort Drucker. Top right: Cover, *Mad* (1969). Art: Norman Mingo. A dig at patriotism at the height of the Vietnam War. Above centre, above and right: examples from *Panic* (EC Comics), a sister comic to *Mad* that never garnered the same following. 'I Touched a Flying Saucer,' *Panic* (1954). Art/script: Jack Davis. Cover, *Panic* (1965). Art/script: Jack Davis. 'Tick Dracy', *Panic* (1954). Art/script: Will Elder.

following. Titles included *Crazy, Eh!* and *Whack*, all 1953; *Flip, Wild* and *Panic*, all 1954 (the latter a sister title from EC) and Harvey Kurtzman's *Trump* (1957) and *Help!* (1960). Later on, they were joined by *Brand Echh* (1967) and *Crazy* (1973). They may not all have been particularly hilarious, but put together they represented a new American comics genre.

Yet despite all these notable comedy titles, and taking the American humour industry as a whole, it was still true that exploitation of artists and writers was as much of a problem as in Britain. The traditional American working method was to split creative task down among artists, writers, inkers and letterers, and this both guaranteed anonymity and militated against collective action. Unions were near impossible to organize (though some attempts were made), and in general comics creators were considered factory workers on an assembly line. Like in Britain, pay was by the page, with no royalties or rights over characters. (The team behind *Mad* were more fortunate than most: standards at EC were relatively high, and artists always signed their work.)

Examples of individuals who were taken advantage of are endless. The only name to appear on the Dell-published Disney comics, for instance, was Disney's, even though the real work was being done by others. The aforementioned Carl Barks, perhaps the greatest of all Disney artists, laboured anonymously for much of his working life, and saw no extra money for the characters he created (a tale that is even more galling when it is remembered that they were to become the subject for lucrative cartoons and merchandising). It is a sad reflection on the industry as a whole that for every Leo Baxendale in Britain there were several Carl Barks-es in the United States.

Before we leave the subject of the British and American comedy comics, it is necessary to take stock of their impact on society's perception of comics as a medium. For put together, the industries of the two nations constituted a major force in children's, and teenagers', leisure, and the immense popularity of their products forced the adult world to come to some sort of reckoning. Put simply, youngsters were involving themselves in something over which adults had no control, and for the reason above there seemed to be a need for people to have an opinion. Comics thus became a discussion topic in newspaper opinion columns and on radio chat shows: the question was, were they 'a good thing' or not?[17]

Unsurprisingly, no consensus emerged, and in time two opposing positions took shape. On the one hand, the criticisms that had once been levelled against the pre-First World War adult comics were now modified for their new juvenile offspring. As ever, stories in pictures were maintained to be innately inferior to those in words, and it was now argued that children's ability to learn to read would be retarded by an over-familiarity with comics. This view was supposedly corroborated by the fact that strips now contained fewer words than ever before (at least the old complaint that close type strained the readers' eyesight was no longer tenable). The pre-1914

prejudice against comics for being 'reading matter for the working class' held fast. Especially in the case of children, it was maintained that comics were not 'improving', were essentially 'lowbrow', and reflected badly on the reader's background and intellect. In the case of the American comics that came to Britain, these were also seen as a manifestation of a vulgar and TV-obsessed culture. It was a short step from here to arguing that comics might actually be harmful: undoubtedly a widespread view, though never theorized to any coherent degree. Thus, many upper- and middle-class families refused to allow comics in the household (a move which only made them more attractive to youngsters, who inevitably found ways of stashing comics outside the home).

Critics also began to attack comics for more specifically ideological reasons. The 1950s backlash that resulted in the Comics Code mainly affected adventure comics, though, as we have seen, *Mad* was briefly a target. In the 1960s, criticism was focused on the humour comics for being violent, sexist and racist.[18] In Britain, *The Beano* was particularly singled out for its lack of black characters, its emphasis on violent confrontations and the prevalence of corporal punishment (especially scenes where mischievous characters ended up being chased by teachers with canes or dads with huge slippers). In the United States, humour comics were similarly attacked, and were additionally prone to criticism from the Left for being conveyors of capitalist propaganda. This was especially true, it was said, of the Disney titles: for example, a quote from one famed critique of the Carl Barks comics: 'So there is really no history in these comics. For gold forgotten from the previous episode cannot be used for the following one. If it could, it would connote a past with influence over the present, and reveal capital and the whole process of accumulation of surplus value as the explanation of Uncle Scrooge's fortune.'[19]

Yet, there was another side to this story of hardening attitudes. For simultaneously, an altogether more liberal approach towards comics developed. In particular, because they were now being produced for an exclusively younger age range, they were tolerated, and even encouraged, as part of 'childhood'. They may have had their faults, the thinking went, but, after all, they were

This page: A selection of covers to *Mad* copyists. Above: *Not Brand Echh* (Marvel Comics, 1968). Art: Marie Severin. Right: *Sick* (Crestwood, 1966). Art: Joe Simon. *Crazy* (Marvel Comics, 1976). Art: Anon. *Arrgh!* (Marvel Comics, 1974). Art: Tom Sutton. None of the more recent titles were particularly inspired, but most did good business nevertheless.

1. Quote from 'Editorial Message', *New Comics* (National Allied Publications, 1935), no 1.

2. Denis Gifford, *The International Book of Comics* (London, WH Smith, rev edn, 1990), p 29.

3. The Amalgamated Press additionally tried to penetrate the nursery market (their biggest hit here was *Rainbow*, 1914, with the character 'Tiger Tim').

4. Leo Baxendale, *On Comedy: The Beano and Ideology* (Reaper Books, 1989), p 9.

5. See Joseph McAleer, *Popular Reading and Publishing in Britain 1914–1950* (Oxford University Press, 1992), Chapter 6 (pp 162–205), and Paul Harris (ed), *The DC Thomson Bumper Book of Fun* (Edinburgh, Paul Harris Publications, 1977).

6. One English publisher, Gerald Swan, emulated the look of American comics in his own line, which included *New Funnies* (1940) and *Topical Funnies* (1940). He did not use American artists, however, and in fact many of his contributors were moonlighters from the Amalgamated Press.

7. The Dirty Comics also included stories about celebrities and gangsters, and could occasionally be subversive by showing criminals in a glamorous light.

8. *New Comics* was the brainchild of one Major Malcolm Wheeler-Nicholson, an ex-cavalry officer. His company, National Allied Publications, later became National Periodical Publications, and after that, DC Comics.

9. Dell took its name from the first syllable of the name of its founder, George Dellacorte, an industry pioneer who in 1929 had published *The Funnies*.

10. See Mike Barrier, *Carl Barks and the Art of the Comic Book* (New York, M Lilien, 1981).

11. Mention should also be made of the various funny animal parodies of superhero comics, (the top American adventure genre – see Chapter 3). These generally dull characters included Super Mouse, Hoppy the Marvel Bunny, Super Rabbit, and Mighty Mouse (adapted from an animated series).

12. There are two excellent sources on Pogo: Norman Hale, *All-Natural Pogo* (New York, Thinker's Books, 1991); and Walt Kelly, *Ten Ever-Loving Blue-Eyed Years with Pogo* (New York, Simon and Schuster, 1959).

13. Which is not to say that adults did not read children's comics. Far from it: although no figures are available, it is well known that titles such as *Little Lulu* and *Pogo* had a large grown-up following. Also, many creators in the children's market bore in mind that parents would be cajoled into reading stories, and so tried to keep them entertained.

14. Ron Goulart, *Over 50 Years of American Comic Books* (New York, Publications International, 1986) p 155.

15. Harvey Kurtzman, *From Aargh! to Zap!* (New York, Prentice Hall Press, 1991), p 41.

16. On *Mad* see Maria Reidelbach's excellent history *Completely Mad* (New York, Little Brown and Co, 1991).

17. It was George Orwell who started the debate in earnest with his essay 'The Boys' Weeklies' in *Horizon* magazine (March 1940). (Incidentally, he was also a classic anti-American, peppering his work with prejudiced comments about American cultural vulgarity.) Since then, the 'value' of comics has been the subject for numerous newspaper articles and radio broadcasts. The best sources in book form are Nicholas Tucker (ed) *Suitable for Children?* (London, Chatto and Windus, 1976), which discusses very sketchily some of the main prejudices, and Martin Barker's superb analysis *Comics: Ideology, Power and the Critics* (Manchester University Press, 1989), which re-evaluates criticisms through close readings of the comics themselves.

18. Racism in comics should be seen in context. Only in the 1960s did complaints really become vociferous: in the 1930s, people rarely batted an eyelid at gross caricatures of blacks, Arabs and Orientals. Denis Gifford's *Encyclopaedia of Comic Characters* (London, Longman, 1987) lists some hilariously un-politically correct entries from the pre-Second World War era, such as Little Black Sambo, Our Nigs, and The Piccininies.

19. A Dorfman and A Mattelart, *How To Read Donald Duck* (New York, International General, 1975, rev edn 1991) p 79. The authors were in fact Chilean and Belgian respectively, though their ideas were taken up enthusiastically by the American left.

20. *Ibid* p 29.

21. Some defenders of the medium were even bold enough to suggest that comics, rather than being a hindrance to reading, were in fact a spur. However, there was no proof for this until serious studies were undertaken later. As a result, comics have increasingly been used in schools as a learning tool in the 1980s and 1990s.

a part of a particular, and special, time in life: a time symbolic of a state of innocence. This romanticism was a legacy from the Victorian era, when children began to be sentimentalized as angelic creatures to be protected from the temptations of a vicious world: later, it was manifested in ways such as the strictly controlled 'Children's Television' of the British Broadcasting Corporation, and, in America, the hokey naivety of the 'Our Gang' cinema serials.

In this way, comics came to be seen as harmless fun: a way for children to let off steam, and to give vent to their 'natural' sense of adventure and mischief. There were limits, of course: it was important that the juvenile reader should not encounter any semblance of the adult world (any hint of sex, realistic violence or adult relationships would have shattered the illusion). Similarly, politics was out: as one comics critic has written, 'Inasmuch as the sweet, docile child can be sheltered effectively from the evils of existence, from the petty rancors, the hatreds, and the political or ideological contamination of his elders, any attempt to politicise the sacred domain of childhood threatens to introduce perversity where once there reigned happiness, innocence and fantasy.'[20] Instead, comics were coopted into a vision of childhood that included climbing trees, flicking catapults and playing tag.[21]

Confusingly, then, comics were sentimentalized one hand, and criticized on the other. Their stock in society could not be said to have risen since their genesis: they still were not 'respectable', and as a result teachers felt perfectly at liberty to confiscate them in schools, and parents to ban them from the home. Yet because they were now orientated towards a juvenile market, they were also 'winked at' and tolerated. It was an odd set of contradictions, and one which children's comics never quite escaped until the present.

Three

Action and adventure

Opposite: 'Dan Dare, Pilot of the Future', from *The Eagle* (Hulton Press, 1959). Art/script: Frank Hampson. Dashing Dan was the archetypal British adventure hero, a symbol, perhaps, of the country's already redundant dream of leading the space race. Right: Covers to *Doomed Division* (IPC, 1968), art: Anon; *Crime Suspenstories* (EC Comics, 1953), art: Jack Kamen; *Spider-Man* (Marvel Comics, 1964), art: Steve Ditko. The adventure genre basically entailed stories aimed at boys and young men.

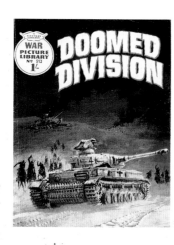

The stereotype of a comic as something inherently 'comical' was one that dominated the initial emergence of the form in both Britain and America. Nevertheless once the psychological leap had been made that an 'adventure comic' was not necessarily a non-sequitur, the effect on the industry was transforming: as a result, any new stereotype would now have to incorporate the 'Biff! Pow!' of fisticuffs and the 'Bratt-att-att!' of machine-gun fire. This being the case, the adventure comics were the next stage in the medium's evolution, and their heyday can be dated to roughly the years between 1940 and 1970: the period we will be covering here.

In Britain, adventure only became widely popular after 1950, even though it had been the basis for a long tradition of British story papers; and had been present in newspaper strips since the First World War. Artistically speaking, the genre made new demands on comics. Invariably, the style would have to be 'realistic' in order to carry the story, and this required a new attention to detail. For young readers, meticulous accuracy was a large part of the spell: as many artists have testified, the sin of getting the turret-shape wrong on a tank, or the type of sword wrong for a particular period, could be greeted by complaining letters. Cinematic techniques also now became appropriate in a way that had not been previously considered: panoramas, close-ups, long-shots and exciting 'cuts' increasingly became the action comic's stock in trade. Whether this was a heuristic development or originated as a steal from the movies is still debated.[1] Whatever the case, when the demands of authenticity and

cinematic structuring were wed together, the results added up to a new level of sophistication in the medium.

Commercially, the genre was dominated at first by the same companies that had made humour their own: DC Thomson and IPC (International Publishing Corporation). They now competed as hard for this sector of the market as anywhere else, and were fortunate in that they had virtually no American competition until the 1960s. As we have seen, official distribution of American comics in Britain did not begin until 1959, though some titles did enter the country via airbases and ports, while others were reprinted in black-and-white by small British publishers (particularly active in the adventure field were Thorpe and Porter, Miller and Son and the Arnold Book Company).[2] In the 1960s, however, the two majors found themselves increasingly challenged by the American companies DC Comics (no relation to the Scottish giant) and Marvel. These would eventually come to eclipse the British publishers altogether: a progression which took several decades, and which corresponded with the overall decline in comics circulations (something we shall come back to in chapters 6 and 7).[3]

The first of the new British comics built on the heritage of the story papers, and proved that action yarns in pictures could be equally successful as humour. As such, they also perpetuated the essentially male market opened up by the story papers (a trend that was only bucked later with the sudden flowering of a sister comics industry orientated towards girls). These papers in the 1920s and 1930s were dominated by the 'Big 5' of *Skipper, The Hotspur,*

Above: Covers to the three most famous inter-war story papers (all DC Thomson): *The Rover* (1929), *The Wizard* (1927) and *The Hotspur* (1937). Art: all Anon. Their imperialist tone so appalled George Orwell that he penned a famous essay denouncing them. Right: 'Morgyn the Mighty', *The Rover* (1929). Art/script: Anon. The tradition of 'muscular Christianity' was a strong influence on stories of this kind.

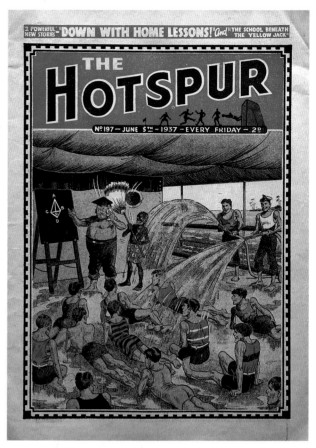

The Wizard, *The Rover* and *Adventure*, which were all published by DC Thomson before they transferred their energies to comics per se, and were 'illustrated text' publications, with the same production values as *The Beano*. They established a formula for the action genre which relied on a clipped, punchy writing style and swashbuckling subject matter. Indeed, war became their single most popular theme: their tone was, perhaps inevitably, xenophobic and imperialist, and fed into a tradition of empire tales, personified by *The Boy's Own Paper* (itself a reaction to the 'penny dreadfuls' discussed in chapter 1). As such, they were famously savaged in a press article by George Orwell for perpetuating conservative values.[4]

The transition to a new form of adventure publication, which emphasized sequential panel narratives, was not simply a question of the story papers adding strips, though this was arguably the major influence. It was also true that increasingly humour comics were featuring adventure stories, in order to add variety. By the 1940s, *The Dandy* and *The Beano* had several, while the outstanding strips 'The Road to Rome' and 'Sons of the Sword', both by Reg Perrott, appeared incongruously in *Mickey Mouse Weekly*. Also, there was the influence of action strip cartoons in the newspapers, which had started to appear during the First World War. Finally, comics from America were becoming more and more popular, which emphasized adventure far more than humour (as we shall see in a moment).

Thus, through the 1940s, small publishers began to experiment with adventure comics in an effort to carve a place in the market. Titles like *The Comet* and *Sun* (both Allen, 1946–7) played with action formulas, and in some cases even mixed in American material and ideas. However, none found significant success, and the story papers continued to be infinitely better sellers. Evidently, it would take something extraordinary to smash the stereotype of what a comic should be.

The breakthrough came in 1950 with the appearance of *The Eagle*, published by the Hulton Press. In many ways it was a revelation: the tabloid size, the unprecedented production values, the high price (3d), the exquisite artwork and, above all, the stunning photogravure colour all marked it out as different in quality both to the comics that had come before, and to the DC Thomson story papers. The other thing that made it unusual was the use of a science fiction drama as its cover story.

This page: More examples from *The Eagle* (Hulton Press). Left and below: 'Dan Dare' (1952 and 1951). Art: Frank Hampson. Below left: A model of the Mekon, Dare's arch-enemy. (Christies Photo Archive). This was one of the many models used by artists on the comic as rendering aids. Below right: centre page spread (1952). Art: Anon. This features one of the very popular 'cutaway' diagrams, plus an episode of 'Tintin' (art/script: Hergé).

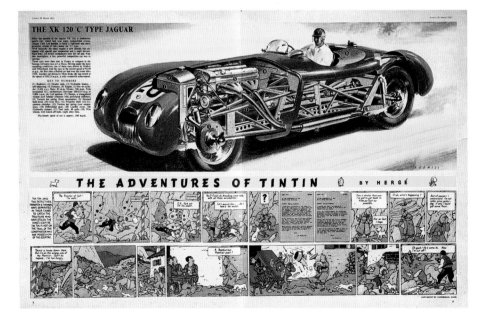

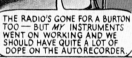
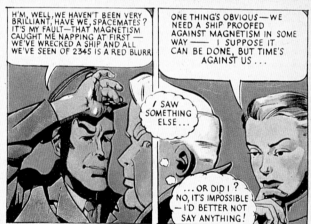

CONTINUED

2

This was the remarkable 'Dan Dare – Pilot of the Future', written and drawn by Frank Hampson, chronicling the galaxy-hopping adventures of a stiff upper-lipped English spaceman. It was Dare's mission to speed through space and do battle with any alien who might have half a mind to colonize earth; a job which, give or take a few punch-ups and necessary acts of extermination, he performed with courtesy and charm. Such was the attention to detail on this strip that models of spaceships and interiors were built specially in order for the artists to have an accurate representation of proportions and shadow to work from, while scientific credibility was provided by the input of space experts such as Arthur C Clarke.

Yet in other ways, *The Eagle* was certainly an heir to the story paper tradition. The tone was basically imperialist (dashing Dan was in the business of 'conquering' the universe, while his enemy, the Mekon, a green alien with a huge head, had a suspiciously Chinese physiognomy), and was steadfastly 'decent' in the mould of *The Boy's Own Paper*. Indeed, religion was never far away, and took centre stage in strips like 'The Road of Courage', about the life of Jesus. Also in common with the story papers, and somewhat in contrast to the moral message, it was war that constituted the single most featured subject, with 'cutaway' illustrations of tanks and battleships proving particularly popular.

Thus it was difficult to avoid the impression that this was a publication with a mission. And indeed it was. For *The Eagle* was co-founded by Hampson and a vicar, the Reverend Marcus Morris, as a response to the emergence of supposedly delinquency-inducing American horror comics (see below), and was intended to provide a wholesome, Christian alternative for the nation's male youth.[5] Interestingly, then, this explanation of the comic's genesis echoes that of the story papers published in response to the penny dreadfuls in the previous century.

Whatever its 'improving' intentions, *The Eagle* was a soaring success. Far from being restricted to a middle-class audience, as its publishers had expected, the comic picked up a sizeable working-class following, and was soon selling nearly a million per issue. In the process, Dan Dare became a national hero, inspiring an enormous quantity of toy merchandising, and even a radio serial: his influence on future science fiction movies, novels and, of course, comics would be very considerable.

In short, *The Eagle* made adventure commercially viable, and in the process spawned a flood of imitators. As DC Thomson and the Amalgamated Press/IPC entered the fray in earnest, so a circulation war was initiated in much the same fashion as had happened with the humour comics. Once again the companies went toe to toe, producing adventure anthologies in *The Eagle* mould. These, however, were typically designed for a more wide-ranging readership. Consequently, they were less expensive, and generally produced in the same format, and on the same cheap paper, as *The Beano* and its ilk. Similarly, the tone tended to be much tougher than *The Eagle*, and more down to earth – in other words, death and destruction without the moralizing.

The Amalgamated Press were first to go on the offensive with *Lion* (1952), which featured 'Captain Condor', an early and very entertaining Dare rip-off, and the sibling title *Tiger* (1954). When the Amalgamated Press became IPC (the International Publishing Corporation), these were followed by *Valiant* (1962), *Hurricane* (1964), *Jag* (1968) and *Jet* (1971), all of which featured a mix of war, sport, western, science fiction, pirate and 'jungle' stories. DC Thomson hit back in two ways: by turning their old story papers into comics (*The Hotspur* and *The Wizard* went this way in 1959 and 1970 respectively, while *The Rover* and *Adventure* were merged into one comic in 1961); and by launching new titles, the most famous of which were *Victor* (1961) and *Hornet* (1963).

All these anthologies were much of a muchness, formularized adventure for a bloodthirsty pre-teen audience. War was far and away the pre-eminent subject, and the key characters were often soldiers: 'Trelawney of the Guards' in *Lion*, 'Union Jack Jackson' in *The Hotspur*, and, perhaps most famously, 'Captain Hurricane' in *Valiant* (a man so hard that he sorts out the enemy with his bare fists). Similarly, intricate cross sections of

Opposite: A page from 'Dan Dare', *The Eagle* (Hulton Press, 1951). Art/script: Frank Hampson. Featured are some of the supporting characters, including Dare's ever-dependable chum, Digby. Right: 'Eagle Club News', *The Eagle* (1952), an article about the fan club, one of the earliest of its kind. Far right: 'Captain Hurricane', *Valiant* (Fleetway, 1966). Art/script: Anon. By the 1960s, adventure comics had gone downmarket: war had taken over as the dominant theme, and obnoxious characters such as this had overtaken the more 'decent' Dan Dare in popularity.

A new bike is waiting to be won!

EAGLE CLUB NEWS
SPOTLIGHT ON COMPETITION WINNER

If anyone tells you that the days of getting a lucky break are dead and gone don't you believe it! EAGLE Club member Bruce Blackburn Elliott can prove that they still come along. Bruce was a prizewinner in one of our recent competitions for which he had to draw a Lockheed Constellation airliner. His prize was a trip in a TWA Constellation and an introduction to Peter V. Nelson, a young designer who builds display fleet models for TWA. Mr Nelson offered Bruce a job and of course he jumped at it! In the photographs you can see Bruce working on the models. Peter Nelson is watching him.

CAPTAIN HERCULES HURRICANE'S FACE TURNED PURPLE AND HIS EYES BULGED AS A TERRIBLE "RAGIN' FURY" TOOK HOLD OF HIM!

GREAT SUFFERING SEA-SLUGS! I'VE HAD ENOUGH! ALMOST ELECTROCUTED... SHELLED BY THE JERRIES... AND NOW PRODDED WITH A SCREWDRIVER! SO HELP ME, SOMEBODY WILL SUFFER FOR THIS!

A FLEETWAY **SUPER** LIBRARY

YESTERDAY'S HEROES

FRONT LINE Series No.10   1/6d

Top Sergeant **IRONSIDE** – tough as they come!

132 PAGES OF ACTION PICTURES!

Above and right: Cover and interior strip, *Yesterday's Heroes* (Fleetway, 1967). Art/script: Anon. Pocket-size titles like this flourished in the 1960s, and refought the Second World War every issue, complete with luridly xenophobic language. Below: Pages from two of the more unusual adventure strips from the period both from *Valiant* (Fleetway): 'Janus Stark' (1973), about a nineteenth-century escape artist (art: Solano Lopez), and 'The Steel Claw' (1966) concerning an independently minded metal hand (art: Jesus Blasco).

weaponry and other military arcana, in *The Eagle* mould, were always popular fillers.

Yet, for all their hackneyed content, the anthologies could provide a home to some surprisingly inventive – nay, surreal – material. For in publishers' eagerness to gain an advantage over each other, creators were occasionally encouraged to experiment. Fresh 'angles' on the adventure theme included: 'The Steel Claw' (*Valiant*), about a disembodied steel hand; 'The Ragged Racer' (*Hurricane*), concerning a 'wild man wonder athlete' who lives in a cave in Wales; and 'Janus Stark' (*Valiant*), chronicling the adventures of a 'rubber-boned escapologist'. For modern-day connoisseurs of British comics, such macabre masterpieces provide endless amusement.

Whatever the appeal of the various titles, it was clear by the mid-1960s that there were too many of them. Though there was some outstanding artwork by individuals like Hampson, Frank Bellamy, Don Lawrence and Ron Embleton, most artists tended to be hacks, and it was perhaps inevitable that the overall standard should suffer. As had happened in the humour genre, the desire by publishers to dominate the market by expanding the quantity of their weekly output led to weaker storytelling and perfunctory art. Weirdness aside, most strips were so clichéd, and so dependent upon 'potboiler' story lines to drag them from week to week, that even the dumbest young reader would not be satisfied for long. If there was a crisis in adventure comics by the 1970s, it was partly the publishers' own doing.

Arguably this situation could have been ameliorated if pay and working conditions for creators had been more reasonable. Unfortunately, however, the same rules applied to adventure comics as to humour. Indeed, if anything, rates of pay were worse on adventure titles

because of the extra attention to detail involved: this took time, for which creators were not paid extra. While DC Thomson were able to exploit their non-union policy, so IPC developed a habit of hiring cheap foreign artists to do the work, which only exacerbated the situation.[6] Understandably, many creators were worn down by the system in the long run: Frank Hampson, for example, left the industry in disgust when he realized he had no control over his creations, and would not earn royalties from them. He said later 'Dare has been, for me, a long and bitter personal tragedy.'[7]

For all the underlying problems, adventure had one major advantage over the humour industry. It was more amenable to diversification. This is what saved it from stagnation in the 1960s, and pushed it on to even greater success. In time, the anthologies were joined by an ever-increasing number of titles devoted to a particular sub-genre.[8]

Inevitably, the subject of war was the main beneficiary of this strategy. It was a logical step for DC Thomson and IPC to launch lines devoted to the theme, since it had long been a mainstay for anthologies. As before, the Second World War was the focus. Particularly popular were: the pocket-size series *Commando Library* (DC Thomson, 1961); and *War Picture Library* and *Battle Picture Library* (both Amalgamated Press /IPC, 1958 and 1961 respectively), which established a formula of longer, often quite complex, stories, with above-average art (commonly by European artists). More specialist war tastes were catered to by *Air Ace Picture Library* (IPC, 1960) and *War at Sea* (IPC, 1962).

All the war comics more or less continued to trade in plot lines that stereotyped Germans as Hitler-worshipping thugs, the Japanese as screeching sadists and the British as whiter-than-white warriors capable of beating off the most fearful odds (Dan Dares in uniform). This formula was never really challenged until the 1970s and the arrival of *Battle* (IPC, 1977), which featured more unorthodox material, such as 'Charley's War', which expressed the horror and fear of the trenches in the First World War through the eyes of a young working-class volunteer.[9]

Sport also took off as a genre. Again, most strips were about dashing British heroes, commonly pitted against

Right and far right: Cover and interior panel from 'Roy of the Rovers', *Tiger and Hurricane* (Fleetway, 1969). Art/script: Joe Colquhoun. Roy was another squeaky-clean British hero, in fact a throwback to the 1950s: an ambassador for the game, he was the natural choice for Rovers captain. The strip helped establish sport as a viable sub-genre. Below and below right: Interior strip and cover from *Battle* (Fleetway, 1981). Art/script for 'Charley's War': Joe Colquhoun and Pat Mills. This late example of a war-based title was remarkable for its downbeat tone: this strip told the grim story of a recruit in the First World War, and eschewed conventional heroics.

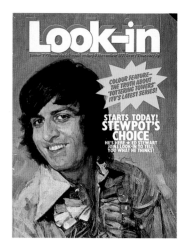

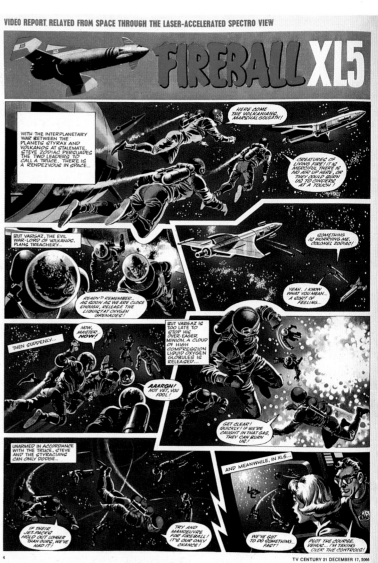

foreign foes (sport as 'war by other means'). Soccer was a mainstay, especially in the late 1960s and early 1970s (due to England's World Cup victory and the successes of various 'classic' league clubs), and giveaway 'league ladders' were a popular gimmick. The most famous soccer hero was 'Roy of the Rovers', he of the unstoppable 'left-foot thunderbolt', who had been a cover star of *Tiger* since the mid 1950s, and who got his own title in 1976 (published by IPC). There were others, including most interestingly those created by Dan Maxted for comics like *Scorcher* (IPC, 1970) – a creator whose crowd scenes commonly featured individuals making comments like 'See the bend on that ball!'.

Educational comics similarly took their own direction. The leader of the pack was undoubtedly *Look and Learn* (IPC/Fleetway, 1962), which owed much to the high-production values, and equally high moral tone, of *The Eagle*. Parents bought it for their children, particularly their sons, because of the strips about classical and historical figures, and the 'How it Works' features on subjects like internal combustion engines. The kids, meanwhile, turned straight to the back pages for the remarkable science fiction strip by Don Lawrence, 'The Trigan Empire', a rip-roaring 'future-past' actioner with plenty of violence.

More populist in approach were the TV-inspired comics that blossomed in the 1960s; a boom that corresponded with the uptake of TV itself in British homes. The best was *TV Century 21* (City, 1965), which was devoted to strips about the Gerry Anderson puppet shows ('Captain Scarlet', 'Thunderbirds', 'Fireball XL5' and so on), and which had a cover made up to look like a futuristic newspaper. The artwork, by Frank Bellamy, Ron Embleton and Don Lawrence, among others, was often astounding, and had the effect of 'breathing life' into the marionettes.

The most popular of the other TV titles were: *TV Tornado* (City, 1967), which boasted 'Bonanza' and 'Voyage to the Bottom of the Sea'; *Countdown* (Polystyle, 1971), which featured 'Dr Who', 'UFO' and 'The Persuaders'; and *Look-In* (Independent Television, 1971), with 'Kung Fu', 'Worzel Gummidge' and 'Potty Time'. It is ironic that the medium later accused of destroying comics sales should simultaneously have provided such a boost.

In America, adventure comics traced to different roots, and were the result of the fusion between newspaper strips and pulp novels. The genesis of the former has been explored in Chapter 2; the latter were essentially books produced for a predominantly working-class readership on pulp paper. Between 1920 and 1930, they supplanted the old dime novels (see p 34), and introduced a new kind of sensationalist genre fiction, with categories like westerns, romance, crime and science fiction becoming particularly popular. Like the comic books that came later, they usually sold for ten cents and sported colourful, often lurid, covers.

Before the 1930s the syndicated newspaper strips were certainly dominated by humorous content, but the influence of pulp-style adventure was increasingly felt. There were sporadic early examples of drama strips,

perhaps the best known being Charles W Kahles's 'Hairbreadth Harry' (1906), which though essentially burlesque, nevertheless took its inspiration from nineteenth-century adventure fiction. Very fast-moving, and with a hero who specialized in hairbreadth rescues, the strip was an early pioneer of continuity: stories would end on cliffhanger situations with words such as 'Looks as if this operation calls for an encore'.

Later, more inventive strips appeared. Two notable examples dated to 1924. Roy Crane's 'Wash Tubbs' was about an optimistic adventurer and his friendship with the hardboiled Captain Easy, and was notable for its punch-ups and treasure hunts in exotic locations. The strip also featured some remarkable new effects, such as the use of mechanically achieved half-tones, which gave the drawings a unique range. Harold Gray's 'Little Orphan Annie' was an adventure variant on the 'kid strip' theme, about a tough little orphan taken under the wing of a rich industrialist. It was based on the movies of Mary Pickford, in content and in look – both stars boasted lustrous curls – though the 'Annie' stories always featured a conservative political subtext, and were commonly used to barrack the pro-welfare policies of the Democrats.

By challenging the notion that strips always had to be funny, these early examples opened the way for more melodramatic fare. In January 1929, the marriage between pulps and comic strips was formalized in spectacular fashion when two characters who had previously been confined to prose fiction appeared in newspaper strips. 'Tarzan', Edgar Rice Burrough's classic story of a primitive jungle hero 'raised by apes', and for many years a staple of the pulps, was transformed

Right: 'Tarzan' (United Feature Syndicate, c1938). Art/script: Burne Hogarth. An American newspaper strip success that helped to establish adventure as a genre in that country. Crucially, it represented the marriage of pulp fiction and comics art.

into strip form by artist Hal Foster, while Dick Calkins did the same for Philip Nowlan's futuristic 'Buck Rogers', about a twenty-fifth-century warrior and his battles with, among others, 'the ferocious tigermen of Mars' (a character who had debuted in the pulp *Amazing Stories*). These two were yarns on an epic scale, and ushered newspaper strips into a new era.

Indeed, other factors were conspiring to produce a boom in adventure material. As one historian has written: 'The stock market crash of Oct 1929, and the long depression that followed, helped guarantee that the new serious note of comics would not be just a passing fad. Readers wanted more than laughs; they also wanted images of strong men taking control of their world.'[10] The 1930s and 1940s thus saw the greatest expansion of the adventure category, accompanied by stylistic innovations which would shape the future comic industry.

Crime fighting was a particularly significant genre, and moved into the funny papers with Chester Gould's grim detective 'Dick Tracy' in 1931. The stories were ostensibly about a pistol-packing charmer and his battles with a roster of grotesque foes, including 'Flyface', 'Rhodent' and 'Mrs Pruneface'. However, they exhibited a new kind of hard-hitting realism dealing with contemporary themes; Gould was motivated by the crime wave during the prohibition era, and was fascinated by characters such as Al Capone and J Edgar Hoover. Pulp-writer Dashiell Hammett got into the act in 1934 with 'Secret Agent X-9', superbly illustrated in a film-noir style by Alex Raymond. Characters from the pulps were also adapted, notably Charlie Chan, the Oriental sleuth, who had already become a screen star when he was transferred to strip form by Alfred Andriola in 1938. Finally, in 1940, *The Spirit* by Will Eisner took the genre to new artistic heights.

Concerning the hardboiled adventures of a mysterious masked crime-fighter and his black sidekick 'Ebony White', the short stories were intelligently plotted and brilliantly drawn, and had an entire pull-out supplement devoted to them.

Other landmark strips included Dan Moore and Alex Raymond's science fiction saga 'Flash Gordon' (1934), about a blond-haired 'saviour of the universe' and his conflict with galactic tyrant 'Ming the Merciless' (the strip was intended as a rival to Buck Rogers, but was artistically in a different league); Milton Caniff's 'Terry and the Pirates' (1934), about a young adventurer in China; Lee Falk and Ray Moore's 'The Phantom' (1936), who had a mask and a secret identity, and was the first comics character to dress in tights; and Hal Foster's 'Prince Valiant' (1937), a handsome-looking Arthurian romance, strong on period detail. Of course, along with the diamonds there was an awful lot of dross; but generally speaking the 1930s and 1940s are seen as the 'golden age' of adventure strips.

Unsurprisingly, therefore, when comic books made their appearance in the mid-1930s, there was very soon pressure to include adventure material within their pages.[11] Indeed, many early examples of humorous anthologies included adventure strip reprints (even the seminal *Famous Funnies* carried Buck Rogers). The influence of the pulps was especially strong because many of the early publishers had started as pulp publishers: this was true of both the big companies that came to dominate comics, DC Comics and Marvel. Similarly, it was true that the writers were often pulp writers, and the artists commonly pulp-book cover illustrators.

Thus, the adventure comics developed a different

This page and opposite: A selection from the 'golden age' of American newspaper strips. Above: *The Spirit*, cover to the pull-out comics supplement of *Detroit News*, 1940. Art/script: Will Eisner. Below: Panel from 'Dick Tracy' (King Features Syndicate, 1949). Art/script: Chester Gould. Bottom left: Detail from 'The Phantom' (King Features Syndicate, c 1936). Art: Ray Moore. Below right: 'Flash Gordon' (King Features Syndicate, 1936). Art/script: Alex Raymond (known as 'the artist's artist'). Opposite: Excerpts from 'Dick Tracy' (1949) and 'The Spirit' (1946). Details as above.

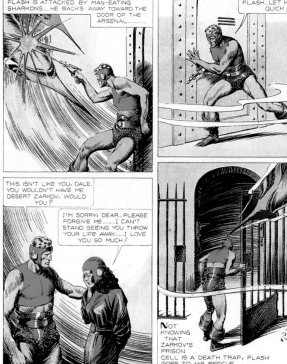

DICK TRACY

Top header bubble: BUT, MR. TRACY, WHY WOULD B.O. HAVE RUN AWAY? I *KNOW* HE DIDN'T SHOOT MR. FREELY.

Panel 1: YOU SAY THIS SAVINGS BOND BELONGING TO SPARKLE WAS LEFT ON YOUR DRESSER DURING THE NIGHT? / YES, YOU SEE B.O. ALWAYS CARRIED IT IN HIS WALLET FOR SAFEKEEPING.

Panel 2: I HEARD A NOISE, BUT WHEN I TURNED ON THE LIGHT NOBODY WAS THERE. / I'M CONVINCED HE ISN'T GUILTY, BUT HIS PANICKY ACTIONS MAKE IT AWFULLY HARD FOR US.

Panel 3: CHIEF PATTON CALLING TRACY— —HELLO, TRACY. I'M AT THE HOSPITAL. TALCUM FREELY IS *DEAD*.

Panel 4: DEAD? / HE NEVER REGAINED CONSCIOUSNESS. WE WERE UNABLE TO GET A SINGLE WORD FROM HIM.

Panel 5: LATER, AT TALCUM FREELY'S MANSION. / HAS TRACY SHOWN UP? HE WAS TO MEET ME HERE AT ELEVEN. / HAVEN'T SEEN HIM, SAM. HE MAY HAVE BEEN WASHED AWAY IN THE CLOUDBURST.

Panel 6: I'LL BE WAITING UPSTAIRS. I WANT TO DO A LITTLE MORE LOOKING AROUND.

Panel 7: PHOSPHATE AND POTASH FOUND ON THE RUG BENEATH THIS WINDOW INDICATE THE KILLER STEPPED IN FERTILIZER IN THE FLOWER-BED BELOW AS HE ENTERED.

Panel 8: HELLO, SAM. / RAIN? THIS IS A WATERSPOUT. / QUITE A RAIN.

Panel 9: HEY! LOOK AT THE WATER BUBBLING IN THROUGH THE CLOSED WINDOW.

Panel 10: IT'S ODD THAT THE EAVES GUTTER SHOULD THROW A STREAM OF WATER LIKE THAT RIGHT OVER THIS WINDOW. / MUST BE A LEAK IN THE PIPE, TRACY.

Panel 11: THERE ARE NO PREVIOUS STAINS OR MARKS TO SHOW IT HAS HAPPENED BEFORE. LET'S TAKE A LOOK FROM THE WINDOW AROUND THE CORNER.

Panel 12: THAT GUTTER ISN'T LEAKING. THAT WATER'S RUNNING *OVER* THE *TOP*! IT'S STOPPED UP! / YEAH, IT'S FULL OF LEAVES, TRACY. / I WONDER?

Panel 1: SATIN! WHAT ARE YOU DOING HERE?... YOU WERE WITH BRITISH INTELLIGENCE WHEN WE LAST MET! / I'M ON A PRIVATE MATTER NOW, SPIRIT!

Panel 2: ...IT'S BEEN A LONG TIME, SATIN! / UH-HUM,—A *VERY* LONG TIME, SPIRIT! / TCH...TCH! AIN'T THAT SWEET?

Panel (Meanwhile): Meanwhile... / AH, AT LAST! I GOT THE DOUGH, PRINCE GLENKO! / CERTAINMENT!! 'ALO, LEETLE WAN!... MON DIEU, WHAT A PRICE MY *CONTACTS* EEN EUROPE WEEL PAY FOR YOU!

Panel: YES, THIS LEETLE GIRL IS NOW THE HEIRESS TO THE GREAT TOVAROFF ESTATES! I—— / ♪ DIEU! ♪

Panel: CHEE, THE BOSS IS DEAD!... WHATLL WE DO NOW? / ? ELLEN! / *SHADDAP!* UNTIE ALL THOSE BUTLERS!

Panel: HELLO....NIFTY!? YEH, THIS IS GRANET! THE WHOLE THING'S WIDE OPEN.... THE *SPIRIT* JUST KNOCKED OFF VAN GILTT?!... NO, WE'VE GOT THE KID—SHE'S STILL WORTH DOUGH! BRING PRINCE GLENKO HERE QUICK!... WHAT?... NO, YOU DOPE! WE HAND HER OVER AND THEN BEAT IT!... YEAH...YEAH...YEH! WE'LL RUB THE *SPIRIT* OUT, TOO! / WELL, SHALL WE STAY, SATIN? / OH, UNDOOBITABLY! UNDOOBITABLY!

Panel: THIS WOMAN... THIS IS HER *MOTHER*!

Panel: WELL, WHAT ARE YOU ALL STARING AT? IT HAPPENS IN THE BEST OF FAMILIES!

Panel (Meanwhile): Meanwhile... / WHAT! HILDIE DISAPPEARED FROM MY HOUSE! WHERE'S ELLEN! / AH, DUNNO, COMMISSIONER DOLAN, SUH! ♪ SOB ♪...THEY BOTH DIS....DIS.... ♪ SOB ♪

Panel: ..AH HAVE FAILED! AH'M GONNA END IT ALL! / OH, EBONY, STOP HAMMING IT UP! ... HELLO. SEND A SQUAD CAR OUT TO VAN GILTT'S AND BRING HIM IN FOR QUESTIONING!

Panel: OH, BROTHER! EVERYTHING HAPPENS AT ONCE.... A LARGE PEANUT EMPIRE TOTTERING AND *I'VE* GOT TO STOP AND LOOK FOR KIDNAPPERS! / CRASH! / SCREE-EEEE-EECHH

Panel: THIS WOMAN WAS IVAN'S WIFE! IS SHE IN CAHOOTS...?

Panel: LOOK, MISTER BONES, I'M NOT PLAYIN' "JACKS"! GIT THE DOUGH OUTA HIS POCKETS AND LET'S HIT THE ROAD!

Panel: AND WE'RE TAKIN' THE KID WITH US!... SO SHE'S AN HEIRESS, EH? OH, HAPPY DAY! AIN'T IT GONNA BE FUN TO BE RICH!

37

Opposite: Panel from *Superman* (DC Comics, 1941). Art: Joe Shuster. The title that more than any other redefined the way comics were perceived in America, and whose star became the quintessential symbol for the country's fortunes. Above: Cover, *Action Comics*, no 1, (National Periodicals, 1938). Art: Joe Shuster. Today, collectors pay upwards of $150,000 for the comic that featured the first appearance of the man of steel. Right: Page from *Superman* (DC Comics, 1941) Art: Joe Shuster/ Wayne Boring. Script: Jerry Siegel. Far right: Cover, *Superman* (DC Comics, 1971). Art: Curt Swan. Below right: Panel from *Action Comics* (DC comics, 1963). Art: Curt Swan. Below: The first-ever edition of *Superman* (National Periodicals, 1939). Art: Joe Shuster.

aesthetic. Most began as anthologies of short stories, but developed into soap operas starring a single character. In the process, the publishers rejected the abstract poetic fantasies that distinguished the more arty newspaper strips in favour of a more representational style: the name of the game was bold, figurative art with strong colours, though as artists became more ambitious, they increasingly challenged traditional 'chessboard' layouts. In terms of content, the emphasis was again on simplicity: the heroic derring-do found in the pulps was perfect, and it is significant that two of the most important examples of early comics that developed original themes, rather than relying on newspaper reprints, were adventure-orientated titles: *Detective Comics* in 1937 and *Action Comics* in 1938.[12]

In the first full decade of American comics, the 1940s, the biggest genre consisted of superhero comics. These were essentially aimed at children, but derived from a pulp tradition, and thus often contained political and social overtones. One character set the template: 'Superman', born in No 1 of *Action Comics* (National Periodicals) in 1938. Created by two teenage fans of science fiction pulp novels, Jerry Siegel and Joe Shuster, Superman represented the ultimate power fantasy: the sole survivor of doomed planet Krypton, this super-powered alien in

57

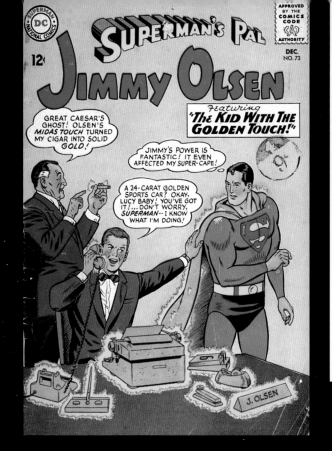

1939

Panel from *Superman*, No 1 (DC Comics). Art: Joe Shuster. Script: Jerry Siegel. The hero was intended to be a composite strongman, part-Samson, part-Hercules: here he meets Lois Lane for the first time.

1954

Cover, *Action Comics* (DC Comics). Art: Wayne Boring. One of the great Superman artists who originally worked as an understudy for Shuster when he was going blind.

1962

Panel from *Action Comics*, (DC Comics). Art: Curt Swan. Unarguably it was Swan more than anyone else who defined Supes' square-jawed 'Charles Atlas' look for the modern period.

Far left: Cover, *Jimmy Olsen* (DC Comics, 1963). Art: Curt Swan. Even the bit-players in the Superman saga got their own comics in due course. Left: Advert for animated shows on CBS Television, including *Superman* (CBS, 1966). Right: Pages from *Superman* (DC Comics, 1971). Art: Curt Swan. Below: Cover, *Superboy* (DC Comics, 1950). Art: Curt Swan. It was decided to make Superboy's adventures part of Superman's boyhood, rather than making the character a junior version, so as not to dilute the original.

1978

Still from *Superman: The Movie* (The Kobal Collection/ Warner Brothers/DC Comics). The first in a string of hit spectaculars. Here, Christopher Reeve, perfect in the role, battles with some dodgy back-projection.

1986

Page from *Superman* (DC Comics). Art: John Byrne. This version, a more human character, was largely inspired by the movies.

1996

Cover, *Superman* (DC Comics). Art: Kiron Dwyer and Denis Rodier. The latest incarnation, with longer hair and muscles looking like walnuts stuffed into a balloon. The age of steroids had dawned.

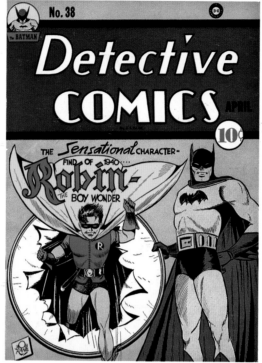

This page: Covers and excerpts featuring the second great costumed hero, Batman. The early stories were remarkable for their gothic tone. Above: Cover, *Detective Comics* (National Periodicals, 1939). Art: Bob Kane. This is the issue that featured the first appearance of Batman. Above right: Cover, *Detective Comics* (DC Comics, 1940). Art: Bob Kane and Jerry Robinson. Here, Robin makes his first appearance. Above far right: Detail from *Detective Comics* (DC Comics, 1950). Art: Anon. Right and below: Page and cover from same issue.

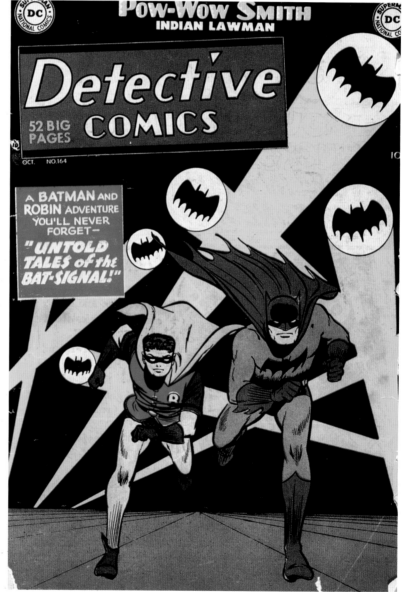

human form could fly faster than a speeding bullet, see through buildings with his X-ray vision, and lift huge objects with his bare hands. 'All of a sudden, it hits me – I conceive a character like Samson, Hercules and all the strong men I ever heard of rolled into one', Siegel later explained. Though it is clear that the writer must also have been aware of the analogies with Jesus: Superman was similarly a man sent from the heavens by his father to use his special powers for the good of humanity.[13] His mythic qualities, combined with his square-jawed features and natty blue and red costume, soon acquired iconic status.[14]

Before long Superman would have his own comic, and be the subject for extensive merchandising and film spin-offs. In the process, the politics of the comic changed. In his earliest outings, he had been a kind of super-social worker, in the comic's words, a 'Champion of the Oppressed', reflecting the liberal idealism of Franklin

Roosevelt's New Deal. Drunks, wife-batterers and gamblers received his attention, while in one famous tale a mine-owner who obliges miners to labour in dangerous conditions is compelled by Superman to experience those conditions himself. Then, when the Cold War came to America, the character evolved into a fantasy guardian of the world order: an all-powerful, and at times slightly portly-looking conservative, fighting for 'Truth, Justice and the American Way'. Later still, he would be revamped again for more cynical times (see Chapters 6 and 7).

Superman's main counterpart, 'Batman', made his appearance in *Detective Comics*, no 27 (National Periodicals, 1939), and embodied a much darker vision – a 'caped crusader' against the criminal underworld that had killed his parents. Created by Bob Kane, Batman had no supernatural powers as such, but in the early stories relied on four things: his athletic ability, his trusty sidekick 'Robin', the cover of night and an array of gadgets housed in his 'utility belt'. In time, he acquired an innovative line-up of enemies (inspired, in part, by the weird villains in Dick Tracy). Most notoriously they included 'The Penguin', 'Twoface', and, most disturbingly, 'The Joker' – a villain so sadistic that he leaves his murdered victims with grotesque smiles on their faces.

Batman too was given his own title, and also generated vast cross-media exploitation. His mythology similarly changed to suit the times. At first, he was a gothic figure: a tortured soul, driven by revenge and most at home in the shadows. The early comics were remarkable for their grim tone and 'noirish' use of bold blocks of black ink. Later though, the stories were progressively 'lightened' in order to draw in a younger readership, a trend which culminated in the 1960s, when the comics became

'camp' comedies to reflect the amazingly successful television series. Later still, there would be a 'return to roots' – the inspiration for the blockbuster movies of the 1980s and 1990s (see p 167 and pp 173–4).[15]

Superman and Batman quickly dominated the American market, selling millions every month, and established National Periodicals – later renamed DC Comics – as the premier publisher.[16] They founded complementary superhero paradigms – supernatural versus super-athlete, strength versus wit and day versus night – which would later be copied by a seemingly endless array of imitators through the 1940s.[17] Publishers realized that big money could be made, but were also aware that the war could be capitalized upon to advantage: after all, real-life super-villains like Hitler and Tojo were ideal foes for the superheroes. Thus, most of the new titles were feeble copyists of Superman and Batman, infused with a wartime spirit, but devoting less thought to the characters than to how to get from one fight scene to another. There were, however, one or two notable additions to the super-roster.

Historians usually identify four significant examples.

The first, Captain Marvel (Fawcett, 1941), by CC Beck and Bill Parker, had an alter-ego as a kid reporter, who becomes a scarlet-clad strongman when he utters the word 'Shazam!' (a moment always accompanied by plenty of thunder and zig-zag lightening). This 'world's mightiest mortal' was a little too like Superman for National Periodicals' liking, and there followed a legal battle over copyright. Fawcett finally gave up on the Captain in the mid-1950s, though not before sales of the comic had briefly outstripped his rival. The second example, Captain America (Marvel, 1941), by Joe Simon and Jack Kirby, was the embodiment of American patriotism during the Second World War. This genetically engineered super-soldier even wore a costume that resembled the American flag, and the first issue had a cover depicting him socking Hitler on the jaw. The title was also remarkable for its artwork by rising star Kirby, which experimented with panel layouts to inject more movement into the balletic fight scenes. Thirdly, there was Wonder Woman (National Periodicals, 1942), a super-strong Amazon princess, and one of the very few female characters to be successful. More about her in Chapter 4.

This page: Covers and excerpts featuring Captain Marvel, an early rival to Superman, famed for his red costume and magic command 'Shazam!'. Above: Cover, Captain Marvel (Fawcett, 1950; British black-and-white edition, L Miller and Son, 1950). Centre: Page from the same comic. Right: Panel from Captain Marvel (Fawcett, 1951), demonstrating other members of the 'Marvel Family'. Art/script for all: CC Beck.

This page: Another big-selling superhero: Captain America. All examples: Marvel Comics. Right, left and below: Cover, page and panels from the first edition of *Captain America* (1941). Art: Jack Kirby. Script: Joe Simon. This super-patriot was sent into action against the Nazis and the Japanese, to devastating effect – on the cover, he even chins Hitler. Bottom left and right: Cover and strip from *All Winners* (Marvel Comics, 1946). Art: probably Alex Schomberg. Script: Anon. Here, the 'Cap' teams up with The Human Torch and Sub-Mariner, among others. The idea was to have a comic with 'all winners and no losers'.

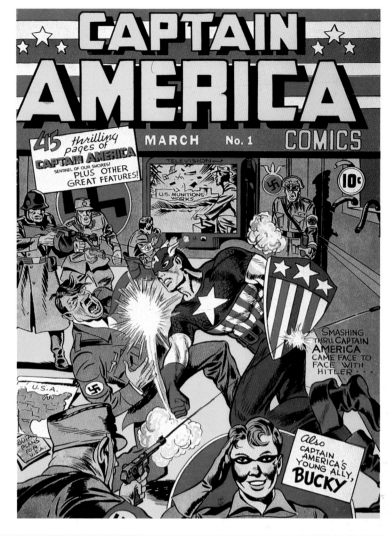

Above and right: Cover and splash pages from *Captain America* (Marvel Comics, 1968). The 'Cap' was revived in the 1960s, but his patriotism seemed decidedly out of tune with the Vietnam era. The artist for this issue was the great Jim Steranko, who would be a major influence on the next generation of superhero creators (as we shall see in Chapter 7).

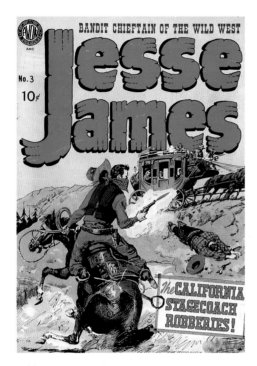

Other genres also thrived in America. Above: Covers, *Jesse James* (Avon, 1951) and *The Lone Ranger* (Dell, 1949). Art for both: Anon. Westerns were extremely popular in the late 1940s and early 1950s, and fed from pulp novels, movies, and television. Below: Cover, *Frontline Combat* (EC Comics, 1951). Art/script: Harvey Kurtzman. War comics were spurred into life by the Korean conflict: the EC examples were exceptional in that they did not take a gung-ho line. Right: Cover, *Crime Does Not Pay* (Lev Gleason). Art: Charles Biro (a criminally underrated artist). Undoubtedly the best of the controversial 1940s crime comics.

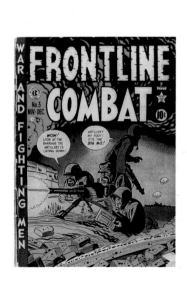

Fourth, and finally, *Plastic Man* (Vital, 1943), by Jack Cole, was about a reformed gangster with extendable limbs. This engagingly odd title did not take itself too seriously, and tapped into the public's current fascination with plastic, then being hyped as 'the miracle material'. Every month the hero would thwart criminals by stretching like a firehose, or flattening himself like a parachute, much to the delight of his substantial readership.

This first wave of superheroes soon gained international fame and distribution. Yet, for all that, it is worth noting that the superheroes were never particularly successful in Britain before 1959. Why not is still a matter for debate: possibly the pulp tradition was not as strong or possibly the prejudice against American culture in general was too pervasive. Nevertheless, small coteries of British fans developed who were passionate about the imported titles, while some British publishers either reprinted them or attempted to introduce strips into anthologies.[18] There were even some (slightly off-key) home-grown efforts to imitate the genre, such as 'Wonderman' and 'The Bat'.[19]

As the 1940s moved on, so too did the American industry: other genres became popular as superheroes waned. The war had ended in 1945, and patriotic supermen temporarily lost their appeal. To try to rejuvenate the market, publishers attempted to target older readers, and as a result the range of subject matter expanded. Many of the genres that had been popular in the pulps now vied against each other for attention on the newsstand shelves, including westerns, detective, crime, war, science fiction and horror.

The westerns featured familiar yarns about cowboys despatching indians, and sheriffs pacifying border towns: the most popular starred characters who were making names for themselves in the movies, such as *Wild Bill Hickock* (Avon, 1949), *Jesse James* (Avon, 1952) and *Wyatt Earp* (Atlas, 1955), as well as movie heroes per se, such as, *Gene Autry* (Fawcett, 1941) and *Roy Rogers* (Dell, 1944).[20]

The detective genre featured a vivid roster of private eyes, eager to discover 'whodunnit' with a combination of brain and brawn. Usually, they were based on newspaper strips: Dick Tracy became a comic in 1939 (Dell), and was joined by *The Spirit* (Quality) in 1944 and *Charlie Chan* (Crestwood) in 1948. Occasionally, sleuths would be created exclusively for the comics, such as *Sam Hill Private Eye* (Close-up, 1950) and *Ken Shannon* (Quality, 1951).

The crime comics were different to the detective titles in that they were more in tune with adult 'true crime' magazines, and the hard-nut heroes of the Jimmie Cagney gangster movies: they were more grown-up and infinitely more violent. Mixing fictional and non-fictional stories about hoods, murderers and other criminal types, they revelled in bloody tommy-gun shoot-outs and underworld sleaze – blowsy dolls were obligatory. None delivered the goods with more style than *Crime Does Not Pay* (Comic House/Lev Gleason, 1942), the market leader for many years, which featured the kinetic artwork of Charles Biro; in fact the comic's sensibility was not a million miles from the 1990s movies of Quentin Tarantino. The crime titles that followed through the 1940s and 1950s were often more extreme: for example, issues of *True Crime Comics* (Magazine Village, 1947) and *Murder Incorporated* (Fox, 1948) are sought after by modern collectors for their spectacular scenes of sadism and torture.

American war comics concentrated on the Second World War, just like their British counterparts, and were just as racist towards the Germans and Japanese (the latter were sometimes referred to as 'Japanazis' for extra effect). They also fed much more from the Korean

conflict in the early 1950s: titles like *War Action* and *War Adventure* (both Atlas, 1952) portrayed the Koreans in the same way as the Japanese – yellow-skinned demons – and generally perpetuated old formulas.

By far the best war comics were two anthologies published around this time by EC (Entertaining Comics), *Two Fisted Tales* (1950) and *Frontline Combat* (1951), which took a more realistic approach. With outstanding, historically-accurate artwork by Wally Wood, John Severin and others, and under the proselytizing influence of contributing editor Harvey Kurtzman (who simultaneously fulfilled the same role on *Mad*), these comics pointedly eschewed gung-ho glamour in favour of an emphasis on war's horrors.

Science fiction also took off. Buck Rogers and Flash Gordon were given their own comics in 1940 (Famous Funnies) and 1943 (Dell), but other titles moved away from simple heroics, and tapped into post-war American fears about UFOs and aliens, which has been interpreted today as a metaphor for the 'red scare'. Once more, EC led the field in terms of quality, with *Weird Science* and *Weird Fantasy* (both 1950) which featured Wally Wood's wild depictions of space hardware and 'borrowed' plots from top science fiction authors like Ray Bradbury.

The final kind of American comic in this early 1950s period were undoubtedly the most notorious – the horror comics. Technically, they had been around since the early 1940s, when individual 'monster' titles had been popular. But they really came into their own in the 1950s, when they became a recognizable genre, notable mainly for their sanguine story lines. Indeed, many titles went further than contemporary horror films, and featured beheadings, eviscerations, gouged eyes and so on, in gleeful detail.

The best were undoubtedly the EC triumvirate of *The Vault of Horror*, *The Crypt of Terror* and *The Haunt of Fear* (all 1950): though no less violent than the rest, they distinguished themselves by the wit of their storytelling (individual tales were introduced by 'horror hosts' like the Old Witch and The Crypt Keeper), and, characteristically for the publisher, superb artwork. Indeed, some EC artists really took to the task – none more so than Graham Ingels, who signed his work 'Ghastly', and who produced some of the most feverishly intense visuals yet seen in comics.

Predictably, the titles that tried to imitate the EC formula usually fell short. They tended to eschew the humour in favour of nastiness, and artistry in favour of hackwork. Smaller publishers were particularly guilty of this: one title, *Mysterious Adventures* (Story, 1951), made a point of featuring violent dismemberments and gross close-ups. There would be a price to pay for such provocative material in the long run.

Of all the adventure genres – war, crime, horror, and so on – it is worth dwelling for a moment on just how outstanding the EC titles were. Most historians point to the artwork as the main bonus (already discussed above), but the care that was taken over the writing was equally impressive: indeed, the word-balloons and narrative boxes were designed first, and then the artwork fitted around them – rather than the other way round. Also, whereas most companies were essentially 'sweatshops', EC was legendarily creator-friendly, and every strip carried credits – virtually unheard of at the time. EC publisher William Gaines later cited this working atmosphere as a major reason for their success: 'The artists had tremendous admiration for one another. Wally Wood would come in with a story, and three artists would crowd around him and faint, just poring over every brushstroke and every panel. Next time around it's his turn to adulate someone … They were all in friendly competition to see who could make everybody faint more than the other guy. And it was wonderful. Just a nice, warm place.'[21]

The increasing trend for violence in American comics

This page: Examples from two of the many horror titles that flooded the shelves in the early 1950s, some of which took comics into new realms of nastiness. They would have a lasting effect on the horror genre, and numbered among their fans future writers and filmmakers Stephen King, George Romero, and John Carpenter. Right: Page from *Uncanny Tales* (Marvel Comics, 1954). Art: Dick Briefer. Below: Cover and interior from *The Vault of Horror* (EC Comics, 1954). Art: Johnny Craig (cover); Jack Davis (strip). One of the excellent EC line, with stories introduced by 'horror hosts' such as The Old Witch.

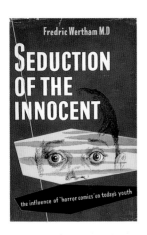

This page: Examples from the backlash against the crime and horror comics. Above: Cover to the influential academic study, *Seduction of the Innocent* (Museum Press, 1955) by the psychiatrist Fredric Wertham. Above: 'Should US "Comics" be Banned?', an article from Britain's *Picture Post* magazine. In fact they were – by an Act of Parliament in 1955. Above right: Photo of a 'comic book burning' in Nebraska in 1954, the sort of scene one associates with Nazi Germany. Below: Cover, *Ivanhoe* (Gilberton, 1946). Art: Anon. One of the Classics Illustrated line, educational comics that automatically escaped censure.

was too much for the 'Guardians of Public Decency' in the long term. Unfortunately for the fans in the United States, and also Britain where there was a slow but steady flow of comics into the country, there was about to be one of the biggest crises in the medium's history. In a few short years, comics became the scapegoat for various forces of reaction and censorship; the result would be the emasculation and re-structuring of the entire American industry. The immediate cause was the objections of sections of the public in America (and to a lesser degree in Britain) to the two obvious genres: crime and horror.

To simplify a long story, these comics – especially those produced by EC – caused a furore. In America, the idea that they were at least partly reponsible for the rise in juvenile delinquency quickly gained ground, fuelled by a book by an eminent psychiatrist, Dr Fredric Wertham. The book, entitled *Seduction of the Innocent* (Rinehart, 1954), attacked most genres of comics, but focused on horror and crime in general, claiming that at best they were 'especially apt to interfere with children's sleep', and at worst led to copycat crimes.[22] In fact, the book was academically unsound, and used illustrations from the comics completely out of context, but its sensationalism – 'The Most Shocking Book of the Year' – and its author's evangelical zeal, were enough to inspire widespread moral panic. This manifested itself in protests, and even in neighbourhood comics burnings.[23]

In Britain, similar fears were whipped up. The EC titles had been reprinted in black-and-white by the Arnold Book Co, and had sold in tiny quantities compared to mainstream comics like *The Eagle*, but had nevertheless caused a scandal. An influential article in *Picture Post* in 1952 asked the question: 'Should US "Comics" be banned?', and answered it by repeating Wertham's claims about delinquency, and getting British experts to back him up. It ended with a 'slippery slope' analogy: 'these books depend on the administration of violent shocks to the nervous system, and just as the drug addict must progressively increase the size of the dose to obtain the same effect, so, as sensibilities become dulled by the repetition of a particular kind of brutal act, the degree of violence must of necessity increase.'[24]

In this way, the public on both sides of the Atlantic were suddenly spurred into taking a stance on comics in a way they had not before. Parents had not taken much notice when Junior was reading other kinds of action or humour titles (or if they did, they were mildly disapproving), but this new horror and crime material was a different kettle of rotting fish altogether. Again, the stereotype of a comic was being challenged (note those inverted commas in the *Picture Post* piece), and there could only be one outcome: censorship.[25]

In America, there were hearings in the Senate, at which both Fredric Wertham and William Gaines testified, after which publishers were compelled to band together into a self-regulatory group, the Comics Magazine Association of America (established in 1954). This association thereafter administered a code of conduct, overseen by a review body called 'The Comics Code Authority'. This 'code' consisted of a list of

prohibitions. There were to be no references to sex, no excessive violence, no challenges to authority, and so on. It was enforced by an arrangement whereby every new title thereafter was submitted for approval. If it passed, it ran with a cover stamp 'Approved by the Comics Code Authority'; if it failed, it did not get distributed.[26] In Britain, Parliament passed a law, 'The Children's and Young Persons Harmful Publications Act' (1955), which effectively banned the offending comics from entering the country, or from being reprinted.[27]

This was a turning point for the American industry. Sales slumped almost immediately as lines of comics were cancelled. Whole genres were virtually destroyed: horror and crime were especially badly hit, but war, westerns, romance and even superhero titles also suffered. EC very nearly went under (and would have, had it not been for the success of *Mad* – see p 38–41), while other publishers were not so lucky. It all added up to disaster. For parents and educators, the Code meant peace of mind, but for kids it signified little except insipidly 'safe' entertainment. The comics world post-1955 looked very different to that before.

The Code certainly marked the end of a phase in American comics development. It was not, however, the end per se. Although many publishers suffered, others were adaptable, and worked round it. They proved that comics could still command viable sales while staying within its boundaries. (The name of the game was now implication rather than explicitness, suspense rather than gore.) In this way, the industry managed to stay alive, though in overall terms sales continued in a downward trend due, arguably, to the rise of television.

In Britain, this process corresponded with the lifting of the ban on the distribution of American comics in 1959. By then, the Code was seen to be doing its job, and the British Publications Act had not had to be called into effect. In other words, there were no more scares. Also, anti-American prejudice was on the wane, and indeed the political 'special relationship' between the two countries seemed to be stronger than ever due to the continuing Cold War.

In terms of publishing, the crushing of EC left the way open for the domination of the market by DC Comics and Marvel (formerly known as 'Atlas' and 'Timely'), and for the rise of smaller companies like Gilberton. The former

two benefited by focusing on superheroes, old and new. It was a genre which stayed within the Code by emphasizing its make-believe core: huge punch-ups were okay, so long as nobody actually bled. Gilberton, on the other hand, were responsible for publishing the 'Classics Illustrated' line, designed to adapt classics of literature into comics form, and were therefore exempt from submitting comics to the Code authority in the first place.

No American publisher was more adaptable to the new conditions than Marvel. The company had previously been heavily involved with war and horror titles, but now reorientated its attention towards Code-friendly superheroes. In a move intended to take on DC Comics at their own game, a new line was masterminded by editor-writer Stan Lee and artist Jack Kirby: between them, they decided that an interesting new direction would be to make the personalities of the heroes more of a focus than the plots. Thus, in contrast to the old formulas, the Marvel superheroes would be humanized, troubled characters ambivalent about their powers.

The art would also be a major focus. Kirby had previously worked on a range of comics genres, including superheroes (*Captain America*) and war (*Foxhole*), but was now to be allowed to give free rein to his flair for spectacle and science fiction. 'I'm very well versed in science fiction and science fact', Kirby said later. 'I used to read the first science fiction books, and I began to learn about the universe myself and take it seriously ... I began to realise what a wonderful and awesome place the universe is, and that helped me in comics because I was looking for the awesome.'[28] 'Awesome' was the word, and if anybody could show that comics need not be hamstrung by the rules on explicitness, Kirby could: his explosive, kinetic style gave the appearance of untold power and energy (rather than of violence per se) and his characters seemed as if they could really could punch through walls. It was this unique talent above all that marked Kirby out as one of the outstanding creators in American comics history.

The first major Marvel success was *The Fantastic Four* (1961), consisting of Mr Fantastic, the Human Torch, The Thing and Invisible Girl. They were, essentially, a 'supergroup', who spent as much time agonizing over beating up baddies as actually doing it. The mix of characters was especially strong: The Thing, looking like a menacing pile of orange rocks, had a quick temper, and

This page: The dawn of the 'Marvel Age'. Above and right: Cover and interior from *Fantastic Four* (Marvel Comics, 1968), Script: Stan Lee/Jack Kirby. Art: Jack Kirby. The title that revived superhero comics in America. Stories exhibited a new level of psychological depth: the 'Four' bickered among themselves like any family, and always found time to agonize over issues of brain versus brawn.

CONTINUED AFTER NEXT PAGE

This page: More *Fantastic Four* (Marvel Comics, top 1970, far left 1965, left and above 1968). Script: Stan Lee/Jack Kirby. Art: Jack Kirby. The character 'The Thing' was the most innovative of the 'Four': a young man trapped in the body of a craggy monster, he was notable for his stoic sense of humour about his plight.

70

Right: Page from *Fantastic Four* (Marvel Comics, 1968). Script: Stan Lee/Jack Kirby. Art: Jack Kirby. Kirby is undoubtedly the key artist in American mainstream comics history; the king of dynamic rendering, as this example shows.

This page: Examples from *The Hulk* (Marvel Comics), about a scientist bombarded with gamma rays, who develops the habit of transforming into a decidedly un-jolly green giant. Above: Detail from *c*1965. Right: Pages from the original story, 1962. Below: Pages from a 1964 edition. Script for all: Stan Lee and Jack Kirby. Art: Jack Kirby.

This page: Examples from perhaps Marvel's best-known title, *Spider-Man* (Marvel Comics), about a shy teenager and his web-slinging alter-ego. Above: Cover by John Romita (1968), making reference to contemporary student strife. Top right, left and right: Pages and panel from a 1964 edition, featuring one of Spidey's most entertaining foes, Dr Octopus. Script: Stan Lee. Art: Steve Ditko.

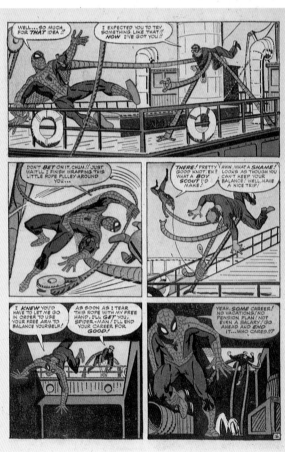

nicely counterposed Mr Fantastic's cool scientific detachment. With the addition of some formidable villains, like the Puppet-Master and Dr Doom, the comic really hit its stride, and garnered a fanatical following.

Fast in its wake, Marvel published *The Incredible Hulk* in 1962, about a scientist, the tormented Bruce Banner, who gets zapped by radiation in an accident and becomes a super-strong green brute. 'Half-man, half monster, the mighty Hulk thunders out of the night to take his place among the most amazing characters of all time!' ran the suitably hyperbolic blurb. The story was inspired by Dr Jekyll and Mr Hyde, and also tapped into current fears about the 'atomic threat'. However, it did not have *The Fantastic Four*'s characterization, and was a damp squib at first, only gathering a significant readership slowly.

More immediately succesful, 1962 saw the introduction of The Mighty Thor (in *Journey into Mystery*, number 83), about a weedy doctor who goes on holiday in Norway and there finds the hammer of the god Thor in a cave. When he picks it up, he is tranformed into a super-Viking, complete with flowing blond locks. In subsequent issues, Norse mythology was introduced to an increasing degree, including the appearance of Thor's traditional nemesis, Loki. Thor was eventually given his own title in 1966.

But the biggest Marvel hit came in 1963: *The Amazing Spider-Man*. This was another Lee-Kirby creation, but featured art by Steve Ditko. It concerned the story of a bookish teenager, Peter Parker, who is bitten by a radioactive spider during a scientific demonstration. Thereafter he finds he is able to climb walls, dangle from ceilings and spin webs. The attraction of this ostensibly very simple story for readers was that they could identify with the protagonist's adolescent angst. He at least tries to do the right thing, even when his life is in a mess (in some stories, Peter Parker's bookshelves are stacked with existential texts). It was a powerful formula, given a final twist with the introduction of a suitably twisted super-villain, the Green Goblin.

Other heroes poured forth from Marvel. Among the most famous were *The X-Men* (1963), about another 'four' (The Beast, Cyclops, Iceman and Angel; later joined by Marvel Girl); *The Avengers* (1963), which teamed up The Hulk and Thor, with less well-known characters such as Iron Man, Ant-Man and The Wasp; and *The Silver Surfer* (1968), about a contemplative surfing alien and his battles with Galactus, a world-devouring giant. Other excellent artist who had stints on these, and the other Marvel heroes, included James Steranko, Neal Adams and John Romita.

This new wave of superheroes were hyped by Marvel in a way that had not been seen before (note, for example, those adjectives 'Fantastic', 'Incredible', 'Mighty' and so on). Indeed, Stan Lee made sure that the company's name became almost as famous as the characters: these were not just superheroes, but 'Marvel Superheroes'. More than this, the comics were designed to be collected: buy one and you had to buy the series (and ideally all the other series as well). Characters would appear in each

other's comics, thus introducing fans of one to all the others, while simultaneously creating a richly populated cosmos that would later become known as 'The Marvel Universe'. In this way, Lee managed to convince readers that they were part of a club of connoisseurs, and so initiated what has become known as comics fandom.[29] 'I think I really treated the whole line as a gigantic advertising campaign', he later confessed. 'I wanted the readers to feel that we were all part of an "in" thing that the outside world wasn't aware of.'[30]

The success of Marvel had the effect of kick-starting the entire industry back into life. DC Comics competed by reviving their two biggest characters, Superman and Batman. Superman had extra elements added to his mythology (such as different types of kryptonite, the concept of a 'phantom zone' and new sidekicks, including Krypto, the super dog), and benefited from some imaginative artwork by Curt Swan. Batman, by contrast, was given a lift by the ratings-busting TV show, with Adam West in the lead role, which debuted in 1966. The new Batman comics featured elements like the Batmobile and Batcave, and in general followed the campy, tongue-in-cheek style of the show, and so picked up a new generation of readers.

Superheroes continued to be successful until the end of the 1960s, and for a time even became 'hip'. This was partly the influence of Pop Art, which frequently referenced and quoted from comics, and partly because the new generation of hippie college students declared themselves fans. As ever, it was Marvel and Stan Lee who made the most of this: Marvel comics ran with the label 'A Pop Art Production!', while Lee went on college tours and proudly reproduced missives from students and

For a short while in the late 1960s and early 1970s, comics were 'hip'. Right: A hippie festival-goer enjoys a copy of Superman. Below: The Hulk makes it onto the cover of *Rolling Stone* (Straight Arrow, 1971).

college professors in the letters pages. It should be noted that this kind of cooption of comics by adults could only have occurred as a result of the more cosmopolitan sensibility of the American titles: it was unthinkable that the same could happen with their British counterparts.

Other genres boomed as well. War, for example, went through a renaissance. Marvel's main title was *Sgt Fury and his Howling Commandos* (1963), which was set in the Second World War, and featured a cigar-chewing Sarge and a group of ethnically diverse commandos ('howling racial stereotypes', according to some). DC Comics' answer was *Sgt Rock*, an old character from *Our Army at War*, given his own title in 1977, which was also set in the Second World War, but which was less 'superheroey'. It was left to smaller publishers to deal with Vietnam, especially Dell, whose main hit was *Tales of the Green Beret* (1967). Despite the lead set by EC in the 1950s, these comics eschewed an anti-war stance in favour of old-fashioned shoot-em-ups.[31]

Even horror made a comeback eventually. Of course, publishers had to tread carefully, because even though the Code was less stringently enforced with time, there was always the lurking possibility of another backlash. Because of this, titles like DC Comics' *House of Mystery* and *House of Secrets* prospered: they had existed since the early 1950s, but had never been in the market for grossness. Similarly, Marvel scored a few notable hits based more on creepiness than old-fashioned gore: *Tower of Shadows* (1969) was an anthology with some

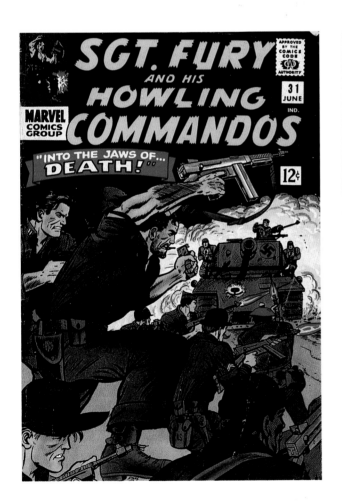

outstandingly atmospheric 'fast-cut' artwork by Jim Steranko.

Other horror publishers avoided the Code altogether by putting out comics in a magazine format (usually in black-and-white). *Creepy* and *Eerie* (both Warren, 1964 and 1965 respectively) harked back to the glory days of EC, and in fact used some of the same artists (newer names included Berni Wrightson and Neal Adams). They featured stories heavily influenced by the 'gothic' films of studios like Hammer and Universal. Warren's third major title, *Vampirella* (1969) was its most original, and starred a sexy vampire from another planet ('A hickey from this vamp is sure worth dying for!').[32] There were many others, some good, some bad: *Nightmare*, *Psycho* and *Scream* (all Skywald, 1970, 1971, and 1973) were not of the same quality as the Warren magazines, but had more interesting narratives, dealing in psychedelic weirdness and imaginative adaptations of Edgar Allen Poe stories.

Finally, no survey of American adventure titles would be complete without briefly returning to the Gilberton 'Classics Illustrated' comics. As mentioned previously, these were intended to introduce children to great works of fiction, which in effect meant books by 'classic' authors. The majority were action-orientated – ripping yarns such as *Treasure Island*, *The Last of the Mohicans* and *The Three Musketeers* – though there were a few romances, such as *Wuthering Heights*. They stood apart from the other comics on the racks because they were lengthy, self-contained stories, and because they were obviously meant to be educational: for this reason they tended to be bought by parents rather than children. They were published in America by Gilberton from 1947, and in British editions by Thorpe and Porter from 1951: they reached their peak popularity in the immediate post-Code period.[33]

American comics may have found their feet again in the 1960s, but the conditions of employment for those

This page: Some horror comics managed to thrive, despite the Code. Below: Pages from *Tower of Shadows* (Marvel Comics, 1969): double-page spread (left) scripted by Stan Lee, art by John Buscema; single page (right) by Jim Steranko, demonstrating his effectively scary 'fast-cut' technique. Bottom: Covers, *House of Secrets* (DC Comics, 1975). Art: Anon; *House of Mystery* (DC Comics, 1975). Art: Anon; and *Tower of Shadows* (Marvel Comics, 1969). Art: Jim Steranko.

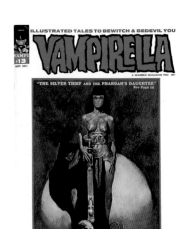

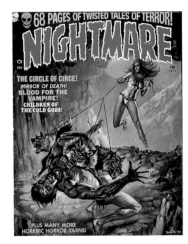

This page: Other horror titles took a magazine format, and were published in black and white, to avoid the Code altogether. Left, below left and bottom left: Cover and interior pages from *Vampirella* (Warren Publications), a comic about a sexy vampire. Cover (1971), art: Anon; centre strip (1971), written by Archie Goodwin, art: Jose Gonzalez; bottom strip (1972), art: Esteban Maroto.

Top right, above right and right: Covers and interiors from the altogether more weird *Psycho* and *Nightmare* (both Skywald). Covers, both 1971, by Boris Vallejo; *Psycho* strip, centre (1971), art: Ross Andru and Mike Esposito; script: Ross Andru; bottom: *Nightmare* strip (1971), art: Anon.

within the industry hardly improved at all. The adventure genre had always been notorious for poor pay and working conditions (a legacy of the pulp industry), and the fact that work was on a freelance 'for hire' basis, and divided between writers, artists, pencillers and inkers, militated against any kind of effective unionisation. It also meant that most comics were anonymous.

True, some publishers were better than others. As we've seen, the staff at EC were relatively well treated, and allowed to sign their work; the same was true of Charles Biro at Lev Gleason. Similarly, some creators made substantial profits from their work: Will Eisner owned everything he did, and reaped the rewards. But the more common story is one of exploitation and disillusion: Siegel and Shuster were financially milked by DC Comics for their work on Superman, while Jack Kirby was similarly treated at Marvel and had to fight a lengthy battle with the company for the return of his artwork. This is the sordid side to the industry that one rarely sees in the history books, yet it must be taken into account when any other, aesthetic, consideration is attempted.[34]

In conclusion, before we wind up this chapter on adventure comics, we need to return to their place in popular culture generally. This is obviously a complex subject, but of one thing we can be certain: adventure broadened the content of comics, but it also broadened the range of targets for criticism. Clearly, the 1954–5 crisis over the American horror and crime titles brought things to a head, but in terms of the 1930–70 period as a whole, a far broader range of opinions were encouraged.

Certainly, there was an ambivalence towards the action genre, much in the same way as there was towards humour. There were basically two opposing viewpoints. On the one hand, many people, particularly adults and parents, saw adventure comics as 'blood-stirring yarns', robust entertainment for boys and adolescents, and therefore as nothing very much to worry about. Indeed, when it came to the 'improving' comics such as the Classics Illustrated line, in Britain and the United States, and *The Eagle* and *Look and Learn*, in Britain, many felt that it might even be possible that they had an educative effect. On the other hand, complaints against the medium intensified, often extending arguments first put forward against publications that were comics' predecessors (in Britain, the penny dreadfuls and story papers and in the United States, the dime novels and pulps), and were increasingly aired in press articles, radio and television broadcasts, and in academic books.[35]

Objections were backgrounded by the feeling that there was something vulgar about the very idea of using the comics form to deal with adventure: it was somehow dragging 'culture' down. For instance, comics dealt in cheap thrills, sensationalism and visual stimulation (even when it came to words, they used slang instead of correct English). How could this possibly be preferable to reading a proper book? From this vantage, even those comics which adapted classic adventure stories (the 'improving' ones, once again, ironically) were merely vulgarizing literature.

Individual issues provoked more intense reactions. The

biggest fear was over violence, and especially the idea that this would brutalize children, and inculcate in them the philosophy that 'might is right'. Thus, war stories with their constant battle scenes and consequences-be-damned heroics were condemned, along with superhero titles and their endless punch-ups. The superhero comics were also attacked because it was feared that kids might try to punch their way through walls, like the Hulk, or fly out of windows, like Superman. As we have seen, the extreme violence in the American crime and horror titles was considered separately and was believed by some to lead directly to delinquency.

Sex in comics was another common bugbear (as ever, sex went with violence like salt with pepper). This was seen as simply too adult a matter for children to be concerned with – regardless of the fact that comics containing sexual material would appeal to an older readership in the first place. Examples included American crime comics, where women were depicted in a deliberately sleazy manner, in keeping with genre conventions, and some superhero titles, where voluptuous females were often a convenient prop to add sex interest. This kind of content was deemed by some to be beyond the pale – almost capable of turning innocent boys into drooling sex maniacs – and commentators on the subject tended to agree with Wertham that comics were 'aggressively sexual, in an abnormal way'.[36]

Later, awareness of other, more specifically political, issues grew, especially with the rise of the movements for Civil Rights and Womens' Liberation in the 1960s. The question of racism in adventure comics was addressed frequently, since stereotypes of blacks as criminals and 'social problems' were common. Even the very few comics that tried to redress the balance, and to reach a black readership, were often politically flawed (the superhero title *Black Panther* drew particular flak). Other racial minorities were similarly badly served. Arabs were 'shifty', conniving and treacherous; Orientals were 'inscrutable' sadists; and native Americans were monosyllabic savages. In some comics, the level of insensitivity could be astonishing: in one British title from the 1960s, the white hero uses the terms 'wog', 'nignog' and 'Gippo' in a single story.[37] Not surprisingly, both in Britain and America, there were only a handful of creators from ethnic backgrounds working in the industry.

Above: The Code stamp of approval, which appeared on the covers of all American comics submitted to the Comics Code Authority after 1955. Right: A member of the Authority explains its censoring effects (1954). Opposite: An exhibition of American horror comics in Britain (1954), organized by the National Union of Teachers at their London headquarters, who felt that some action should be called for to prevent their publication.

1. Certainly, many comics storytelling techniques pre-date the cinema, and often the influence may well have been the other way round (especially with regard to cutting, perspective and close-ups). See David Kunzle, *History of the Comic Strip: the Nineteenth Century* (Berkeley, University of California Press, 1989), Vol 2, Chapter 15 'Movement Before the Movies: the Language of the Comic Strip', pp 348–74.

2. It should also be said that, as with the comedy comics, some American strips did appear in British titles, eg The Hulk, Spider-Man, Superman, etc. See Denis Gifford, *Encyclopaedia of Comic Characters* (London, Longman, 1987).

3. Two useful general studies of British comics are: K Carpenter (ed) *Penny Dreadfuls and Comics* (London, Victoria and Albert Museum, 1983) and Gifford, *Encyclopaedia of Comic Characters*.

4. George Orwell, 'The Boys' Weeklies' (*Horizon*, March 1940). (These story papers were sometimes marketed as 'comics', and indeed, Orwell's piece is commonly remembered as an attack on the same.)

5. Contrary to popular belief, it was not just the violence of the American comics that Morris objected to. His religious beliefs were also offended by what he saw as the supernatural elements in many titles.

6. One such famous foreigner was Hugo Pratt, later to be a huge star in Europe (see p. 222).

7. Frank Hampson, speaking at some point in the early 1970s, quoted by Jonathan Glancy, in 'Sufferin' Satellites, the Comic is Dead' (*The Independent*, 6 March 1993, p 36). (Additionally, it is not widely known that Hampson reached such a low ebb that he attempted suicide.)

8. Though it was true that comics split into genres in the 1960s, in some cases there were predecessors: sport, for example, was represented in *Sports Fun* (Amalgamated Press, 1922) and *Football Comics* (1953).

9. *Warlord* (1974), published by DC Thomson, is sometimes portrayed as a precursor to *Battle*. However, it did not have the same 'edge'.

10. Les Daniels, *Marvel: Five Fabulous Decades of the World's Greatest Comics* (Virgin Books, 1991), p 16.

11. Some early strips were collected into reprint collections in the form outlined on p.53 (for example, Little Orphan Annie and Dick Tracy were featured in the Cupples and Leon hardcover series).

12. On American comics, the best general histories are L Daniels, *Comix: A History of Comic Books in America* (New York, Bonanza Books, 1971); M Benton, *The Comic Book in America* (Dallas, Taylor Publishing, 1989); R Goulart, *Over 50 Years of American Comic Books* (New York, Publications International, 1991). Also recommended are Les Daniels' twin histories of the two biggest publishers in America: *Marvel*, London, and *DC Comics: Sixty Years of the World's Favorite Comic Book Heroes* (1991 and Virgin Books, 1995).

13. Jerry Siegel, quoted in Benton, *ibid* p 22.

14. It is instructive to compare images of Superman in this period to contemporary Russian posters of heroicized workers.

15. The best in-depth study of Batman is R Pearson and W Uricchio (eds), *The Many Lives of the Batman* (London, BFI Publishing, 1991).

16. 'DC' was short for 'Detective Comics', also the name of the first title put out by the company.

17. For an academic look at superheroes, see Richard Reynolds' excellent book *Superheroes: A Modern Mythology* (London, Batsford, 1992).

18. The reprint history of *Captain Marvel* is particularly noteworthy. The comic was republished in various forms in the UK by Miller and Son from 1944. When the stories dried up, due to the legal dispute between Fawcett and National Periodicals, Miller, along with the Mick Angelo Studios, started their own new title, *Marvelman*, (1954). This anglicized version of Captain Marvel had the new hero's alter-ego change into Marvelman by uttering the word 'Kimota!' ('atomik!' backwards). The comic was moderately successful; the character has recently been revamped by Eclipse Comics under the name *Miracleman* (1985).

19. To be specific, 'Wonderman' appeared in in *Wonderman* (Paget, 1948) and 'The Bat' in *Thrill Comics* (Swan, 1940).

20. As noted earlier, some titles were reprinted in black-and-white by British companies, while western strips were a staple of British anthologies. In the main, these western strips were by British artists. The most famous example was 'Riders of the Range' by Charles Chilton and Jack Daniel in *The Eagle*.

21. 'An Interview with William M Gaines', conducted by Dwight Decker and Gary Groth (*The Comics Journal*, no 81, May 1983, p 66).

22. *Seduction of the Innocent* (Museum Press, 1955), p 70.

23. On Wertham, see J A Gilbert, *Cycle of Outrage: America's Reaction to the Juvenile Delinquent in the 1950s* (New York, Oxford University Press, 1986) and also M Barker's introduction to the new edition of Wertham, *Seduction of the Innocent* (Kitchen Sink), forthcoming. It is also important to note that the intellectual refutation of Wertham is not a recent phenomenon: many psychiatrists spoke out against him at the time.

24. See Peter Mauger, 'Should US "Comics" be Banned?' (*Picture Post*, 17 May, 1952). It is no coincidence that *Picture Post* was published by the same people that published *The Eagle*: the Hulton Press. Indeed, this notorious article included a passage contrasting *The Eagle* with the 'pernicious' American titles.

25. It is helpful to note that moral panics tend to be cyclical, and usually involve a process of scapegoating wider issues. Other examples of panics include the penny dreadful scare of the 1860s, and the 'video nasties' debate of the 1980s. For an introduction to the historical context for the subject, see G Pearson, *Hooligan: A History of Respectable Fears* (London, Macmillan, 1983).

26. Not every publisher had to submit comics for Code approval. The main exceptions were Dell and Gilberton (see below, pp 68-9 and 76).

27. On the campaign in Britain, see M Barker, *A Haunt of Fears* (London, Pluto Press, 1984).

28. 'Jack Kirby: Interview with Gary Groth' (*The Comics Journal*, no 134, Feb, 1990, p 92).

29. Some historians trace the origins of fandom to different sources. Certainly the role of Julius Schwartz as Editor-in-Chief at DC Comics was important in this respect, especially for his attention to fan-mail. Similarly, EC had a fan-mail service (answered by 'horror hosts'), plus a number of fanzines devoted to the company.

30. Stan Lee, quoted in Daniels, *Marvel*, p 105.

31. Some titles made limp reference to the anti-Vietnam War movement. For example, *Sgt Rock* ran with a 'Make War No More' label.

32. Warren were also responsible for a short-lived war comic-magazine, *Blazing Combat*, which was notable because it contained a number of anti-war stories in the EC tradition.

33. Gilberton originally started the line in 1941, calling them 'Classic Comics': they changed their name to 'Classics Illustrated' in 1947 in a search for a classier logo. The British editions were sometimes straight reprints, sometimes reprints with new covers, and occasionally entirely new comics.

34. The career stories of Siegel, Shuster and Kirby are complicated because at certain points they were earning relatively high page rates. However, when it came to royalties, they were treated the same as any other creator. They certainly never got the recognition they deserved.

35. A round-up of many of these criticisms can be found in N Tucker (ed) *Suitable for Children*, (Chatto and Windus, 1976).

36. Dr Wertham, *Seduction*, p 85.

37. 'The Nile Flows Red' (*Espionage*, no 8: Brugueditor, 1967).

38. Again, readers are reminded of Martin Barker's important work *Comics: Ideology, Power and the Critics* (Manchester University Press, 1989).

Sexism was seen as an even bigger problem. Most adventure comics were created by men for a male audience, and women generally came off very badly. There were three main objections to the images put forward: that women performed subordinate roles, typically as 'helpers' (nurses, mums, housewives); that they were used as plot devices, commonly as 'victims' (there to be rescued, and the subject for violence); and that they were portrayed as sex objects, all plunging necklines and endless legs (see above). The new awareness that feminism brought in the late 1960s initiated calls for the complete reassessment of the industry's treatment of women characters. However the publishers were unwilling to mess with (so far successful) genre conventions, and in fact very little was done until the 1980s, and even then the changes were largely cosmetic.

All these worries concerned the perceived 'effects' of adventure comics on readers, and on children especially. Although the level of theory was often very rudimentary, youngsters were thought of as empty vessels, unable to think for themselves: the idea that a visual medium like comics would have a lasting effect seemed like common sense. But in fact there was no empirical data to support this case, which rested on long-standing fears: as we saw in our last chapter, it can be traced back to the cult of the 'innocent child', somebody who should be kept away from vicious temptations of adult world at all costs. More recent analysis has been much more sophisticated, and shown, among other things, that children interpret comics according to their circumstances, and often 'set their own agenda'. The evidence is still inconclusive, however, and the debate on effects continues to be far from dead.[38]

Girl

Companion to EAGLE, SWIFT and ROBIN

28 JANUARY 1961
VOL 10 No 4
EVERY WEDNESDAY

5d

Win a holiday in ITALY

Susan of St. Bride's *in* **TIME FOR STUDY**

Student nurse Susan Marsh, having fun with her gay new friend, Fenella, neglects to help new student Charity Smith with her studies. Then, because Fenella forgets to pass on a message, Charity's mother is rushed into hospital. Later, Fenella is brought in unconscious, after a car smash. Susan and Charity fail their exam and must start again with the junior nurses.

ALL BECAUSE I WENT OUT WITH FENELLA INSTEAD OF WORKING WITH CHARITY...

AWAY FROM MY FRIENDS, AMONG THE NEW STUDENTS...

SERIOUSLY ILL
Miss Jackson
Mrs Thomas
Miss Darcy
Mrs Campbell
Miss O'Sullivan
Miss French

POOR FENELLA — I WONDER HOW SHE IS?

AND SO...

COULD I SPEAK TO FENELLA, PLEASE SISTER?

MISS DARCY? I'M TO TELL ANYONE WHO ASKS THAT SHE'S 'QUITE COMFORTABLE' NOW.

OH, GOOD! I'LL GO AND SEE HER, THEN.

SPEAK TO HER? DON'T YOU KNOW...?

Four

Something for the girls

Opposite: Cover, *Girl* (Hulton Press, 1961), a sister comic to *The Eagle*, with the same high production values. 'Susan of St Bride's': Art: Peter Kay, script: Ruth Adam. Far right: An idealized, middle-class vision of a little girl and her comic (1957). Right: A less innocent, working-class female strip star, 'Beryl the Peril', *The Topper* (DC Thomson, 1953). Art/script: David Law. Below: Cover, *Wonder Woman* (DC Comics, 1960), featuring the number one female American superhero. Art: Anon.

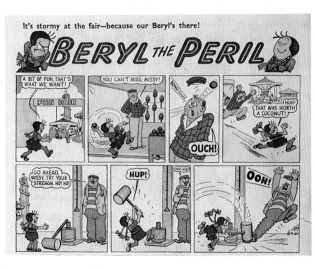

The period from the 1930s to the 1960s saw enormous advances in the genres of humour and adventure in comics, yet the audience was perceived to be primarily boys between the ages of eight and twelve. Girls, although they had been catered for by some of the early humour titles, were increasingly overlooked, and this left publishers with a problem: how to appeal to the other half of the juvenile market? On both sides of the Atlantic, new strategies were tried, some of which were so successful that they reshaped the medium forever. Despite these innovations, however, it is a sad fact that titles for girls rarely feature in histories of modern comics: the 1990s collectors' market is essentially uninterested in them, and therefore they remain a forgotten story.[1]

In Britain, comics for girls were the final aspect of the drive towards diversification within the industry, and in many ways the most interesting. The adventure boom had been spectacular, with *The Eagle* being followed by a wave of titles devoted to war, science fiction and sport. From 1950 onwards, these were joined by an increasing number of girls' comics, which often followed their format, but which reflected notions of 'female interest' current at the time (which typically meant role stereotyping every bit as crude as in the boys' comics). What was remarkable about the new titles was that a significant number managed to notch up sales that matched their male counterparts.

But before looking at these, we need to backtrack for a moment. For, in fact, comics for girls and women had a much longer history in Britain. Even during the initial boom of comic sales before the First World War, there

had been attempts to appeal to this market. *Ally Sloper's Half Holiday* had included several female characters, most notably Tootsie Sloper, daughter of the famous derelict, who became the focus for jokes about votes for women and other political issues. Other early comics included fashion pages, with sketches of the latest dresses, hats and so on.

The children's humour comics, which were the successors to these adult titles, also made a play for female readers, with characters like Keyhole Kate, Beryl the Peril and Minnie the Minx becoming national institutions. If many of these publications had readership profiles that were split roughly fifty-fifty along gender lines, there were other comics in the period from the 1920s to the 1950s which were targeted at more specific audiences. For younger readers, for example, there was *Playbox* (Amalgamated Press, 1925), which featured the adventures of the sisters of *Rainbow*'s Tiger Tim (among them Tiger Tilly and Olive Ostrich).[2] Also, for slightly older girls, there were story papers, which increased the amount of space that they gave over to comic strips from the 1930s onwards.

In Britain the first of the 'boom' comics of the 1950s had links with the earlier story papers. *School Friend* (Amalgamated Press, 1950) was a revival of long-defunct title, and was an instant success (in large part due to the popularity of its cover strip, 'The Silent Three at St Kit's', about a secret fourth-form conspiracy to combat a 'tyrannical head prefect'). The tone of the content was essentially middle class, picturing a world where boarding schools were the centre of social definition;

GIRL 1 February 1952

THE NEW SUPER-COLOUR WEEKLY FOR EVERY GIRL

Girl

EVERY FRIDAY

4½d

SISTER PAPER TO EAGLE.

VOL. 1 No. 14 FEBRUARY 1, 1952

WE'VE NO TIME TO LOSE. WE MUST GET THE TREASURE FROM THE PRISON-WELL BEFORE MARLOS FINDS WE'VE ESCAPED.

Above: Detail and cover, *Girl* (Hulton Press, 1952). Art/script: Ray Bailey. A pioneering girls' title, somewhat upmarket in tone. The strip 'Kitty Hawke' was about a remarkably well-heeled all-female aircrew (the navigator's name was the Hon Patricia D'Arcy). Below: Cover, *Romeo* (DC Thomson, 1968), one of the early British romance comics. Art: Anon. Below right: Cover, *Bunty* (DC Thomson, 1963). Art: Anon. A huge success with eight to twelve year olds which frequently included 'free gifts' such as the 'pretty party bracelet'.

Romeo

BEST FOR LOVE STORIES

where awfully nice 'gels' stuck up for their chums, disapproved of sneaks and rotters, and were ever so good at swimming. It was a seductive formula, and *School Friend* ran as a weekly for sixteen years, inspiring other story-paper conversions in its wake (most notably *The Girl's Crystal*, Amalgamated Press, in 1953).

Very much in the same vein, and an even bigger hit, was *Girl* (Hulton), a sister comic to *The Eagle*. Launched in 1951, it boasted the same high production standards, tabloid format and high moral tone as its counterpart. Furthermore, the original idea was to ape the kind of stories that made *The Eagle* so popular. Hence, the cover strip, 'Kitty Hawke and her All-Girl Crew', was a Dan Dare variant set in the skies rather than space ('Well, here we go again, gang, one more job chalked up to prove to Dad that we can operate his planes as efficiently as the glorious males!'). This was backed up by various other blood-stirring yarns, and by *Eagle*-esque personality profiles of heroines such as Marie Curie and Joan of Arc. However, this strategy did not prove popular, and within two years *Girl* was featuring more sedate tales about ballet, showjumping and valentines, and featuring on its front page a more traditional series about a boarding school ('Wendy and Jinx'). A valuable lesson had been learned: stock adventure formulas were not translatable from boys' to girls' comics.

The 'jolly hockey sticks' tone of *Girl*, *School Friend* and their ilk was not overturned until the late 1950s, and the advent of romance comics. In Britain the boom was started by *Marilyn* (Amalgamated Press, 1955) and was followed by the more famous duo of *Romeo* (DC Thomson, 1957) and *Valentine* (Amalgamated Press, 1957). These titles went for an older readership, and hinted at the immensely exciting adult world of sex. They could hardly be described as 'steamy', however,

and in most respects were as much a reflection of their era as any of their predecessors. The stories were about 'true love' and the moral rectitude of marriage, and typically ended in nothing more shocking than a clinch. They express the kind of innocent, virginal sensibility we might now associate with Mills and Boon novels. However, these comics were followed by a spate of pocket-sized romance titles from 1957–63, such as *Picture Romance Library* (Arthur Pearson, 1958) and *Romantic Confessions Picture Library* (Fleetway, 1961) that were typically more racy, having been influenced by the pulp-style romance comic books being imported from America, which we will discuss later.

If some British publishers were looking to older girls for their market, others realized that the eight to twelve age range was being neglected. DC Thomson took its chance. *Bunty* (1958) forged a different path to its predecessors by going for a 'cheap and cheerful' look. It was printed on the same low-quality paper stock as *The Beano* and it targeted a more working-class readership. It also hit upon an entirely new formula, typically involving a child alone in the world, away from fondly remembered parents, trying earnestly to do the right thing. Characters tended to be stereotyped in a way which was not a million miles from the formulas employed by Enid Blyton in her novels. They included the Cinderella figure, the wicked stepmother, bullying girl, gossip and swot. Occasionally stories would be set in Victorian times, thus providing a setting for sub-Dickensian tales involving pickpockets, orphans and toffs.

The psychology of *Bunty* stories could sometimes be almost cruel. A great deal of time was spent in feuds:

No. 300–OCTOBER 12, 1963.

BUNTY

32 PAGES EVERY WEEK

EVERY TUESDAY. Price 5d.

FREE Inside

PRETTY PARTY BRACELET

YOU'LL BE THE ENVY OF ALL YOUR FRIENDS

petty bickerings and misunderstandings between friends, punctuated by purse-lipped jealousies between enemies ('Now Nancy Smithers was netball captain, I hated her even more!'). The most popular strip, 'The Four Marys' was ostensibly a traditional tale about rivalry at a boarding school, but was much darker than anything that had appeared in *Girl*. Other stories centred on predicaments: aspiring ballerinas kept from their vocations by evil stepmothers and would-be nurses who have to deal with a crisis. What the story lines all had in common were heroines that were victims – everyone and everything was out to get them. Sometimes supernatural elements would be introduced to heighten tensions. In one story a 'magic mirror' makes any girl that looks into it obsessively vain.

These formulas proved immensely appealing. *Bunty* was a massive seller, and came to define the style for comics aimed at this age range. DC Thomson followed it with *Judy* (1960), *Diana* (1963) and *Mandy* (1967).[3] In the 1970s IPC (International Publishing Corporation) joined the fray, and started to make the running with titles like *Tammy* (1971) and *Jinty* (1974). It seemed for a while that there could not be enough titles to satisfy demand, and such was the competition between them that new launches were accompanied by an array of free gifts – rings, brooches and bangles – to snare the first-time buyer. If anything, these newer titles tended to emphasize the darker story lines – especially the IPC line which did not have to hold to the kind of Scottish Presbyterian moralizing that characterized the Thomson comics. In fact, creators at IPC would sometimes amuse themselves by taking things to extremes. 'Becky Never Saw the Ball', in *Tammy*, for instance, told the heart-warming story of a blind tennis player. Sexual innuendo was another common in-joke.[4]

The creation of a huge market for younger girls made publishers aware that there were no longer any suitable comics for teenagers (by the mid-1960s, the boom in romantic comics was effectively over). If the momentum was to be maintained, new strategies had to be tried. Again, DC Thomson took the lead. Recognizing that

Britain had become the centre of the 'hip' 1960s world, with Carnaby Street and the Beatles symbolizing a new phase in youth culture, the publisher attempted to produce a publication which mixed comics, women's magazines, and the 'pop' papers. The result was a new kind of swinging title for swinging times, *Jackie* (1964).[5]

The name 'Jackie' was itself very 'modern', and the comic's mix of beauty tips, pop-star pin-ups, and strips starring Mary Quant-attired teenagers was a daring new direction (in fact, much of *Jackie*'s more adult content was due to the fact that it originated out of the branch of Thomson's that published women's magazines, rather than from its comics department). Other aspects were also new. Unlike *Bunty* and its competitors, the characters in *Jackie* did not go to school: they were wage earners, enjoying their 'freedom', and commonly shared accommodation with other hip wage earners in some large metropolis. They were physically and mentally more mature than the intended readership, and this was undoubtedly a major attraction.

The strips themselves tended to be romantic in an essentially traditional way, but with a 'sophisticated' veneer. 'Catching a man' was a top priority, and stories typically ended in the conventional final-panel snog. However, the artwork was more cinematic than most comics (there were a large number of foreign artists who were allowed to indulge in European styles), and the plots usually had some measure of psychological depth. Later, the addition of romantic black-and-white 'photo stories' would become one of the comic's most

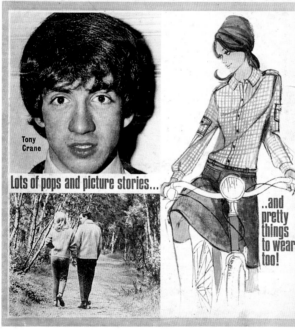

This page and opposite: Girls' comics get trendy. Above: Cover, Jackie (DC Thomson, 1965), the quintessential 'swinging sixties' title. Art: Anon. Above left: Cover, Diana (DC Thomson, 1973). Art: Anon. A less illustrious predecessor, and a sort of half-way house between the old romance titles and Jackie. Both comics had more in common with women's magazines than with traditional comics. Opposite: Page from 'Words of Love', Jackie (DC Thomson, 1965). Art/script: Anon. This demonstrates a more 'adult' rendering style, plus a storyline about the love-life of an independent (wage-earning) woman.

popular features. As for the text content, this varied from lightweight articles about pop stars ('Who's Your Favourite Rolling Stone?') to more serious advice columns ('Can Kissing Make You Pregnant?'), though increasingly more space was given to consumer-style pieces about beauty products, as advertising became more important.

With sales of over a million per issue by the early 1970s, *Jackie*'s place in the market was unassailable: it became the natural 'next step' for girls who had previously read *Bunty* and its like. However, its dominance was challenged in the 1980s by the appearance of much more uninhibited publications for young women such as *My Guy*, *Oh Boy* and *Blue Jeans*. These were more magazines than comics, and included subject matter including rape, AIDS and how to put on a condom. They made *Jackie* look very old hat indeed, and when the comic finally folded in 1993 the then-Managing Editor of DC Thomson commented with some understatement: 'Girls today are that bit more sophisticated, the questions they ask are more informed ... *Jackie* has become an old lady.'[6]

Jackie was the final major success of the British boom. Why girls' comics should have declined after this point is a moot point. We shall see that the rise of television was doubtlessly a factor. However, it was also an unrewarding environment for the creators. Increasingly it became the norm for talented writers and artists to move over into boys' comics, simply because here at least there might be a possibility of being head-hunted by the American companies, which paid better and allowed credits. Those creators that did stay with girls' titles thus tended to be second-rate, and unable to live up to the expectations of the 1960s and early 1970s.

By way of a postscript, it is also interesting to note that despite the diversity of British titles from this period, they all had one thing in common: they were all written and drawn by men. Female creators did not have a place in the industry, and men hired by the bigger companies tended to work on two or three comics simultaneously, boys' and girls'. True, it is possible to identify one or two successful women artists: for example, Marie Duval on *Ally Sloper's Half Holiday* (the wife of Sloper's creator, Charles Ross), Evelyn Flinders on *School Friend* and Pamela Chapeau at *Diana*. However, they were exceptions. In the late 1960s things started to improve, but it remained the case that women with creative talents were still much more able to 'get on' in other fields, such as children's book illustration and advertising.[7]

In the United States, the girls' comics industry was less well defined. It did not occupy such a major place in comics culture as in Britain, but nevertheless gave rise to some groundbreaking titles.[8] From the earliest years of comic books, girls had been understood to make up part of the audience for certain genres. The early comedy titles, for example, attracted a wide female readership, while the Disney comics and other 'funny animal' titles were certainly unisex. There had also been a tradition of newspaper strips aimed at women and girls, and as these became comic books in their own right, so they took that

Continued on page 23.

The newest of the DC magazines

SENSATION COMICS

10¢

Featuring THE SENSATIONAL NEW ADVENTURE STRIP CHARACTER— Wonder Woman

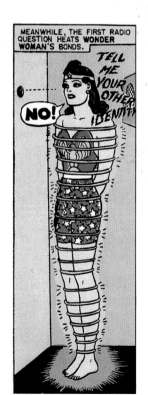

This page and opposite: American comics' premier heroine, *Wonder Woman* (all examples DC Comics). The early stories were notable for her willingness to reform rather than punish criminals. Above: Cover, *Sensation Comics* (1942), featuring her first appearance as a lead strip. Art: Jon Blummer. Below: Panel from *Sensation Comics* (1945). Art: HG Peter. With our stoic star in bondage.

audience with them. Having a female character as the star was an effective way of achieving this, and examples included, in the early years, *Little Orphan Annie* (McKay, 1937), *Tillie the Toiler* (Dell, 1941), and, undoubtedly the most popular of all, *Little Lulu* (Dell, 1945).

The dominant genre in American comics at this time, superheroes, started off as a resolutely male preserve. That is, until 1941, when a character who made her debut in *All Star Comics* (National Periodicals, 1940), overturned the trend in spectacular fashion. She was to gain worldwide fame as Wonder Woman. Given her own title in 1942, this female riposte to the success of Superman was designed specifically with girls in mind, and embodied feminist politics in a way that was unprecedented. Yet at the same time, the comic also managed to appeal to boys due to its undisguised eroticism.

Created by William Moulton Marston, Wonder Woman was revolutionary in a psychological sense. Indeed, Marston had previously had a distinguished career as a doctor of psychology: he discovered the blood-pressure device that would later lead to the invention of the lie-detector test. His theory at the time was that women were more honest than men, and he turned to writing comics as a way of expressing this and other ideas about the female mind. Wonder Woman would be the bearer of the message that women should realize their potential, should fight for equal rights and that a feminized society would be more caring than the prevailing patriarchy. She would be concerned not so much with the punishment of crime, but with the re-habilitation of criminals. Above all, she would only use force as a last resort, if the appeal of reason failed.

Top and above: Pages and panels from *Wonder Woman* (1960). Art/script: Anon. Opposite: Cover, *Wonder Woman* (1967). Art: Anon. By this time, the heroine was more prone to sort things out with her fists, and was being referred to as 'The Amazing Amazon'.

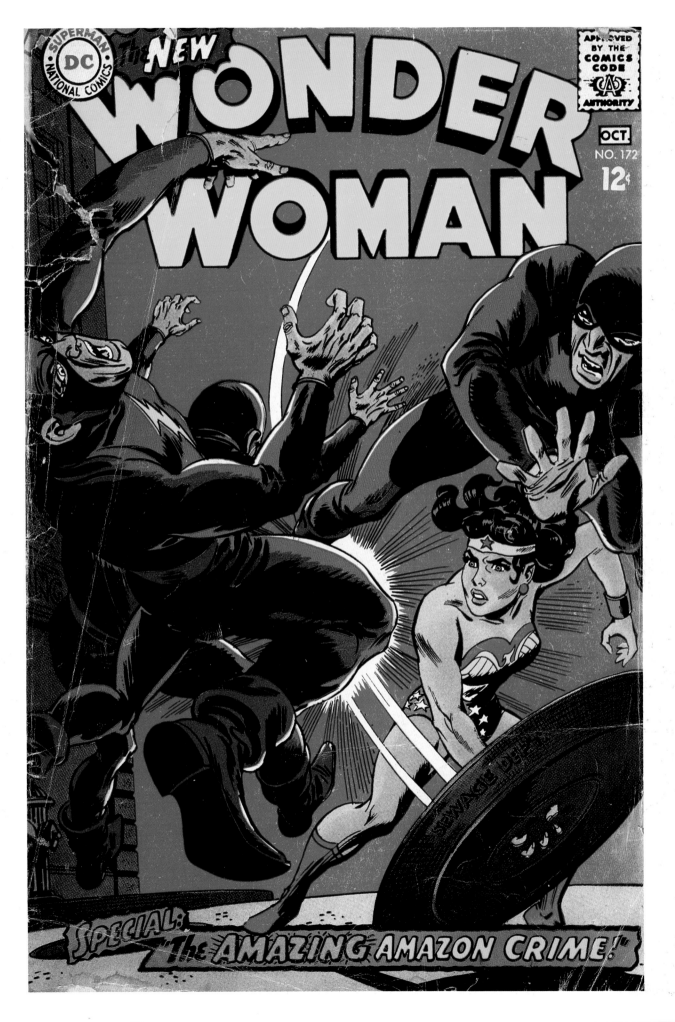

Although Marston wanted the comic to be current, and to reflect the changing political situation in America (he foresaw the inevitability of involvement in the Second World War, and perceived the resurgence of the women's movement on the home front as a consequence of the drafting of the male workforce), he also realized the need for *Wonder Woman* to have a mythological dimension. So, to this end, he invented an origin story set on Paradise Island, the secret twentieth-century home of the Amazons where no man may set foot. This race of immortal super women is ruled by Queen Hippolyte, who has a daughter, Princess Diana: 'as lovely as Aphrodite, as wise as Athena, with the speed of Mercury and the strength of Hercules'.

The Princess eventually leaves the island to become 'Wonder Woman', in order to help America, and in particular, American women. She is armed only with a costume resembling the American flag, and a magical lasso: a device which not only compels anybody it binds to obey her, but also to confront their innermost feelings and motivations (again, an incentive to reform). In a story from 1943 entitled 'Battle for Womanhood', she uses the lasso to rescue a woman whose life has been shattered by her scheming husband. The wife tells Wonder Woman, 'What can a weak girl do?' She replies, 'Get Strong! Earn your own living – join the WAACs or WAVES and fight for our country!'

The men in these early stories typically came off very badly. They were either misogynists, like the evil villain 'Dr Psycho', or helpless and ineffectual creatures needing to be rescued, such as Wonder Woman's own boyfriend,

Steve Trevor. This kind of role reversal was quite deliberate on the part of Marston. 'Not even girls want to be girls,' he wrote in 1943, 'so long as our feminine archetype lacks force, strength and power.'[9]

Yet, Marston was a psychologist, and he must have realized that male readers would be attracted to the comic by its Freudian sexual imagery. Most notoriously, scenes of bondage were everywhere, not just those involving the lasso, but also stories including whips, chains and manacles. The editor of the comic, Sheldon Mayer, was suspicious of this, but chose to play along. He commented later, that: 'There was a certain symbolism that Marston engaged in which was very simple and very broad ... I suspect it probably sold more comic books than I realized.'[10]

After a period of spectacular sales in the early 1940s (mostly, it has to be said, to male readers), *Wonder Woman*'s star began to wane. The political climate changed after the war: servicemen returned from overseas and there was a drive to push women back into the home. Moreover, the death of Marston in 1947 meant that thereafter the stories became more ordinary. Under successive writers, the heroine became just another superhero ('The Amazin' Amazon', as one strapline rather tackily put it), dependent on fists and gadgetry, and more inclined to become romantically distracted. In other words, although *Wonder Woman* has continued to be popular until the present day, and is one of the very few titles to have been continuously published since the 1940s, she was never really the same.

There were several *Wonder Woman* copyists over the

Above: Panel from *Wonder Woman* (1960). Art/script: Anon. A wonderfully curt brush-off for a suitor. Right: Pages from 'Supergirl', *Action Comics* (DC Comics, 1963). Art/script: Anon. It was stressed that Superman's counterpart ('The Girl of Steel') was in fact his cousin from Krypton, in order to pre-empt any notion that they might be potential mates, and so not to interfere with his ongoing affair with Lois Lane. But she never really caught on, and stories could sometimes become word-heavy soap-operas, like this one.

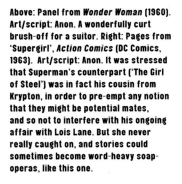

"Sheena" ©1939 Real Adventures Publishing Co., Inc.

Above and right: Page and panel from *Sheena, Queen of the Jungle* (Real Adventures Publishing, 1939). Art: probably Mort Meskin. Script: W. Morgan Thomas (pen-name for Jerry Iger). The first of the 'jungle queens', Sheena's costume was pretty racy for the time. This particular strip is in black and white because it was originally intended for export to the British Empire.

years. In the 1940s, these included *Miss Fury* (Marvel, 1942), *Mary Marvel* (Fawcett, 1945) – a counterpart to Captain Marvel – and *Black Cat* (Harvey, 1946). Later, Supergirl, Superman's teenage cousin, made her debut in *Action Comics* (1959), and was eventually given her own title in 1972.[11] The 1960s wave of Marvel super-heroes was complemented in the 1970s and 1980s with *Ms Marvel* (1977), *Spider-Woman* (1978) and the *She-Hulk* (1980). None, however, had the same mythical qualities, or panache, as their progenitor.

The so-called 'jungle queens' were close relatives with the superheroes. Popular in the 1940s and 1950s they were ostensibly aimed at a female audience, but also attracted substantial adolescent male followings, largely due to the fact that the heroines tended to wear little other than leopard-skin bikinis. The most famous of all was Sheena, Queen of the Jungle, given her own title in 1942 (Fiction House). She was a sort of female Tarzan, who would befriend animals and swing through the jungle on vines to confront wrongdoers. Others included *Nyoka the Jungle Girl* (Fawcett, 1945), and *Rulah* and *Zegra Jungle Empress* (both Fox Comics and both 1948). The stories were all pretty similar, and usually incorporated racist sub-texts: the typical reaction of the superstitious 'wild' tribespeople to these white goddesses was to bow down in awe and fear.

Superheroines and jungle queens aside, American publishers were finding other ways to capitalize on the female market. For youngsters, a number of 'wholesome adventure' comics appeared, the foremost titles among them published by an organization called The Parents' Institute. Their most popular offering, *Calling All Girls* (1941), was half-comic and half-magazine, and mixed strips centred around 'morally proper' role models, such as nurses and historical heroines, with articles on etiquette and 'back to school fashions', and comments from 'Advisory Editors' such as Shirley Temple. The idea behind the title was to offer an 'educational and uplifting' alternative to other comics on the shelves, much in the same way as Britain's *Girl* in the 1950s.[12] Other Institute hits for girls included *Polly Pigtails* (1946) and *Sweet Sixteen* (1946).

For slightly older female readers, there developed a market in what became known as 'teen comics'. The leaders in this field were undoubtedly Archie Publications. Their *Archie* comics had been a big hit, especially among adolescent boys (see p 38), and in the 1950s they were not slow to diversify with titles aimed at girls in a similar age range. In particular, the supporting characters were given comics of their own: thus, *Suzie* in 1945, *Katy Keene* in 1949 and, most popularly, *Betty and Veronica* (the blonde and brunette rivals for Archie's affections) in 1950. These were all created on similar lines, starring cute women in bobby sox, and concentrating on 'dating' disasters and misunderstandings. They pictured an idealized adolescence wholly obsessed with the issue of lust versus true love – though always within a highly moral context. Only *Katy Keene* offered something slightly different due to the comic's emphasis on clothes and fashion. The star's nickname was 'the Pin-Up Queen',

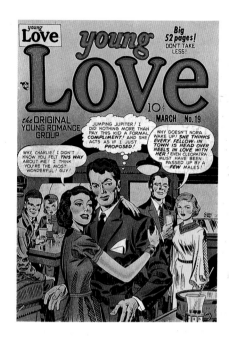

and her wardrobe was as much the focus of attention as the plots. Readers were encouraged to send in their own fashion designs for Katy to wear.

The Archie titles were joined by a host of competitors over time. The more traditional were matched by *Candy* (Quality, 1947), *Dotty* and *Vicky* (both Ace, 1948) and *Kathy* (Standard, 1949), while 'fashion model' titles included *Millie the Model* and *Patsy Walker* (both Marvel, 1945). Such comics prospered in the 1950s, but started to die out in the 1960s. Though they were joined by further additions that were more pop-literate, such as *Josie* (Archie Publications, 1963), *Bunny* (Harvey, 1966) and *Tippy Teen* (Tower, 1965), it was increasingly clear that their heyday had passed. Not only were bobby sox and innocent romance out of fashion, but teen-orientated television shows and movies had effectively taken over.

The final sector of the American female market to be conquered was that of mature women, or at least girls over sixteen. These were catered for with a boom in romance comics from the late 1940s. An extension of the teen comics craze, they were also an attempt to cash in on the popularity of the confession-style pulp magazines. At one point in 1950, more romance comics appeared on American newsagents shelves than any other genre.

The most influential title was *Young Romance* (Prize, 1947) written by Joe Simon and drawn by Jack Kirby, who brought the same intensity of feeling to tales of love, adultery and revenge as he would later inject into the Marvel superhero comics. The pulpy narrative also had a unique energy: 'As she fought to free herself, I tightened my hold on her arms ... Lola's face suddenly arched upward – her full red lips directly beneath my own!' This was erotic stuff indeed, and marked out new territory in romantic storytelling: within a few months, the comic was selling over a million copies.

Other titles followed, few of which were technically in the same class. Publishers such as Fox and Fawcett jumped in with both feet. Titles like *Sweethearts* (Fawcett, 1948), *My Love Story* (Fox, 1949), *Exciting Romances*

(Fawcett, 1949) and *My Private Life* (Fox, 1950) seemed to multiply by the day. Content-wise, they ran the gamut from 'innocent' to 'steamy', and commonly tried to distance themselves from other juvenile comics by featuring photo-covers that were reminiscent of magazines. The Fawcett line never even used the word 'comics', while some titles carried special labels to warn off youngsters: even *Young Romance* carried one saying 'For the More ADULT Reader of Comics'.

As the boom gathered pace, so there was a curious period of crossovers with other genres. For example, *Cowboy Love* (Fawcett, 1949) and *Western Love* (Prize, 1949) ('He rustled my heart!') were joined by *Wartime Romances* (St John, 1951) and *GI Brides* (Superior, 1954). There was also a slide into sleaze, as some publishers attempted to pack their comics with as much sex as they could get away with, which was not much by today's standards. The advent of the Comics Code in 1955, however, meant toning things down, and thereafter romance comics were never really the same. Most publishers cut back their lines, and although there were still nearly forty different titles on the shelves in the 1960s, they were less innovative, and less sexy, than their predecessors, and the market for women craving cheap thrills had largely shifted back to magazines.

This survey of American comics for girls and women would not be complete without making the important point that almost all the comics were produced by men. As in Britain, the gender balance within the industry was overwhelmingly skewed in their favour, though in America far more women were involved in 'behind the scenes' work such as colouring, lettering and editing. It is true that there was a brief period during the Second World War when more women became active as writers and artists, due to the drafting of the old workforce. Indeed, some publishers became especially dependent upon women, such as Fiction House. Paradoxically, this was a company known for titles starring scantily-clad sex objects; their jungle queen comics were often created by women using male pseudonyms. Nevertheless this aberration was short-lived, and afterwards women disappeared into the background again until the late 1960s, when things started to improve. This return was only a very gradual development, as we shall see.[13]

Controversy was never far away for the girls' comics. During the boom years between the 1940s and 1960s in Britain and America, society exhibited a heightened sense of protectiveness about female children – indeed females in general – and this led to their comics being scrutinized in, if anything, a more detailed manner than the boys' titles. In the early years, the few feminists who were inclined to speak out complained about the kind of role models that the comics offered – if female characters had aspirations, they were rarely to do with taking on traditional male roles or occupations. Right-wingers also picked up on any 'dubious' elements in the stories which might 'pervert' the idyllic juvenile world they evoked. Dr Wertham, for example, spent time attacking *Wonder Woman* for the lesbianism implicit in the idea of an island of Amazons.

The romantic comics came in for particular criticism. In the 1950s, the American titles were hammered for being immoral, salacious and un-Christian, and, as we have seen, suffered badly when the Code was introduced. Later, with the rise of Women's Liberation in the late 1960s, the romance titles that remained in existence were attacked from another perspective, with feminist critiques emphasizing that there might just be more to life than 'catching a man'. Similarly, in Britain, *Jackie* became the focus for feminist scorn.

In the 1980s, these various controversies were reassessed, and new theories about reading comics were suggested – especially with regard to female audiences. It was shown, for example, that readers develop a relationship with 'their' comics, and that stories can be interpreted in wildly differing ways. For example, a plot that may have appeared to be 'sexist' according to traditional feminist viewpoints may in fact have been empowering for the reader, depending on how it was received. Also, it was argued that by looking closely at the comics themselves, rather than starting from an entrenched ideological position, it was possible to see how storytelling changed with time, and thus how it was impossible to generalize about stereotypes. This new theorizing did not imply by any means that feminist critiques were no longer valid, merely that the debate surrounding comics for girls and women has become more sophisticated.[14]

As we shall see later, the position of women in comics has changed a great deal in the post-1960s period. Today, there are more women creators than ever before, and more positive images of women depicted. Paradoxically, there are also more sexist titles than ever, and the gender profile of the industry is still overwhelmingly male. Meanwhile, the new mainstream comics market has become confined to specialist 'fan shops', which are male enclaves, and the traditional 'girls' comic' on the news-stands has virtually disappeared. So far as this latter market is concerned, in the age of cheaply produced, high-quality 'pop' magazines, a revival of this once-thriving genre seems very unlikely.

1. This is indicated by the fact that most collectors' 'price guides' exclude girls' comics altogether.

2. *Playbox* was, in fact, a failure, and within two years of its launch was being re-marketed to a mixed-sex readership.

3. DC Thomson cannily adapted the *Bunty* formula for a nursery-age readership with *Twinkle* (1968).

4. One creator who worked on girls' comics later recalled a number of risqué cover straplines, including 'Knit Yourself a Dutch Cap!' Interview with Kevin O'Neill, *Comics Journal*, no 122, June 1988, p 89.

5. The nearest precursor to *Jackie* in terms of referencing pop culture was probably *Boyfriend* (City Magazines, 1959), in which pop stars were the inspiration for strips.

6. DC Thomson managing editor Harrison Watson, quoted in: Helen Renshaw, 'Darling, how can you leave me this way?', *Today*, 29 May 1993.

7. Even newspaper cartooning was more welcoming. There are far more examples of successful women writers and artists in this field than in comics (such as Mary Tourtel, who created Rupert the Bear for the *Daily Express*).

8. Although American comics were not officially distributed in Britain until 1959, there were two main kinds of title that made an impact before this date: the superhero comics and the romance genre. Both gained entry into Britain via military bases and ports, as had been the route for the comedy and boys' comics.

9. William Moulton Marston, writing in *The American Scholar*, 1943, quoted in Mike Benton, *Superhero Comics of the Golden Age* (Dallas, Taylor Publishing, 1992), p 140.

10. Sheldon Mayer, quoted in Les Daniels, *DC Comics: Sixty Years of the World's Favorite Comic Book Heroes* (London, Virgin Books, 1995), p 61.

11. Lois Lane, Superman's girlfriend, had been given her own title in 1958.

12. Parents' Institute publisher George Hecht made this attitude clear in an editorial to another title, *True Comics* (1941): 'We believe that by offering comic readers a magazine that looked like the others, but was informational as well as entertaining, we could fight fire with fire. In other words,... a substitute for less desirable comics. Psychologically, such substitution is better than a prohibition of all comics while they are so very popular.'

13. For more on the contribution of women to American comics, see Trina Robbins and Catherine Yronwode, *Women in the Comics* (California, Eclipse Books, 1985), and Trina Robbins, *A Century of Women Cartoonists* (Princeton, Kitchen Sink, 1992). Both books represent valuable exercises in the 'recovery of history'.

14. The key title in this revision is Martin Barker, *Comics, Ideology, Power and the Critics* (Manchester University Press, 1989). For a feminist critique of *Jackie*, see Angela McRobbie, 'Jackie: An Ideology of Adolescent Femininity' in *Popular Culture: Past and Present* (Routledge/Open University Press, 1989), pp 263–83.

Five

Going underground

Opposite: Cover to the high voltage title that jump-started the underground, *Zap* (Apex Novelties, 1968). Robert Crumb's hilariously subversive masterpiece. In fact, issue no 0 was to appear after no 1 on account of lost artwork. Right: Panel from 'Mr Natural' (Print Mint, 1970). Art/script: Robert Crumb. Far right: Cover, *Slow Death Funnies* (Last Gasp, 1978), a protest against atomic power. Art: Greg Irons. Below: Back cover, *Deviant Slice* (Print Mint, 1972). Art: Greg Irons. A *Time* magazine parody referring to the Vietnam War.

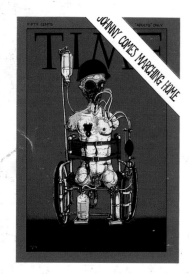

The late 1960s saw the emergence of 'underground comics', a new wave of humorous, hippie-inspired comic books that were as politically radical as they were artistically innovative. As the name suggests, they had nothing to do with the mainstream – in fact, in many ways they were antithetical to it. Instead of pandering to a kids' market, these titles spoke to the counter-culture on its own terms, which meant dealing with subjects like drugs, anti-Vietnam protest, rock music and, above all, sex. For this reason, the new comics became known as 'comix', both to set them apart, and to emphasize the 'x' for X-rated.

The underground was basically an American phenomenon, which was then imitated in Britain. It originated from a variety of sources, which can be traced back to the 1950s. First, and perhaps most importantly, there was the influence of the *Mad* tradition. Harvey Kurtzman had liberated comedy in comics with this seminal title: along with its more inventive imitators, it was to inspire a new generation of cartoonists to push back the boundaries of satire even further.[1] More directly, in his post-*Mad* magazine *Help!*, Kurtzman provided pages devoted to 'amateur talent', where many future undergrounders got their first break.[2]

Secondly, there was the college magazine route. These publications were more sophisticated than their British 'rag mag' counterparts, and came out on a regular basis. They were a focus for localized, campus-satire, but also took in more wide-ranging political issues. Again, they were highly influenced by *Mad*, and gave many comix

cartoonists their first exposure. Certain titles were particularly important in this respect, such as the University of Texas's *The Texas Ranger* and the University of Wisconsin's *Snide*.[3]

Thirdly, there was an anti-Comics Code reaction, which provided a kind of negative impetus to underground creators. As children, these were the very people who had been worst hit by the 1950s scare – sometimes having their comics collections torn up by their parents, or thrown on the playground fires. Now it was time for payback: where the Code had stipulated 'no violence', 'no sex', 'no drugs' and 'no social relevance', the underground comix would indulge themselves to the maximum in every category. If the Code meant, essentially, that a comic was prevented from saying anything meaningful about the real world, then by defying it this possibility was reawakened.

But the underground was also an expression of its time politically, and the final essential ingredient in its make-up was a new kind of political awareness. In the mid-to-late 1960s, the hippie movement in America was engaged, to a greater or lesser degree, with protest against the Vietnam War, the Civil Rights struggle, Anarchism, Socialism, Women's Liberation and Gay Liberation. Add to this an interest in the spiritual value of taking drugs (marijuana and LSD being the favourites), and of 'free love' (the pill had become widely available a few years before), and you had – very simplistically speaking – a thriving 'counterculture'.

Of course, a counterculture had always been present

in American society, but at no point in history had it been so focused, or so large, as at this moment. The comix mirrored – albeit distortedly – this unique development, and were at the same time conveyors of the hippie creed. They became a place where the counterculture could debate with itself, and could flex its muscles. In fact they were as much a product of events as the many, and much better-remembered, rock bands that emerged in the same period.

It is this convergence of influences that caused the comix explosion to happen when it did. The boom lasted from about 1968 to 1975, when many thousands of comix were produced, mostly on a self-published basis. Unlike conventional comics, underground strips were not created in a production-line environment. Writers and artists, inkers and letterers were not teamed up to work under the control of one editor. Instead, the underground creator controlled every facet of his or her individual creation. This meant, among other things, that creators worked at their own speed, without regard for deadlines, which had the frustrating result that some comix only ran to one issue, while continuing titles often suffered huge gaps between instalments. Even so, in the words of one creator: 'We believe it's better for all concerned to spend a year producing one gem than it is to have to hump-up behind deadlines just to produce a lot of crap on a regular basis.'[4] Also, in tune with the hippie ethos, creators kept copyright over their work, and received royalties. Thus, they benefited financially in proportion to the success of their labours, which could mean, of course, earning nothing at all. The idea of a flat fee per page was unknown, and in the early days at least, there was nothing so unseemly as a contract.

Finally, in terms of marketing, the comix were ideally placed to take advantage of the existing network of hippie shops, or headshops, which were a feature of most big towns in the USA and Canada. These sold trendy clothing and jewellery, plus drugs paraphernalia, such as pipes and reefers, as well as a selection of psychedelic posters, which were a major influence on the look of the comix.[5] The content of the comix meant they could not possibly be sold via the traditional newsagent route, so this was a perfect alternative.

Chronologically speaking, the underground experienced a number of false starts. In the early and mid-1960s, sporadic comics appeared with very small print runs, usually produced with friends in mind and concerning personal subject matter. (Though it should be mentioned here that some more political titles also appeared at this time, such as *Harry Chess*, Trojan Books, 1966, the first gay comic.[6]) Then there were compilations of hippie cartoons drawn from the alternative newspapers. These papers were an integral part of the scene, and were typically tied to specific towns. They included *The Barb* in Berkeley, *Yarrowstalks* in Philadelphia and *The East Village Other* in New York. They were very important in giving creators their first professional 'gigs' and were often a 'next step' after the college magazines.

In spite of these publications, the story does not really begin until 1967. By this time, San Francisco had

become the undisputed 'hippie capital'. It acted like a magnet for America's disenfranchised youth, and quickly certain districts, such as Haight-Ashbury, were completely colonized. The New York coffee-house circuit had become passé, and all of a sudden this was the place to be. 'Frisco' headshops thrived and there were a number of local alternative newspapers, all of which carried strips. If the comix revolution was going to happen anywhere, it would happen here.

One creator in particular became synonymous with the San Francisco comix boom, and later with the underground as a whole: Robert Crumb. Crumb moved to the city in 1967 and immediately started to produce strips for the alternative papers. (His previous experience included a stint working for Harvey Kurtzman on *Help!*) In 1968, his first solo comic appeared, the seminal *Zap* (Apex Novelties). This was to be the title that started the whole comix ball rolling.[7]

Why *Zap* became so important is not difficult to explain. The artwork was tremendous, and mixed influences from *Mad* (Basil Wolverton especially), Disney and the 'bigfoot' style of American newspaper strips, to generate an old-fashioned, almost 'sweet' effect. This was in total contrast to the content of the strips, which included LSD-fuelled fantasies, libertarian politics and sex – plenty of sex. As if to underline the fact that this was no kids' comic, the Code seal of approval was parodied on the cover.

Crumb published *Zap* with a friend at first, selling issues out of a pram on street corners in Haight-Ashbury. However, such was its popularity that it wasn't long before more professional hippie publishers took it over (namely, The Print Mint). Quite unexpectedly, it had opened up a market, proving that there was room for alternative comics as well as newspapers within hippie-dom. *Zap*'s sales, as well as its revolutionary style,

This page: Robert Crumb, king of the underground – and arguably this century's greatest satirist. Above: Panel from *The People's Comics* (Golden Gate, 1972), featuring the artist in typically paranoid frame of mind. Right: Sketch made by Crumb in 1992, depicting him and his pregnant wife in 1968, selling copies of *Zap* on the corner of Haight Street, San Francisco.

A Historic Moment: R Crumb sells ZAP #1 from a baby carriage in Haight-Ashbury, 1968.

This page: More Crumb. Top: Pages from *Zap* (Print Mint, 1969), satirizing racist stereotypes and incest within the all-American family. This was strong stuff indeed and this particular issue (no 4) was prosecuted for obscenity in New York. Above: Panel from *Home Grown Funnies* (Kitchen Sink, 1971), featuring 'Angelfood McDevilsfood' aka 'Angelfood McSpade'. Right: Sleeve to the album *Cheap Thrills* by Big Brother and the Holding Company – Janis Joplin's band (Columbia Records, 1968).

became a rallying cry for a scene waiting to happen.

Zap itself developed into a continuing anthology, with other cartoonists contributing, while Crumb himself upped his workload to include other solo comix. These tended to last for only one or two issues, but were nevertheless incredibly numerous: they included *Despair* (Print Mint, 1969), *Big Ass Comics* (Rip Off, 1969), *R Crumb's Comics and Stories* (Rip Off, 1969), *Motor City Comics* (Rip Off, 1969), *Uneeda* (Print Mint, 1970), *Home Grown Funnies* (Kitchen Sink, 1971) and *Hytone Comix* (Apex Novelties, 1971). He also found time to initiate two infamous porn anthologies: *Jiz* and *Snatch* (both Apex Novelties, 1969).[8] He later justified their typically controversial content thus: 'People say "what are underground comix?" and I think the best way to define

them is to [talk in terms of] the absolute freedom involved. I think that's real important. People forget that that was what it was all about. That was why we did it. We didn't have anybody standing over us saying "No, you can't draw this" or "You can't show that". We could do whatever we wanted.'[9]

In them, his most famous strips sent up the establishment ('Whiteman', about an office 'suit' who secretly dreams of rampant sex), racist stereotypes ('Angelfood McSpade', about a totally sexual, pidgin-English speaking black amazon), and, most frequently, the more idiotic aspects of the hippie counterculture ('Fritz the Cat', about a hip feline who becomes a political revolutionary out of ennui, and 'Mr Natural', about a capitalistic guru). Crumb would also feature himself as a character, usually portrayed as a self-loathing, sex-obsessed intellectual – which was, in fact, just how others saw him at the time.

Crumb always claimed that he was never a 'hippie' as such, and disliked being counted as part of the subculture. However, his strips give the lie to this: they show how, despite the fact that he never grew his hair, he was deeply involved with life in Haight-Ashbury. He did, in fact, hang out with rock stars like Janis Joplin, and he took hippie ideals very seriously. There is a socialist/anarchist/libertarian sensibility to all his work, and however critical he was of flower power in his strips, he was certainly very defensive of it in interviews with the straight press.

His weak spot was sexism. Like just about every 1960s icon (with the possible exception of John Lennon), he thought of women as 'chicks', second-class citizens whose function was the entertainment of men (ideally in a sexual sense). To say he was slow to recognize the aims of Women's Liberation would be an understatement: his

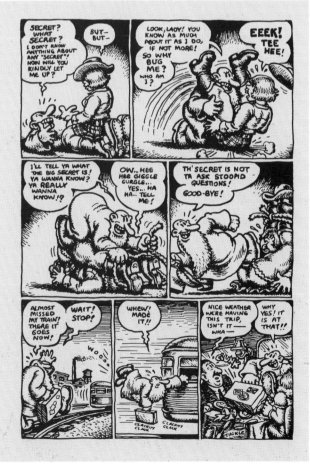

This page and opposite: Pages featuring some of Crumb's best-loved characters. Above left: Crumb himself, in one of his intense confessionals (*The People's Comics*, 1972). Above: Fritz the Cat, a 'hep cat', literally, here trying to impress a female ostrich (*The People's Comics*, Golden Gate, 1972). Left: Mr Natural, a bearded sage, spiritual leader and conman (*Mr Natural*, Print Mint, 1970). Opposite: Whiteman, the archetypal American Mr Straight (*Zap*, Print Mint, 1968).

Pages from *Zap*, (Print Mint, 1973), featuring the grotesquely compelling work of S Clay Wilson. If anyone pushed the envelope of what was acceptable in a comic, Wilson did. This tale of demons, angels, 'nymphs' and of course, sex and violence, was fairly typical.

This page: Two more of the great *Zap* artists. Below: Cover, *Zap* (Print Mint, 1973) by Gilbert Shelton, the hippie king of comedy. The cover is in fact a homage to *Mad* artist, Basil Wolverton. Bottom left: page from *Zap* (Print Mint, 1969), featuring 'Wonder Wart-hog', one of Shelton's most popular creations.

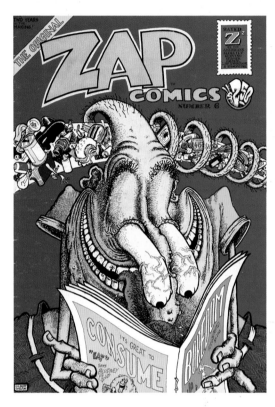

Above: Page from *Zap* (Print Mint, 1974), featuring a fetishistic story by Spain Rodriguez. Right: Panel from *Subvert* (Rip Off, 1970). Art: Spain Rodriguez. This features 'Trashman', the tough-as-nails anarchist and 'Agent of the Sixth International'. Trashman became a symbol for much of the 'street action' of the period.

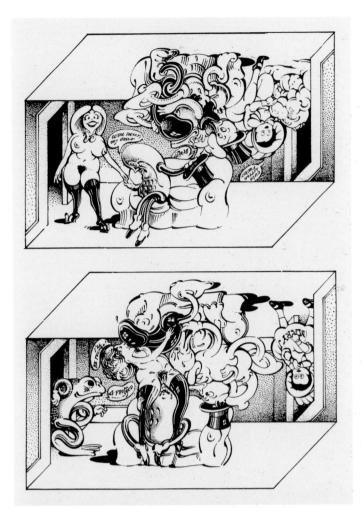

This page: A selection from two of the more psychedelic *Zappers*. Above: Wraparound cover to the notorious *Zap*, no 4 (Print Mint, 1969). Art: Victor Moscoso. This shows 'Mr Peanut' on the front transforming into 'Mr Penis' on the back. Left and far left: Pages and panel from *Zap* (Print Mint, 1969 and 1974). Art: Victor Moscoso. Below left: Pages from *Zap* (Print Mint, 1973). Art: Rick Griffin. Below: Poster for a Jimi Hendrix concert by Rick Griffin (1968). Poster art had a significant influence on the comix and both Griffin and Moscoso were leading practitioners.

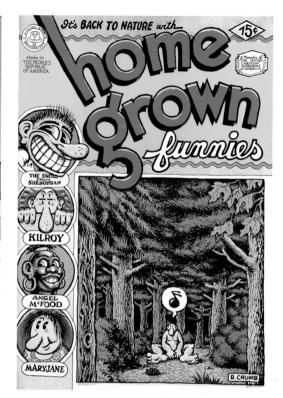

Above: Covers to four solo comix by
Robert Crumb: *Despair* (Print Mint, 1969),
Mr Natural (Print Mint, 1970), *Home Grown
Funnies* (Kitchen Sink, 1971) and
The People's Comics (Golden Gate, 1972).
Bearing in mind how prolific Crumb was,
the consistent quality is astonishing.
Right: Page from *The Collected Adventures
of The Fabulous Furry Freak Brothers*
(Rip Off, 1971). Art/script: Gilbert Shelton.
The eponymous heroes were three
endearingly drug-obsessed hippie
degenerates, who inevitably became
big heroes of the counterculture.

strips are crowded with misogynist images, often involving violence. His excuse was that he was expressing his innermost feelings, as every artist has a duty to do; but this did not satisfy feminists. As one female creator put it: 'It's weird to me how willing people are to overlook the hideous darkness in Crumb's work ... What the hell is funny about rape and murder?'[10] Later in his career, Crumb would have second thoughts, and create some of the most rounded female characters in comics; but at the time when his influence was at its height, this aspect of his work remained a nagging problem.

Despite his flaws, every would-be underground cartoonist in the land wanted to copy Robert Crumb. So many tried to, in fact, that Crumb's style is indelibly stamped on the era: he both invented and shaped the movement. Others who found more original ways to express themselves still owe a debt to him for his pioneering spirit. As one creator later reminisced: 'Could comix have happened without *Zap*? Probably, but why bother with "what ifs"? The fact is, *Zap* kicked it off in grand style and gave the movement a kind of energy that hasn't yet spent itself. When future historians of the comic book medium look back at the results, Crumb's genius will shine through and the offerings of the mainstream industry will pale beside it. You can take that to the bank, folks.'[11]

The underground did not, however, begin and end with Crumb – far from it. There were many other excellent cartoonists, and *Zap* in particular became a focus for some of the most original work in the movement. It pulled together the best creators from within San Francisco (many of whom had migrated there in much the same way that Crumb had), and in its anthology-incarnation set standards for the rest of the underground to follow. The '*Zap* artists', as they became known, are thus worth mentioning in turn.

Gilbert Shelton was perhaps the funniest. He had worked for Kurtzman's *Help!* and on college magazines,

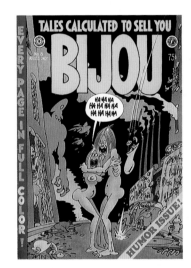

and had become one of the early stalwarts of the alternative newspapers. His style was much less confessional than Crumb's, and more slapstick: his characters were often goofy, but with pretensions which landed them in ever more disastrous situations. Contrary to many critical assessments of Shelton's work, he also possessed the same underlying political intelligence and would sometimes attack individual politicians directly. Along with his contributions to *Zap*, his most famous comix were *Wonder Wart-Hog* (Millar, 1967), a parody of superhero comics starring a 'hog of steel'; *Feds 'n' Heads* (self-published, 1968); and *The Fabulous Furry Freak Brothers* (Rip Off, 1971), about three bored hippies ('freaks') who spend their time scoring drugs and avoiding 'the pigs'.

S Clay Wilson was another original, but of an altogether darker nature. His strips were not particularly funny, and relied instead on shock impact – sex and violence being their stock-in-trade, usually mingled to stomach-churning effect. Wilson took the ethic of 'freedom of expression' to its furthest extreme, and his tales of sadomasochistic pirates, outlaw-biker lesbians, and cruel demons provoked enormous controversy, especially from feminists, who pointed out that the majority of the violence was directed against women. As well as *Zap*, his comix included *Bent* (Print Mint, 1971), *Pork* (Co-Op Press, 1974) and *The Checkered Demon* (Last Gasp, 1977).

'Spain' Rodriguez was different again. His idea of an underground strip involved pushing political issues to the fore, and his in-your-face 'urban guerilla' style had already proved very popular in the alternative papers. His character 'Trashman' (a machine-gun toting anarchist avenger) became a symbol for the more radical elements of the anti-Vietnam protest movement, while 'Manning: Police Detective' told the story of a cop who uses his badge as a cover for murder and sadism. *Zap* showcased some of his best work, though popular solo outings included *Zodiac Mindwarp* (East Village Other, 1967) and *Subvert* (Rip Off, 1970).

Finally, there were three lesser-known *Zap* contributors who added their own particular flavour to proceedings. Victor Moscoso and Rick Griffin made their names originally on the San Francisco poster scene – the latter especially having originated an intricately 'mystical' psychedelic style. Both used cartoon motifs in their poster work, and were to be responsible for some of the most memorable, and most colourful, *Zap* covers. The third, Robert Williams, previously worked as a T-shirt designer and oil painter on the West Coast, and was greatly influenced by legendary hotrod artist Ed 'Big Daddy' Roth. Williams's cartooning style was clean and distinctive, and unlike Moscoso or Griffin, he had a talent for telling a funny story. All three contributors additionally put out comix of their own.

Though *Zap* may have been the premier showcase for the movement, there were certainly some other top-notch comix, and some quality creators outside the *Zap* circle. *Bijou Funnies* (Bijou Publishing, 1968) was perhaps the second-best known anthology, and hailed from Chicago.

Much influenced by *Mad*, it was edited by Jay Lynch, whose 'Nard 'n' Pat' told the story of two friends (one a bourgeois man, the other a radical cat) who bicker over everything from politics to who's going to do the shopping. Another key contributor was Skip Williamson, whose 'Snappy Sammy Smoot' chronicled the adventures of a besuited ingenue and his surreal encounters with the counterculture. Williamson believed in 'comix as propaganda', but though his strips often featured politicians, such as Richard Nixon and Spiro Agnew, and had serious themes, the laughs were always paramount: one of his better gags involved an alien that eats only policemen.

Young Lust (Company & Sons, 1970) was another San Francisco-based anthology. It was a parody of the 1950s romance genre, which predictably upped the sex. (One spoof of a 1950s cover depicted a distraught woman pondering: 'Last week he was dry-humping me in the lift; now he can't even remember my goddamn name!'). It featured, among others, the remarkable work of Bill Griffith, whose dry, observational wit was complemented by a semi-realistic art style, and Art Spiegelman, whose often very risqué strips were laced with liberal helpings

Above: Pages from *Bijou Funnies* (Bijou Publishing, 1971), featuring Nard 'n' Pat, an update on a vaudevillian double act. Art/ script: Jay Lynch. Below: Covers to two more top anthologies: *Young Lust* (Company and Sons, 1977) with art by Jay Kinney/Larry Todd; and *Bizarre Sex* (Kitchen Sink, 1972), art by Denis Kitchen. Below right: Cover, *It Ain't Me Babe* (Last Gasp, 1970). Art: Trina Robbins. The pioneering women-only anthology, dedicated to 'Women's Liberation'.

of Jewish black humour. Spiegelman was one of the great experimenters of the underground, and on other titles, such as *Ace Hole, Midget Detective* (self-published, 1974), he developed a revolutionary approach to panel layouts.

Bizarre Sex (Kitchen Sink, 1972), from Milwaukee, was another successful anthology (unsurprisingly, with a name like that). It too contained copious quantities of graphic copulating, and similarly looked back to the 1950s, this time to the science fiction genre. One strapline, for instance, announced: 'The Giant Penis That Invaded New York!' Contributors included Denis Kitchen and Richard 'Grass' Green, one of the few black contributors to the underground.

These anthologies were certainly important, but there were contemporaneous developments in the underground that were equally as groundbreaking, though for different reasons. The early 1970s, in particular, saw a boom in comix by and for women, and the growth of a subgenre of horror titles. Both forged new paths, and allowed an opportunity for creators to get involved with the comix movement who might otherwise not have had the chance or the inclination.

The women's comix were revolutionary in the sense that they were the first time, generally speaking, that women creators had been given the scope to produce stories by themselves. It was true that in the past there had been a few examples of female newspaper cartoonists, but in the comics industry, the writing and drawing had been done almost exclusively by men. If women were involved at all, they were relegated to back-stage roles such as colouring or lettering.

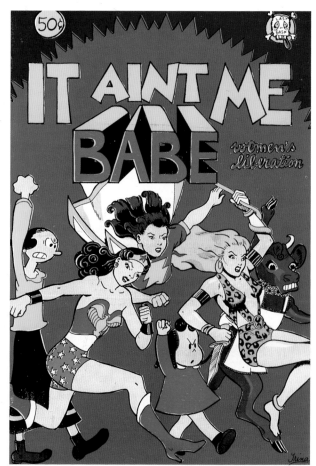

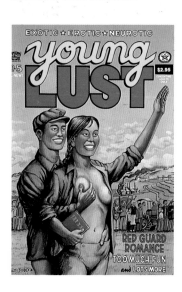

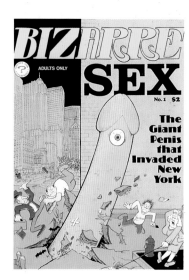

The pioneering female comix creators were Trina Robbins, Willy Mendes and Lee Marrs. Robbins was the most influential of the three, nicknamed the 'Queen of the Underground', and put together the seminal all-women anthology *It Ain't Me Babe* (Last Gasp) in 1970. The statement of intent on the cover, 'Women's Liberation!', indicated a radical political slant, though Robbins' own art style was essentially traditional: uncluttered, glamorous and sometimes almost 'art deco'. The same year, Robbins collaborated with Mendes, whose style was contrastingly psychedelic, on *All Girl Thrills* (Print Mint). At the same time, Lee Marrs was working on *Pudge, Girl Blimp* (Last Gasp), about an overweight office worker, and her neuroses about men, which was eventually published in 1974.

These early women cartoonists were using their strips to protest about a number of related issues: obliquely, about being excluded from the male-dominated underground (especially the big anthologies, which they claimed had a 'Boys Only' atmosphere) and about the sexism that was rife in the movement (particularly comix by Wilson, Crumb and Spain); and more directly about women's politics generally – subject matter included rape, sex, abortion, babies, working conditions and housework.

The individual comix did not command anything like the sales of *Zap* and *Bijou Funnies*, but nevertheless they were successful enough to inspire others. They were followed by a string of women's anthologies which were generally better organized and produced, the best-known titles being: *Wimmen's Comix* (Last Gasp, 1972), designed as a platform for new creators; *Tits 'n' Clits* (Nanny Goat Productions, 1972), intended to 'bring a sense of humour to the women's movement'; and *Wet Satin* (Kitchen Sink, 1976), a collection of stories about women's erotic fantasies. They featured a number of very talented creators, including Melinda Gebbie (dark sexual fever dreams), Lynda Barry (ratty cod-schoolgirl hilarity), Aline Kominsky (Jewish humour and self-loathing) and

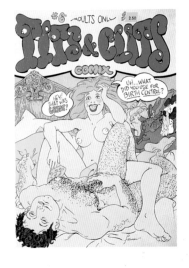

This page: The comix also included horror, and in so doing redefined the genre. Above: Covers, *Skull* (Rip Off, 1972) with art by the underrated Greg Irons; and *Gory Stories* (Shroud, 1972), art by J Pound.

experimental ('The Clean-Up Crew', by Veitch and Irons, about a gang that scrapes human remains out of car wrecks on the road), to the altogether more traditional (issue four was devoted entirely to versions of HP Lovecraft tales). Other horror titles from the period include *Bogeyman* (San Francisco Comic Book Company, 1969), *Fantagor* (Richard Corben, 1970), *Insect Fear* (Print Mint, 1970), *Up From The Deep* (Rip Off, 1971), *Snarf* (Kitchen Sink, 1972), *Death Rattle* (Kitchen Sink, 1972), *Gory Stories* (Shroud, 1972), *Deviant Slice* (Print Mint, 1972) and *Two Fisted Zombies* (Last Gasp, 1973).

Certain artists excelled in this kind of material. At one end of the spectrum, there was Rory Hayes, whose primitive, and, frankly, badly-drawn, art relied on energy and excess for its impact. He even rivalled S Clay Wilson on occasion in this respect. Unfortunately, women came off very badly in Hayes's work, typically appearing only to be dismembered or sexually degraded. At the other end of the scale, there was Richard Corben, whose 'professional', superbly crafted strips were in the style of 'Ghastly' Graham Ingels (Corben signed his name 'Gore' as a tribute); though it should be said that he too suffered from the curse of sexism, and his women tended to be melon-chested bimbos. Corben was a master of shadow and lighting, but was also skilled when it came to colour work with an airbrush. Thus, his cover artwork was much in demand.

Horror also brought out the best in certain writers. After all, any story based in such a genre framework demanded more than abstract psychedelia or dumb scatology, and the EC comics had always made plot a

Shary Flenniken (sex, politics and cute characters).[13]

The second major sub-genre, horror, was popular with the comix crowd because it offered opportunities to challenge the anti-violence censorship of the Code. The titles that resulted were taboo-breaking, first and foremost, and although they acknowledged their debt to the EC comics of the 1950s, they took explicitness to levels that even these gory forerunners could not have hoped to aspire to.

The best-known early example was probably *Skull* (Rip Off, 1970), which came complete with a mock EC logo and the EC-style strapline, 'Tales Contrived To Flip You Out Of Your [Skull]'. It included work by Rory Hayes, Richard Corben, Jack Jackson, Greg Irons, Tom Veitch and others, which veered from the disturbingly

Horror subject matter was broadened to include the after-effects of Vietnam, the sex war and psychedelia, as well as more conventional monster stories. Above and right: Panel and cover from *Deviant Slice* (Print Mint, 1973). Art: Greg Irons. Script: Tom Veitch. Top far right: Panels from *Skull* (Rip Off, 1970) by the idiosyncratic Rory Hayes. Bottom far right: Cover, *Fantagor*, (Last Gasp, 1972) by master of creepy lighting Richard Corben.

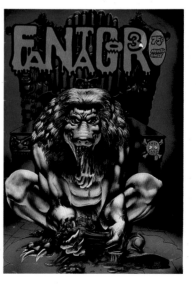

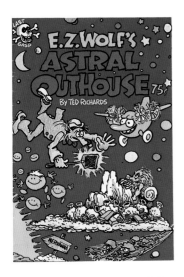

This page: Two relative obscurities, both excellent comics. Above: Cover to *EZ Wolf's Astral Outhouse* (Last Gasp, 1977). Art/script: Ted Richards. Below: Pages from *Inner City Romance* (Last Gasp, 1972). Art/script: Guy Colwell.

priority. Many of the new comix made explicit reference to this, and included figures similar to the Crypt Keeper to introduce stories. Jack Jackson in particular was responsible for some remarkably-told satirical horror strips, taking EC's black humour to even blacker levels, while partnerships were hatched which placed an emphasis on the writing, like that between Tom Veitch and Greg Irons (whose work for *Skull* and *Deviant Slice* was among the most memorable to come out of the entire underground).[14]

This emphasis on new kinds of storytelling, plus the extreme nature of what was drawn – every unfurling entrail lovingly depicted – meant that the horror genre as a whole was turned on its head. Nothing was suggested anymore, everything was shown. At the same time, writers' forays into existential terror was something new. Obviously, there were problems with this approach, especially regarding the role of women, but even so, it is fair to argue that the comix anticipated the trend for 'body horror' in the cinema by several years.[15]

If we can identify this phase, including the funnies, the women's comix and the horror titles, as the first of the underground, then it is possible to conclude that by only a few years after *Zap*, the movement had become an industry to be reckoned with. There were comix communities all over America, mainly based in the big cities, producing hundreds of titles each month. Certainly, most were small beer: typical print runs were in the hundreds – smaller still would be their distribution. Yet there were also a few major publishers – Krupp Comic Works (later Kitchen Sink), Rip Off, The Print Mint, The San Francisco Comic Book Company and Last Gasp – which between them had the power to take things to a new level of commercialism. With their help, the most popular creators, like Crumb and Shelton, could hope to sell hundreds of thousands per issue.

Thus, although the underground was not a challenge to the mainstream – it was never intended to be – it was nevertheless thriving on its own terms. When it was in full flow, in the early 1970s, it generated its own momentum, with new surprises in art and narrative every month. Strips ranged from cartoony, Crumb-like images, to radical abstract expressionism – often within the pages of the same comic. They were commonly created in a completely spontaneous fashion, with the creator not knowing how it would end: sometimes 'jams' would take place involving many creators at once, mixing up styles in a crazy melange.[16] The covers were especially important, because in contrast to the innards, they were in full colour, and thus could show off particular artists' styles to their optimum extent. One of the few ideas that the comix borrowed from the mainstream industry was that a striking cover was the key to high sales: here more than anywhere the influence of the poster scene was in evidence, with LSD-inspired, explosion-in-a-paintshop, graphics becoming a favourite option.

Integral to this boom, there were many more great early undergrounders, which unfortunately space forbids us from discussing here. They included Jay Kinney, Kim Deitch, Frank 'Foolbert Sturgeon' Stack, Justin Green, Dave Sheridan, Ted Richards, Vaughn Bodé, Guy Colwell, Joel Beck, Diane Noomin and Roberta Gregory, to name a few.[17] However, with more comics being produced, there was inevitably going to be more rubbish. In fact, if anything, the underground actually encouraged poor work because its central ethic that 'anybody could do it' meant that anybody did. Its main strength was also its main weakness in that comix were often amateurish, misogynistic and not very funny. 'Self expression' could also mean 'self indulgence', and it should be borne in mind that for every *Zap*, there were a hundred comix by rank amateurs doing their growing up in public.

The development of an underground in Britain echoed that of the United States. The American comix had been imported into Britain from the beginning, and gleefully consumed. Indeed, bootleg versions of early titles were published, sometimes before they appeared in the States.[18] Crumb and Shelton were particular favourites, though other creators developed cult followings, depending on whether Customs would allow their work into the country.[19]

It was not long before an indigenous underground began to take shape, and although the comix were highly influenced by the American example, both in terms of content and format, they did exhibit a local flavour. It should be remembered that the British counterculture had developed in subtly different ways to its American counterpart, and that the concerns were not always the same. Edward Heath, for instance, was almost as much of a hate figure as Richard Nixon. Similarly, the mainstream comics tradition was unique, and instead of looking back to *Mad* and the ECs, British creators also referred to titles such as *Film Fun*, *The Eagle* and *The Beano*.[20]

Although there was no equivalent to the *Zap* crowd in Britain, there was a London scene based around the hippie publications *IT* (*The International Times*), a

This page and opposite: The British underground had a flavour all its own. Above: John Lennon relaxes with a copy of *The International Times*. Right: Covers to *The International Times* (Lovebooks Ltd, 1967) and *Oz* (Oz Publications Ink, 1968), the two archetypal hippie publications. Art: Anon and Martin Sharp. Below, below right and opposite: Cover and strips from *Cyclops* (Innocence and Experience, 1970). Cover: Edward Barker; 'The Unspeakable Mr Hart', written by William Burroughs (*the* William Burroughs), art by Malcolm McNeill; and 'True Meat Tales' by Ray Lowry. The first of the British comix and artistically speaking, the most experimental.

TRUE MEAT TALES

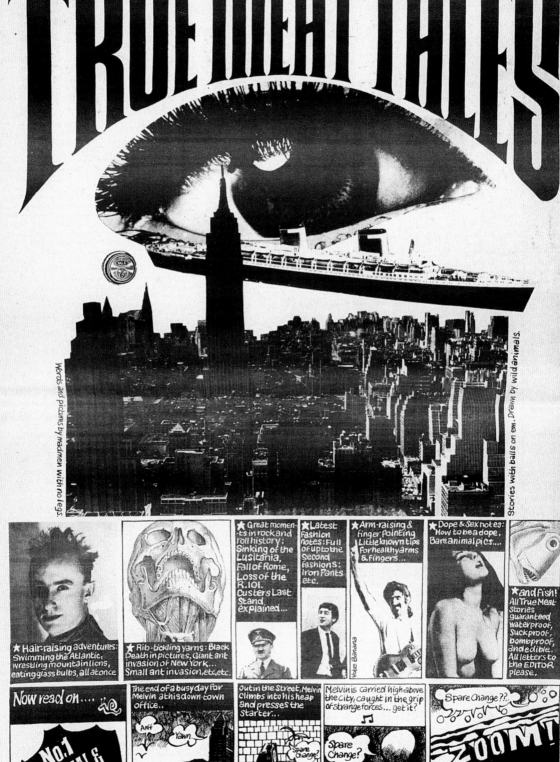

Words and pictures by madmen with no legs.

Stories with balls on em. Drawn by wild animals.

news-based tabloid, and *Oz*, a glossy magazine famed for its psychedelic design. These were essentially the voice of the British counterculture, and were closely linked, sharing journalists and cartoonists. They also both reprinted strips from America. By the early 1970s, however, they were past their peak, and their publishers decided to experiment with launching comix offshoots in the hope that they would make enough money to keep them afloat.

The results were the *IT*-based *Cyclops* (Innocence and Experience, 1970) and *IT*-financed *Nasty Tales* (Bloom, 1971) and the *Oz*-funded *Cozmic Comics* (H Bunch), which ran under twenty-one different subtitles from 1972. As well as reprinting American material by Crumb, Shelton, Spain, Irons and others, they showcased a roster of British strips – not all of which, it has to be said, were in the same league. They were able to reprint so much American material because it was essentially and controversially free. Without contracts the underground artists had no claims on their work and British editors could draw on it as much as they wanted.[21]

The London (or, more precisely, 'London-associated') creators included Chris Welch, whose 'Ogoth and Ugly Boot' was a violent science fiction satire (a mix of Conan the Barbarian and London Hell's Angel culture); Edward Barker, whose sketchily rendered long-haired lowlifes lent his strips a pleasingly seedy quality; Mike Weller (aka 'Captain Stelling'), whose angry stories about industrial relations had real political bite and were a highlight of the *Cozmic* line; Ray Lowry, whose Dadaist collages for *Cyclops* pushed the envelope of artistic innovation; Malcolm Livingstone, whose cockney funny animals debated the decline of hippiedom; William Rankin (aka 'Wyndham Raine'), whose detailed 'kids' comics' style harkened back to British titles from the 1930s; and finally Dave Gibbons and Brian Bolland, mentioned together because their superb Americanized style – clean, precise and 'professional' – betrayed their love of Marvel/DC comics.

Yet some of the best British creators came from the regions and were associated with other comix. Three in particular were outstanding. Bryan Talbot, originally from Preston in Lancashire, made his name on the London-published *Brainstorm* (Alchemy, 1975): his art was impressively accomplished, while his main character 'Chester Hackenbush, Psychedelic Alchemist' became something of a hippie hero due to the sheer quantity of illegal chemicals he consumed; Angus McKie, from Newcastle, whose obscure *Either Or Comics* (Junior Print Outfit, 1977) demonstrated a range of styles, from Crumb-like slapstick to more Kirbyesque rendering (McKie also contributed to the *Cozmics* with the latter technique); and Hunt Emerson, from Birmingham, who contributed to and edited the *Street Comix* line (Arts Lab, 1976), and whose bold, cartoony linework evoked a sense of enormous speed and energy. Emerson drew on a mixture of influences from Leo Baxendale via Crumb to Tex Avery's madcap animation, and he is generally agreed to have been the most important of all the British comix creators.

Top: Covers to *Nasty Tales* (Bloom, 1971), art by Dave Sheridan, and *Cozmic Comix* (H Bunch, 1974), one of the Cozmic line, with art by Joe Petagno. Above: Pages from *Cozmic Comics* (H Bunch, 1972). Art: Dennis Leigh. Right: Page from same comic (H Bunch), reprinting an American strip by Jay Kinney.

Below: Page from *The Firm*, (Cozmic Comix, 1972), a vicious satire of office and factory life, and one of the outstanding titles of the British underground.
Art/script: Mike Weller. Bottom right: Page from *Cosmic Comix* (1974), about a visit to London by a 'miracle crusade'.
Art/script: RC Moody.

This page: More examples from the extensive Cozmic line (all H Bunch). Top left, top right and above: Cover and strips from *Zip Comics*, 1973. Cover by Rand Holmes ('Achtung Decadent Hippies!' Laughter is Against the Law!'); panel by Thomas Warkenin; pages by J Jef Jones (script) and Martin Sudden (art). British comix could be as sexist as their American counterparts.

Britain also had its share of 'wild men' – home-grown equivalents of S Clay Wilson and Rory Hayes. The two names that fit the bill most closely were Antonio Ghura and Mike Matthews. Ghura was one of the funniest of all the undergrounders, but his humour could veer into some extremely sick areas: rape, incest and necrophilia were all fit subjects for his gags. He was a frequent contributor to the anthology *It's All Lies* (Gemsanders, 1973), and followed up with his own *Bogey* (Vicar's Raw Balls Co, 1975), *Truly Amazing Love Stories* – a sort of British *Young Lust* – and *Raw Purple* (both Beyond the Edge, 1977). Matthews was a better artist than Ghura, but lacked his wit. Nevertheless, his work was just as extreme, evidenced by his notorious *Napalm Kiss* (self-published, 1977).[22]

Britain similarly had female creators. There was never really a 'women's scene' like there was in America, but some notable comix did emerge. They served the same twin purposes of providing a platform for women creators, and a venue for women's issues to be aired. Thus they included similar protests against the sexism of the male underground, in this case directed at people

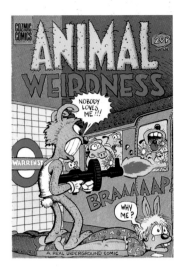

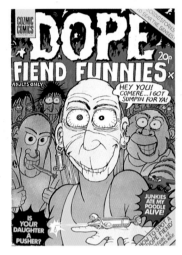

This page and opposite: More Cozmic material. Opposite; Pages from 'So-realist Cartoons', *Zip Comics* (H Bunch, 1973) by William Rankin, one of the real stylists of British comix; and 'Rats' Tails', *Animal Weirdness* (H Bunch, 1974) by J Wesolowski. Left: Cover, *Animal Weirdness*. Art: Anon. Below: Cover and pages from *Dope Fiend Funnies* (H Bunch, 1974). Cover and 'How to Spot a Dope Fiend' by Edward Barker; bottom strip, about some historical dope fiends, by William Rankin.

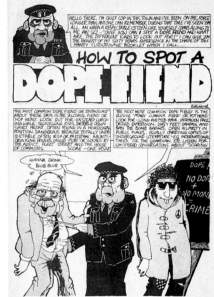

Right and below: Cover and pages from *Brainstorm* (Alchemy), the title that revived British comix in the mid-1970s. Cover, *Brainstorm Comix* (1975), promising a 'Journey into Delirium' (with 'Chester Hackenbush', visible bottom left), by Bryan Talbot; 'Odmund', *Brainstorm*, 'Mixed Bunch' (1976). Art: Chris Welch. Script: Chris Rowley.

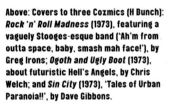

Above: Covers to three Cozmics (H Bunch): *Rock 'n' Roll Madness* (1973), featuring a vaguely Stooges-esque band ('Ah'm from outta space, baby, smash mah face!'), by Greg Irons; *Ogoth and Ugly Boot* (1973), about futuristic Hell's Angels, by Chris Welch; and *Sin City* (1973), 'Tales of Urban Paranoia!!', by Dave Gibbons.

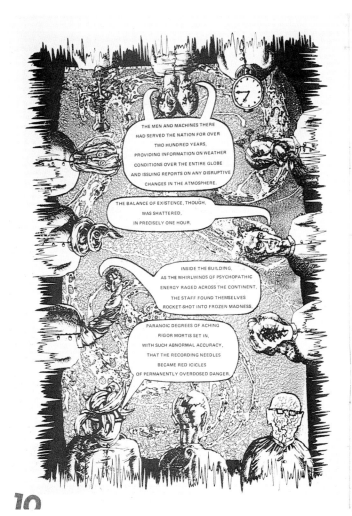

Above and left: Pages from *Street Comix* (Arts Lab), a late British title. Above: 'Ice Age' (1977). Art: Nick Blake. Script: Robin Sendak. Below: 'Old Grey Whistle Face' (1977) by Pokkettz (aka Graham Higgins). Below: Cover, *Raw Purple* (Beyond the Edge, 1977) by 'wild man' Antonio Ghura.

Heröine

AR:ZAK
WOMENS COMIK
45p

This page: The British women's comix.
Above and below left: Cover and pages
from *Heroine* (Arts Lab, 1977). Cover,
featuring a defiant 'punkette'
by Suzy Varty; strips by Paula Williams
(left) and Judy Watson (right). Right and
below right: Cover and pages from *Sour
Cream* (Sour Cream, 1980). Cover by Ingrid
Emsden; strip by Les Ruda.

like Ghura and Matthews. *Heroine* (Arts Lab, 1978)
featured the highly stylized artwork of Suzy Varty,
the best-known female creator, and was followed by
a handful of others, including the most high profile title
Sour Cream (Sour Cream, 1980).

The British underground was certainly far smaller in
commercial terms. Figures are hard to obtain, but the
best sellers were the *Cozmics* and *Brainstorm*, whose top
individual issues sold between ten and twenty thousand;
most others sold in the hundreds or low thousands, and
only lasted for one or two editions. Yet, the comix made
their mark, and for a few years at least they represented
a vibrant alternative to the mainstream. There were even
two 'Konventions of Alternative Komix', KAKs, in 1976
and 1977. Underground art fed into other media in much
the same way as it did in America. Posters, album and
book covers, and more obscure areas such as tattooing
and custom-bike art, were all influenced in one way or
another. Hunt Emerson was the name most closely
associated with this kind of extra-curricular activity.
Understandably, the British story has been overshadowed
by events in America, but this does not mean that it was
any less interesting.

By the mid-1970s, a decline in the underground
generally was already in evidence, and this is where the
final phase begins. Chronologically, the British scene had
been late to flower, and across the Atlantic things had
started to go wrong around 1973–4. The right-wing press
in America had been running negative articles about the
comix since the late 1960s, claiming that they were
socially irresponsible and intent on glorifying violence,
perverted sex and drug taking: now they stepped up
their campaign by eliciting the support of the anti-
pornography lobby. Partly due to this pressure, the
Supreme Court handed down a ruling in 1973 whereby
local communities could decide their own First
Amendment standards with reference to obscenity.
At around the same time, there were a series of 'anti-

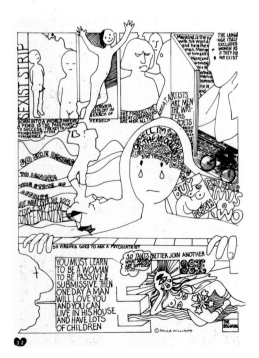

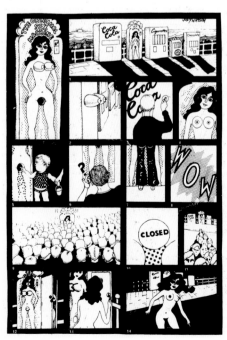

paraphernalia' laws passed which outlawed the selling of drug-related items.

The inevitable busts followed. *Zap* no 4 was ruled obscene in the State of New York, and withdrawn from sale. Another title, *Air Pirates Funnies* (Air Pirates, 1971), was successfully sued by Disney for depicting Mickey Mouse involved in sex and drug taking. There were many more similar instances. At the same time, headshops were prosecuted and closed down: the anti-drugs laws were a convenient way to attack the comix, posters, magazines and other items that were sold.

The consequences of this assault by the establishment were far-reaching. Court actions were expensive, and publishers who were already on tight budgets simply could not keep up. Those that did not close down often took the decision to soften the content of their comix to make them more acceptable. Similarly, for headshop owners, prosecutions were costly, and many shut down of their own accord. Those that stayed open often refused to stock the more dodgy comix due to the risk. This whittling down of the network was obviously of major significance for the future of the entire movement.

In Britain, a similar backlash took hold. Articles in the press took an almost identical stance, with the added complaint that the underground was an import from America: evidently, anti-American prejudice was not quite dead. Customs re-doubled their efforts to keep the American titles out of the country, while at home there was a campaign in the courts against the alternative press as a whole. In time most of the alternative papers were busted, usually for sexual content. The most famous trial in this respect was that regarding *Oz*, which became something of a *cause célèbre* within the

counterculture, with protest marches and meetings being organized, and 'celebrity' witnesses agreeing to appear for the defence. (They included John Peel and Marty Feldman.) Much of the trial was involved with a discussion of the merits of the magazine's cartoons, specifically work by Crumb and Shelton. It ended with the editors being jailed (though they were soon released on appeal).

The most high-profile comix trial in Britain was that concerning *Nasty Tales* in 1973, when the editors appeared at the Old Bailey accused of obscenity. After some earnest legal discussions of such gems as Crumb's 'Grand Opening of the of the Great Intercontinental Fuck-In and Orgy Riot', the court surprised everybody by letting off the accused with a caution. This happy result probably pre-empted any more trials on a similar scale, and was promptly celebrated in a further issue of *Nasty Tales* which gleefully reprinted the 'Riot' cartoon.

Nevertheless, the resulting decline in the British underground was almost as serious as that in America. *Nasty Tales* was effectively killed by the trial, while the *Cozmics* ran out of steam in 1975: the publications that they were designed to rekindle did not fare any better. *IT* stopped in 1973, though there were sporadic attempts at resuscitation, while *Oz* bit the dust in the same year. Other comix creators and publishers began to self-censor their stronger content (those that refused to compromise, like Ghura and Matthews, had great difficulty getting their titles distributed). A revival of sorts occurred post-1975, led by the *Brainstorm* line, but, by then, the British underground was already past its best.

There were also other forces conspiring to kill off the movement. Considering it as a whole, it is evident that

Above: Cover, *Konvention of Alternative Komix (KAK)*, London, (Arts Lab, 1977). Art: Hunt Emerson, perhaps the best loved of the British comix cartoonists. Below: The establishment hits back. Left: Panel from *Oz* (Oz Publications Ink, 1971), the infamous 'Schoolkids issue', (so called because it was put together by kids still at school), which was busted for obscenity. Panel shows a Crumb strip modified by the addition of the head of Rupert the Bear. Centre: The three *Oz* editors in suitable attire. Right: Cover, *The Trials of Nasty Tales* (Bloom, 1973). Art: Dave Gibbons. A comic produced to celebrate the acquittal of *Nasty Tales* in the courts.

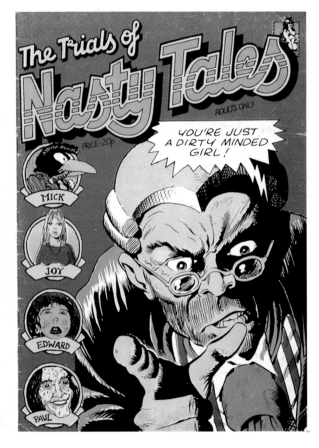

certain sectors brought on their own downfall by getting too commercial. The days of laissez-faire business transactions were over. Now, many publishers were trying to make as much money as possible in as short a time. It was as if they felt they had to cash in before it was too late, and some behaved in a way that put the worst 'bread heads' in the mainstream comics industry to shame. Part of this process involved copying the mainstream by diversifying into other areas, particularly merchandise. Not surprisingly, the mid-1970s onwards was marked by a rush by comix creators to copyright everything they had ever done.

Concurrently, the underground was being co-opted by straight culture. Film companies in particular started to sniff around for ideas, and the most symbolic capitulation was the appearance of two movies based on Robert Crumb's Fritz the Cat. *Fritz the Cat* (1972) and *The Nine Lives of Fritz the Cat* (1974) were made by Ralph Bakshi as big budget animated features for adults.[23] They

were undoubtedly pioneering in terms of cinema – *Fritz* was the first animated movie to receive an X-certificate – and despite some savage reviews, both films did reasonably well at the box office. But in terms of translating the subtleties of Crumb's comix, they were sadly lacking. Crumb himself disowned them, and went to court to get his name removed from the credits. Nevertheless, the very fact that he had signed the movie contract in the first place was enough for some purists within the comix movement to cry 'sell out'.

Television also caught on. In Britain, the comedy show 'Monty Python's Flying Circus' was notable for its animated sequences, which had an underground feel in the sense that they were psychedelic and very sexual. Interestingly, they were the brainchild of Terry Gilliam, who had at one time been a comics cartoonist, and had worked with Robert Crumb and others on *Help!* He was also later to become one of Hollywood's top directors, with movies such as *Brazil*, *The Fisher King* and *Twelve Monkeys* to his name.

Finally, the mainstream comics industry itself began to take notice. Underground-style art and humour had been seeping into mainstream magazines like *National Lampoon* and *Playboy* since the early 1970s. Now, Marvel stepped in, and offered to put out a regular comic, entitled *Comix Book*. The price that comix creators would have to pay in order to be involved would be that they would have to tone down their material to make it news-stand friendly. An impressive number agreed – including Spiegelman, Williamson, Robbins and even S Clay Wilson – and the title debuted in 1974, and lasted for five issues (see also p 151). Certainly, the underground was in trouble by this time, and to some creators, the Marvel venture must have seemed like a way to survive. However, to others, it was the final symbolic defeat.

Cumulatively, these trends were all very disillusioning for those involved. As Art Spiegelman put it some time later: 'The flaming promise of underground comix – *Zap*, *Young Lust*, and others – had fizzled into cold, glowing embers. Underground comics had offered something new ... unselfconsciously redefining what comics could be, by smashing formal and stylistic, as well as cultural and political, taboos. Then, somehow, what had seemed like a revolution simply deflated into a lifestyle. Underground comics were stereotyped as dealing only with Sex, Dope and Cheap Thrills. They got stuffed back into the closet, along with bong pipes and love beads, as Things Started To Get Uglier.'[24]

Things certainly were getting uglier, but it was not all gloom. The underground was suffering, but it was more adaptive to change than the pessimists imagined. The movement in the latter half of the 1970s was nowhere near as moribund as some histories have suggested, and two areas in particular are worthy of comment: the continuing success of the comedy-orientated titles, and the rise of a new(er) sub-genre of more politically focused material.

The humorous comix survived by a process of natural selection. One of the more positive outcomes of the slump in America was that weaker material was gradually

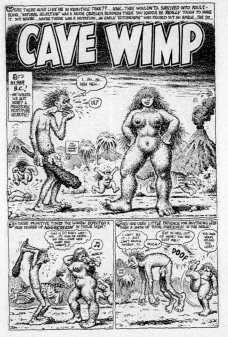

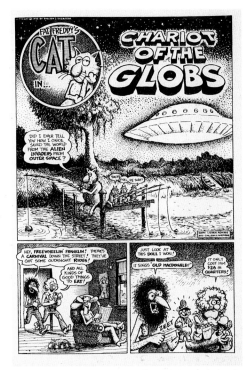

This page: Humour comix that survived the downturn. Above: Pages from the redoubtable *Zap* (Print Mint, 1989) by the ever-popular Robert Crumb. Above right and left: Page and cover detail from *Fat Freddy's Cat* (Rip Off, 1978), a huge seller, by Gilbert Shelton. Below: Cover and page from *Zippy* (Rip Off, 1980), an unlikely hit about a pin-headed savant, by Bill Griffith.

Following pages: Spread from *The Legion of Charlies* (Last Gasp, 1971). Art: Greg Irons. Script: Greg Irons and Tom Veitch. The end of the era of peace and love is horrifically pictured as GIs in Vietnam are equated with the Manson 'Family'.

weeded out. In particular, the surge of opportunistic cash-ins was slowly halted as it became apparent that surviving headshops were not stocking new and untried material. This left the original creators to continue in the vein they had started, and they now went on to produce some of their best, and most commercially successful, work.

Crumb, Shelton and Griffith were the most prominent examples of the comix survivors. Robert Crumb had been through a lean patch since the early 1970s as a result of problems with the IRS (Tax Office) and personal depression over exploitation, but now bounced back with some outrageous contributions to *Zap*, *Bizarre Sex* and *Snarf*, plus his own *Snoid Comics* (Kitchen Sink, 1979), about the evil 'snoids' (manifestations of the id) that live in men's brains. Gilbert Shelton had never been out of the running, and by the late 1970s found that his *Freak Brothers*, which was always extremely popular, had ascended to cult status: his *Fat Freddy's Cat* (Rip Off) series collected stories about the obnoxious feline pet of one of the Brothers, and was a major seller from 1976. Finally, Bill Griffith became more successful than ever, with three new titles in particular, *Zippy Stories* (Rip Off, 1977), *Yow* (Last Gasp, 1978) and *Griffith Observatory* (Rip Off, 1979), cementing his reputation. His character, 'Zippy the Pinhead', a free-associating idiot savant who can see through America's consumerist obsessions, became almost as well known as Crumb's finest creations.

Mention should also be made of an important late satirical anthology, *Arcade* (Print Mint, 1975). This was put together by Griffith and Art Spiegelman as a 'life-raft' for underground creators in the slump, the idea being to try to open up a market on the news-stands, to be achieved by putting it out in a slightly larger, magazine, size, and on better stock paper. Unfortunately, despite attracting the cream of artistic crop, including all the

This page: Examples from *Arcade*, the best of the late anthologies (all Print Mint). Above: Cover (1975), by Robert Crumb. Right: Pages (1976), by Aline Kominsky. Below left: Cover (1976), by Crumb. Below centre: Page (1976), by Crumb. Below right: Page (1975), by Art Spiegelman. In many ways, *Arcade* represented a half-way house between *Zap* and the outstanding 1980s title, *Raw* (see Chapter 8).

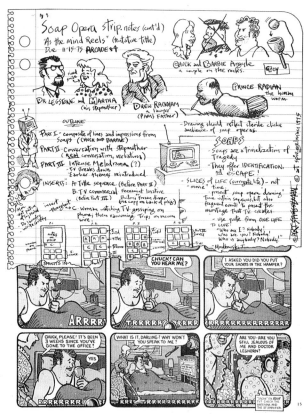

This page: More *Arcade* material
(all Print Mint). Right: Page (1976),
featuring a toad community with political
problems, by Bill Griffith. Below: Page
from 'Stalin' (1975) a documentary piece
by Spain Rodriguez. Bottom left: Panel
from 'Arnold Peck' (1976) by Willy Murphy.
Bottom right: 'Some of My Best Friends
Are' (1976) by Diane Noomin.

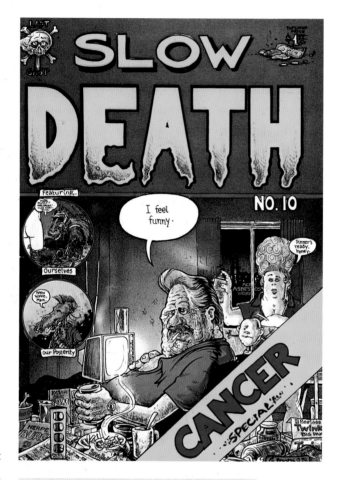

Zappers bar Griffin, it confused newsagents, who did not know where to shelve it, and found itself in competition with Marvel's *Comix Book*. The raft sank after only seven issues.

The political comix that appeared in this late period were fresher in tone than the strictly comedy titles, and tended to be tied to particular causes or ideologies – which is not to say that they couldn't also be funny. There had been precedents, of course. The women's comix, for example, had pioneered a new direction in the early 1970s, and were now followed by other, similarly committed, titles.[25] In the same way that Women's Liberation had been an inspiration to creators, so now Gay Lib was performing the same function. It was true that titles with gay characters and themes had appeared throughout the 1970s, popular examples being *Harold Hedd* (Georgia Straight, 1972) by Rand Holmes and *Barefootz* (Kitchen Sink, 1975) by Howard Cruse, but the official 'coming out' for the subgenre did not happen till later.

Lesbian titles led the way. They were as much an offshoot of the women's comix as an expression of something new, and included Roberta Gregory's *Dynamite Damsels* (self-published, 1976) and Mary Wings' *Dyke Shorts* (self-published, 1978). Finally there was the establishment of the *Gay Comix* anthology (Kitchen Sink) in 1980, which brought together the best of the gay and lesbian crowd. Edited by Howard Cruse, whose 'cute and cuddly' art often masked much darker themes, it featured outstanding work by Holmes, Gregory and Lee Marrs, as well as by less well-known names like Robert Triptow.

There was also a boom in other kinds of politics. Three lines were especially important: *Slow Death Funnies*, *Edu-Comics* and *Anarchy Comics*. *Slow Death* (Last Gasp) had been the first to strike out in a politically specific direction, dating from as early as 1970, thought it

This page: New political avenues. Above and below left: Cover and pages from *Gay Comix* (Kitchen Sink, 1987), the foremost gay anthology. Cover: Anon. Strip: Howard Cruse. Right and below right: Cover and page from *Slow Death* (Last Gasp, 1979), a 'committed' and very funny anthology, both by Greg Irons.

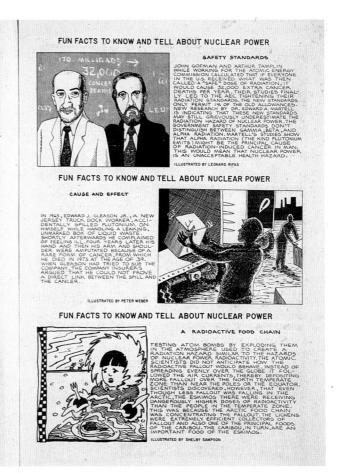

ILLUSTRATED BY LEONARD RIFAS

STORY CONTINUED AFTER NEXT PAGE

Above and above right: Cover and pages from *All-Atomic Comics* (Edu-Comics, 1976), complete with facts and figures about the nuclear threat. Art: Various. Script: Leonard Rifas. Below and right: Cover and page from *Anarchy* (Last Gasp), a comic with an obvious agenda. Cover (1978) by Jay Kinney; strip (1979) by Jay Kinney and Paul Mavrides. Comix like these had an openly proselytizing aim, and worked on the basis that the comic form was a cheap and effective means of getting ideas across.

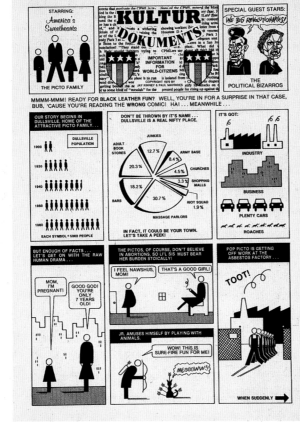

did not come into its own until late in the decade. Individual issues were devoted to nuclear power, the 'medical-industrial complex', Greenpeace and the anti-War movement. It included pages of facts and figures alongside some highly amusing satirical strips by Greg Irons, Jack Jackson and others. The 'Edu-Comics' (published under the same name) were in a similar vein, with *All-Atomic Comics* (1976) and *Energy Comics* (1980), again attacking nuclear power, and *Food Comix* (1980), which supported non-destructive farming methods.

Both *Slow Death* and Edu-Comics developed a 'Green' bent, whereas *Anarchy* (Last Gasp, 1978) was different in that it held to a specific ideology, featuring in its own words, 'comix inspired by or based on anarchist ideas and history in the belief that the true terrorists are governments and corporations who hold us hostage with their armaments, militaries, and intelligence activities.' Contributors included Spain Rodriguez, Melinda Gebbie, Jay Kinney and the Englishman Cliff Harper (whose solo *Class War Comix* (Kitchen Sink, 1979) had a similar agenda).

Britain too had its political titles, though these did not sell as well as their American counterparts. *The Optimist* (Comic Collective, 1976) was a short-lived tabloid, and had strips that made reference to squatting, the dole and even hypothermia among old-age pensioners (in one strip, 'Jinnie the Jinx', the eponymous heroine – not unlike a certain *Beano* character – gets pregnant, has a close shave with a back-street abortionist, and ends up joining the National Abortion Campaign). *Committed*

This page: More politics. Above and right: Cover and panel from *The Optimist* (Comic Collective, 1976), a British tabloid that, frankly, wasn't very optimistic. Cover by Cary Richardson; panel by John Thomas. Right: Page from *Committed Comix* (Arts Lab, 1977), one of the British Street Comix line, warning of the rise of the National Front. Written by David Edgar (also a radical playwright), with art by Clifford Harper. Below: Pages from *The Communist Manifesto* (Quixote Press, 1975), an adaptation that was pretty faithful to the original, by Mexican cartoonist Rius. Opposite: Page from *Knockabout* (Knockabout, 1981). Art/script: Graham Manley. A title that continued the British underground tradition into the 1980s.

Comix (Arts Lab, 1977) was one of the 'Street Comix' line, and had a similar radical agenda: strips made reference to the situation in Northern Ireland, the rise of the National Front, and gay rights, and included work by Cliff Harper, Hunt Emerson, Suzy Varty and newcomer Steve Bell.

But whatever their merits, this late wave of comix was still not enough to keep the underground alive, and as the 1970s progressed, the decline intensified. The movement had been intimately associated with the hippie subculture, but now that subculture itself was dying. For one thing, historical events were fast making many of its original aims irrelevant: the Vietnam War, the original focus of countercultural protest, ended in 1975 when the Americans withdrew from Saigon, while one by one the most hated politicians faded from the picture (Nixon went after Watergate in 1974, and Heath lost the election in the same year).

In addition to this, sections of the counterculture itself were not doing themselves any favours. In the late 1970s, heroin was taking over from marijuana and LSD as the hip substance of choice, and although it is difficult to generalize, it is possible to argue that because of this, the energy of the original movement was sapped. (The Haight Ashbury district became a centre for heroin, as did certain parts of London.) Indeed, the new hard drugs were killers, and many members of the counterculture died at around this time – including some of the underground's finest cartoonists.[26]

As if these problems were not enough, hippiedom's self-image took another blow in 1976–7 with the arrival of punk. This was a different kind of counterculture, more of a howl of protest than a movement based on a coherent agenda, and one which characterized all hippies as 'the enemy'. Suddenly, it was no longer cool to have long hair, smoke dope, wear flares or, more to the point, to read comix. As Hunt Emerson put it, when talking about *Street Comix*: 'In '77 we were overtaken by the punk thing. Before that, quality was what we were looking for – in artwork and production. And, of course, punk ended all that, and we found that all the things we'd been struggling for for three or four years were suddenly negated. People weren't taking comix seriously any more, or didn't think they were important'.[27] We shall look at punk in more detail in Chapters 6 and 8, but it is sufficient to say here that it was the *coup de grâce*. It marked a spiritual break with the past, and afterwards there could be no going back.

What happened to the underground in the succeeding couple of decades is hard to sum up in a few words, and is something we shall be returning to. Essentially, it was overtaken by the appearance of new adult comics, which made the comix look even more time-warped. These new titles were sold from specialist 'fan' shops, which emerged in the 1970s and 1980s as yet another retail network.[28] They became known generically as 'alternative comics', and built on the achievements of the underground. On the one hand, there was a boom in 'alternative' science fiction and horror, while on the other, a new kind of avant-garde emerged, typified by

a title called *Raw*, which was the brainchild of Art Spiegelman. Similarly, a new generation of creators blossomed, including names like Gary Panter, Dan Clowes and Peter Bagge, who were more influenced by punk than the old counterculture.

In this environment, the old underground creators had to decide which way to go. Some were welcomed as contributors to the new alternatives. In fact *Raw* included work by Crumb, Griffith and others. Some went on to work for the American mainstream companies. This was the career path chosen most notably by the Britons Brian Bolland, Dave Gibbons, Angus McKie and Bryan Talbot, and the American Richard Corben. Other artists went on to even greater fame by way of newspaper cartoons: in Britain, Steve Bell worked for *The Guardian* and Ray Lowry for *The Independent*, while in America, Bill Griffith's 'Zippy' became one of the most widely syndicated satirical strips in the country.[29]

By contrast, many creators continued in the same vein as before, though inevitably some of their work began to look very dated. Crumb, Shelton, Spain, Emerson and others put out a range of new comix, which, ironically, sold in much greater quantities in the 1980s and 1990s than the pioneering titles they had produced in the 1960s and 1970s. Similarly, some publishers persevered, and managed to carve themselves a niche in the new comics market. Last Gasp, Rip Off and Kitchen Sink all did well, while in Britain, underground publishing was dominated by the relatively new Knockabout Comics.

But even if the undergrounds now occupied a different position in the marketplace – at best, another variety of alternative comic, at worst, an awkward anachronism – then it is also true that the legacy of the original movement lived on. The underground had shown that a comic need not be restricted to any particular age group, art style or subject matter, and had established a completely new economic rationale for creators. Both these

achievements revolutionized comics, alternative and, to an extent, mainstream, forever.

Yet even if the comix's contribution to the history of the medium is indisputable, there still remains one nagging question. Namely, what was the underground's contribution to politics? After all, the comix were unique for the fact that they had pretensions to changing the world: the very word 'underground' suggested an oppositional stance, and their links with ideological causes were a defining influence.

It is deceptively easy to shoot holes in the movement's idealism. For example, from an historical perspective, 'underground' networks had been an honourable way of resisting oppression in occupied or fascist-controlled countries; they had been effective against the Nazis and more recently in dictatorships in South America. The United States and Britain in the 1960s and 1970s, however, were not in the same political category, no matter how hard some creators protested that they were. Thus, taken at face value, the idea of working for 'the underground' was a glamorous, and ultimately self-deluding, notion.

It is also undeniable that a significant number of comix merely paid lip service to any wider political ideals. We have seen how many were designed almost solely as commercial ventures; similarly, many were openly sexist, and there has to be a question mark over how depicting such activities as drug taking and wild sex were 'revolutionary' in the first place. As historians Reinhold Reitberger and Wolfgang Fuchs put it: 'Underground comix are polemics in comics format. But instead of leading to new objectives or really breaking new ground, they exploit the state of mind of a reactionary subculture and shock by their unconsidered portrayal of drug-addicted drop-outs'.[30]

However, subversion comes down to definitions, and it could equally be argued that the comix were part of the counterculture, which was 'what it said it was': a movement which offered an alternative to mainstream culture based on libertarian and Utopian ideals. In the words of philosopher David Bouchier, the counterculture rejected 'the very forms of thought and existence which have been created by advanced industrial societies. It was the most fundamental and original kind of challenge to industrial capitalism, and potentially the most subversive.'[31]

If one accepts this line of thought, then the underground could not be anything less than revolutionary: a tool of the counterculture, and as coherent or incoherent as the counterculture's wider aims. Indeed, if nothing else, the many police raids, court actions and so on that were undertaken against the comix suggest that the establishment considered them to be a real threat.[32] Of course, the establishment won in the end: this was the result of being both strong enough to fight off the attack, and flexible enough to co-opt and legitimize what was once regarded as outrageous. But ultimately, does the underground's failure make it any less subversive? The answer has to be in the negative.

Right: Page from *Knockabout* (Knockabout, 1981). Art/script: Paul Bignell. By this time, punk was having an influence on art style.

Right: 'Large Cow Comix', *Knockabout* (Knockabout, 1981) by Hunt Emerson. Emerson's fluid line and upbeat stories made him a perennial favourite. His popularity would survive with ease, as we shall see in Chapter 8.

1. Harvey Kurtzman is credited by some historians for giving the underground its name. In the immediate aftermath of the creation of the Comics Code Authority, the sixteenth issue of *Mad* had an image of Kurtzman on the cover peddling his magazine to kids on a street corner. Above him was the strapline, 'Comics go Underground!'.

2. To be specific, *Help!* (1960), included work by future undergrounders Robert Crumb, Gilbert Shelton, Skip Williamson and Jay Lynch. (If it had lasted one more issue, it would have included Art Spiegelman.)

3. Contributors to *The Texas Ranger* included Gilbert Shelton, Frank Stack (aka 'Foolbert Sturgeon') and Jack Jackson (aka 'Jaxon'). The most famous contributor to *Snide* was Denis Kitchen.

4. Jack Jackson, 'Comics or Comix?', *Blab!* (Kitchen Sink, 1989), no 4, p 38 .

5. The link between the poster scene and the headshops was a crucial one. In fact, in many senses the success of the former established the viability of the latter. By 1967, however, the poster boom was past its peak. It had become over-commercialized, and had lost its originality. Counter-cultural artistic communities were thus ripe for turning their energies to something new – which, of course, was provided by the comix.

6. Some historians have chosen to identify certain of these early comics as the 'first underground'. Candidates have included Gilbert Shelton and Frank Stack's *Adventures of Jesus* (Gilbert Shelton, 1962) and Jack Jackson's *God Nose Adult Comix* (self-published, 1964). It is likely that the latter coined the term 'comix'.

7. Robert Crumb has recently been the subject of an award-winning movie-documentary, *Crumb* (1995, Artificial Eye), directed by Terry Zwigoff.

8. *Jiz* and *Snatch* were produced in a smaller format than usual comix as a homage to the 'Dirty Comics' or 'Tijuana Bibles' that had been produced in America from the 1920s to the 1940s. (See p 35)

9. Robert Crumb, speaking in the documentary-feature *Comic Book Confidential* (Canada, Castle Hendring, directed by Ron Mann, 1989).

10. Trina Robbins, 'Comments on Crumb', *Blab!* (Kitchen Sink, September 1988), no 3, p 93.

11. Jack Jackson, 'Comments on Crumb', *Blab!*, (Kitchen Sink, September 1988), no 3, p 80.

12. Gilbert Shelton, quoted in 'Sking, Squalid and ? to the Eyeballs', by Charles Shaar Murray, Q Magazine, July 1988.

13. See Trina Robbins and Catherine Yronwode, *Women and the Comics* (California, Eclipse Books, 1985) and Trina Robbins, *A Century of Women Cartoonists* (Princeton, Kitchen Sink, 1992).

14. One other name was very important to this horror boom in a behind-the-scenes capacity, bookstore owner and publisher, Gary Arlington (founder of the San Francisco Comic Book Company). He was the driving force behind the creation of *Skull*, and later of *Slow Death*, and would often swap copies of original EC titles from his collection with people like Jack Jackson and Greg Irons in exchange for original artwork.

15. This move into horror created a certain amount of friction among other underground creators. Bill Griffith in particular was very vocal, and explained his reasons thus in 1973: 'I ask myself ..."Why is there a tendency for some undergrounds to resemble slightly altered aboveground comics? What's this business with TITS and MONSTERS and WEREWOLVES?" ... "I wanta know what's 'underground' about rotting corpses! Besides buryin' 'em, huh?" ... Aside from the explicit sex and naughty words, [the comix] fall into the "above-ground" category with ease. Which is where [they] belong, and most probably will end up.' *San Francisco Phoenix*, 1973, reprinted in *The Comics Journal*, March 1993, no 157, pp 56–8.

16. Interestingly, some of the most famous jams included a special guest, Harvey Kurtzman.

17. For a more extensive account of the underground movement see Mark Estren, *A History of Underground Comics*. Estren's book is certainly the best on the subject, though is not a complete record because it was published in 1974 and only deals with the USA. Other histories that are worth investigating include *Uncovering the Sixties: The Life and Times of the Underground Press* by Abe Peck (New York, Pantheon, 1985); and *Kitchen Sink Press: The First 25 Years* (Massachusetts, Kitchen Sink, 1994), which focuses solely on the publisher's story. My own *Adult Comics: An Introduction* (London, Routledge, 1993) contains lengthy sections on the underground.

18. To be specific, the most widely available early bootlegs were two editions of *Yarrowstalks*, and *Zap* nos 0 and 1, this is according to Mal Burns' *Comix Index* (Brighton, John Noyce, 1978). There were also various Dutch imports, similarly bootlegs, by the Real Free Press.

19. For the best survey of the British scene, see David Huxley's 'The Growth and Development of British Underground and Alternative Comics 1966–86', PhD thesis, University of Loughborough, 1990. Huxley was himself the editor of an underground, entitled *Blood, Sex, Terror* (BST Comics, 1977.)

20. It should also be noted that Britain had a tradition of radical illustrated publications that was quite different to that in America. These included illustrated poetry magazines, and 'artworks'. (See Huxley, *ibid*, p 21.) Additionally, there was a tradition of satirical magazines that were anti-establishment, if not counter-cultural, the main example being *Private Eye* (founded in 1961).

21. This process was facilitated by the existence of the Underground Press Syndicate (UPS), a free, alternative wire service. (*IT* and *Oz* had previously taken advantage of it, and republished many American strips within their pages.)

22. On Ghura and Matthews, see David Kerekes' excellent 'Thrill to Stories of Graphic Lust!' in *Critical Vision* (Cheshire, Headpress, 1995), pp 1–54.

23. The tireless Bakshi went on to make a number of other movies with a countercultural flavour, including *Heavy Traffic* (1973) and *Coonskin* (1975), both of which mixed animation with live-action.

24. Art Spiegelman and Francoise Mouly, 'Raw Nerves' in *Read Yourself Raw* (New York, Pantheon Books, 1987), p 5.

25. Of the women's comix founded in the early 1970s, by now only *Wimmen's Comix* had managed to keep to a regular schedule.

26. The number of underground creators who are not alive today is quite staggering. Of course, not every death can be put down to drug abuse, but in general the on-the-edge lifestyle that many chose to lead was a contributing factor. Major names no longer around include: Mike Matthews, Rick Griffin, Rory Hayes, Vaughn Bodé and Greg Irons.

27. Hunt Emerson, quoted in Huxley, '*The Growth and Development of the British Underground*', p 33.

28. The new shop network was indebted to the old headshop system in the sense that the latter had demonstrated that a market outside of the mainstream (newsagents) could be viable. Some of the new shops actually used to be headshops: the most famous early example in London, a shop called 'Dark They Were and Golden Eyed' spanned the two subcultures.

29. In Britain, Zippy was serialized in *The Guardian* in the 1990s.

30. R Reitberger and W Fuchs, *Comics: Anatomy of a Mass Medium* (London, Studio Vista, 1972), p 222.

31. David Bouchier, *Idealism and Revolution: New Ideologies of Liberation in Britain and the United States* (London, Edward Arnold, 1978), p 141.

32. A quote by Robert Williams is instructive here (though how much of it is down to personal paranoia is debatable): 'We just thought that we were all going to get arrested because there'd never been material like this before ... In 1969, 70, 71, there was a very, very solid and plausible fear of the government going extremely right-wing and startin' to round people up. In fact, the internment camps were being refurbished at this time and there was photographic evidence that these camps were being reconditioned.' Quoted in: *The Comics Journal*, August 1993, no 161, pp 48–51.

Picking up the pieces

THIS *DAYSTICK* ONLY HAS **ONE** SETTING — BUT IT'LL STILL BREAK YOUR FACE !

THAT'S WHY THEY CALL ME THE **LAW!**

Things started to go wrong for the mainstream comics industry after the end of the 1960s. British titles quickly declined in circulation, and either folded, merged together, or became reliant on reprint strips. American comics had rallied well after the Code, but had never reached pre-Code levels of sales: now they too went through a slump. It was a crisis, and indeed, remains a crisis to this day – despite the growth of a new market in the 1980s based on specialist 'fan-shops' (the subject for Chapter 7), the newsagent market has yet to recover. Sad to report, in the mid-1990s, comics constitute a barely noticeable presence on newsagents' shelves.

One possible reason for this depression was the rise of television. The connection is hard to prove, but it has been argued that the advent of the various stages of television's evolution (black-and-white TV in the 1960s, colour in the 1970s, home video and interactive computer games in the 1980s and 1990s) corresponded with the decline in comics. Of course, the rise of one medium does not automatically spell the wane of another (any more than the growth of comics destroyed the traditional novel), but at the very least it meant that there were more leisure options for people to choose from.[1] There were, however, other reasons for the malaise, and these largely came down to the nature of the comics themselves.

In Britain, the rot was quick to set in. The humour industry got stale due to over-production: the great comics of the Reid/Baxendale era had given rise to a plethora of pale imitations, and the glut inevitably

meant mergers (*Buster* with *Cor!!*, *Sparky* with *Topper*, *Whoopee!* with *Whizzer and Chips* and so on). Even *The Dandy* and *The Beano*, which continued to do well commercially, lost their spark. The adventure genre also ran into problems: its main subject matter, the Second World War, was receding into history, and young readers found more recent wars less interesting (*Battle* attempted a strip about The Falklands, but it was not popular). Here too the way of death for many comics was to merge: *Tiger* with *The Eagle*, *Lion* with *Valiant*, *Hotspur* with *Victor*, etcetera. Finally, the British girls' comics either disappeared, or turned themselves into female-interest magazines: as we have seen, heirs to the tradition included *Blue Jeans* and *My Guy* (glossy, sexually aware publications designed for a teen market).[2]

With this alarming background in mind, British publishers were forced to try other strategies to pick up the pieces. Occasionally – very occasionally – they were successful, and there were individual comics in the period from 1970 to the present that managed to buck the downward trend. After all, there were numerically more newsagents than ever before, and they still represented potentially a very profitable network. If there was to be any chance of exploiting it, publishers could no longer rely on old formulas. As a result, they tended to take two paths: one was to 'tie in' new comics with other media (movies, TV shows, computer games, even the toy industry), and the other was to attempt to open up new audiences among older (teenage and adult) readers.

The first option provided its share of one-off successes, though sales peaks only lasted as long as the particular fad itself. Links with other media had always existed (even *Ally Sloper's Half Holiday* had influenced, and been influenced by, music hall and early movies) and we have seen in chapters 1–5 how important this cultural overspill had been in comics' development. But in the post-1970 period, with the decline in sales generally, this idea of cross-fertilisation became perceived as something of a life-raft – a case of 'if you can't beat 'em, join 'em'. The comics companies could no longer take risks, and they argued that only by cashing in on already recognizable characters could profits be made.

The movie industry was the most obvious source for exploitation, and virtually every new movie released for a children's or teen audience had its comic counterpart. British companies were slow to move at first: perhaps the most interesting example of a film tie-in was *House of Hammer* (1976, Top Sellers/Quality), which adapted old Hammer horror movies (*Dracula*, *The Mummy*, etc) into strip form. However, the pace speeded up with the founding of Marvel UK, a subsidiary of the American giant, in 1982. The company had a brief to reprint American material (thus avoiding freight costs), and to generate titles of its own, and from the start movie adaptations were high on the agenda. The hits were most notably *Star Wars* (1982), which expanded the plotlines of the original films, and *Indiana Jones* (1984).[3] These were joined in the 1990s by a series of titles

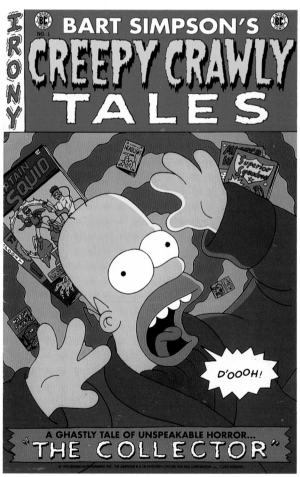

published by Dark Horse UK, another British subsidiary of an American company, which included *Aliens* (1991), *Terminator* (1991) and *Jurassic Park* (1993).[4]

TV also provided a rich seam to be mined. Unarguably the biggest success in this respect was *Teenage Mutant Hero Turtles* (Fleetway, 1990) which fed from the publicity surrounding the hit animated series of the same name, and which at one point had a print run of 700,000. This was a tale for youngsters about four turtles with martial arts skills ('heroes in a half-shell'), who combat crime from their base in the sewers. In actual fact, the idea originated in a comic (a small-scale, American, independently produced satire for adults), but was re-conceived for a children's audience: as such it became the basis not just for the TV show and the Fleetway comic, but also for a massive toy merchandising campaign and a series of big budget live-action movies (see also pp 174–5). Later, animated shows like 'Ren and Stimpy', 'The Simpsons' and 'The Batman Adventures', all had comics devoted to them in British editions, while live action series like 'Power Rangers' and 'Red Dwarf' also led to spinoffs.

Slightly more imaginatively, but still with something of a sense of desperation, the comics companies turned to computer games and toys. The most successful spin-off from the former was *Sonic the Comic* (Fleetway, 1993), about the character 'Sonic the Hedgehog', while there were also a number of titles to tie-in with 'slugfest' martial-arts-style games such as 'Streetfighter' and 'Mortal Kombat' (which themselves became movies in due course). Comics which piggybacked on to the toy market included: *Transformers* (Marvel UK, 1984), about a group of robots (which also became an animated TV series); and less successfully, *Sindy*, which brought the girls' doll to life; and *Action Man*, which did the same for the boys' 'GI Joe' toy (both Tower Magazines, 1995). Marvel UK were undoubtedly the publisher most seriously involved with the toy industry, leading one exasperated commentator to write: 'They have opted to become an extension of the toy companies' public relations departments. They let the companies buy up the Saturday morning TV advertising, and when it gets profitable enough, they buy the license and start to clean up. It's all Transformers, Zoids, Masters of the Universe and the bloody Getalong Gang. The quality or even the content become unimportant when you've got the name of the latest hyped-up toy all over the shiny covers ...'[5]

In spite of the sporadic victories of publishing for the crossover market, it was, and is, a strategy that has natural limitations. The comics produced in this way rarely garner a readership on their own merits, and thus do not develop personalities of their own, or any sense of 'reader loyalty' in the traditional fashion. They tend not to last long. Of more interest to us here were those titles introduced with new markets in mind, which at least represented the comics industry taking a proactive role.

Some publishers in Britain, in particular, decided to try to appeal to older readers. They gambled that the teenage and twenty-something market had more

disposable income than children, and that therefore prices could be raised in the hope that the effects of falling circulations could be combatted (at least to some extent). This entailed getting away from traditional subject matter, and adding more sophisticated material – both in terms of storytelling and artwork. Concomitantly, it also meant taking more care over presentation and packaging, and this heralded a move away from the traditional newsprint comics in favour of more glossy magazine formats.

In terms of the British industry, there were three news-stand comics that were outstanding in the post-1960s period, either because of their sustained commercial success, aesthetic style, or influence on other comics: *2000AD* (IPC/Fleetway, 1977), *Deadline* (Tom Astor, 1988) and *Viz* (House of Viz, 1979) each of which generated characters that were equally as ingenious as any produced by the medium in the past.[6] The three contradicted the economic trend for different reasons, though they had definite similarities: each was an anthology; each was designed for an older readership; each would increasingly distance itself from its origins in comics in favour of being thought of as a magazine; and each was influenced to a degree by the punk movement of the late 1970s.

This last point may seem like a subtlety, but in fact it dictated the tone of the comics in a way that was every bit as important as the underground's links with the hippie scene. Defining that sensibility is a little more difficult, because although punk was certainly an ideology that extended beyond Johnny Rotten screaming his head off, it had no set goals in the way that hippie culture did.

All we can say is that, at its core, it stood for a distrust of any kind of authority; a romanticized belief in working-class culture (street credibility); the worth of rebellion for its own sake; and the fetishization of violence (real or imaginary). It also started out as a peculiarly British phenomenon, only to be taken up in America and other parts of the world later.

2000AD was by far the most influential of the British threesome, and exhibited a definite punk edge, despite being science fiction based. It would be a flagship comic for IPC/Fleetway through the 1980s and 1990s, and borrowed much from its predecessor, *Action* (IPC, 1976) – a comic founded with the intention of adding some zip to the traditional adventure formula, which in some senses succeeded too well. *Action* strips were typically based on themes popular in films and on TV, but given a violent and anti-authoritarian twist: the saintly heroes of yesteryear were now more complex characters, often bitter and morally ambiguous (even the obligatory war strip featured a sympathetic Nazi). For these reasons,

the comic tapped into the very earliest stirrings of punk, and was soon selling over 100,000 to a readership that stretched into late teenage.

Inexorably, *Action* ran into problems with parents, and with the media: *The Sun* branded it 'The Seven-penny Nightmare', and led the campaign to have it banned. Calls for censorship were ostensibly predicated on the quantity of violence, but in fact there were more political objections: this was, after all, a subversive comic in more ways than one. IPC eventually buckled under the pressure, and neutered *Action* amid much protest from fans. It died a lingering death a few months later.[7]

2000AD was intended to plug the gap left by *Action*, and was launched in 1977. It would have the same punk attitude, but would be set in the future so as to avoid the possibility of a similar controversy. The science fiction angle had two other advantages: first, it meant the title could borrow movie ideas in much the same way as its pre-decessor had done (roughly contemporaneous Hollywood hits included *Rollerball, Close Encounters of the Third Kind* and *Star Wars*). Second, it made it more possible for artists to imitate American comics, which at the time were more popular than British product: *2000AD* is remarkable for the fact that it was the first mainstream comic to exploit Kirbyesque splash-panels and dynamic rendering.

Yet, the new comic did not find its personality immediately. One major mistake was to try to revive Dan Dare: *The Eagle* had gone under in 1969, but IPC was keen to link their new comic with a science fiction past.[8] The company announced its intention to revamp the character for the punk era thus: 'Dan Dare will have a leaner jaw, more piercing eyes, and a disposition rather less blandly goody-goody'. But Dare was already a period-piece in 1977, and after the radicalism of *Action*, there was no way that he could be brought back – 'leaner jaw' or not. He was a dismal failure, and was soon dropped.

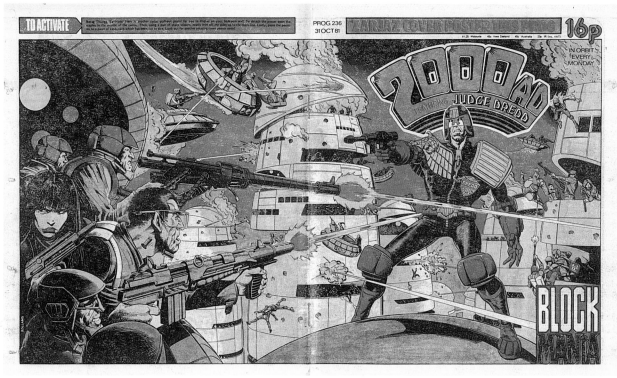

This page and opposite: Various takes on Judge Dredd, arguably the biggest action star in British comics, a character who managed to be both an utter tyrant and very likeable for his refusal to compromise. (All examples Fleetway). Cover, *2000AD* (1981). Art: Mike McMahon. Above: Pages from *2000AD* (1986). Art: Cliff Robinson. Script: TB Grover. Right: Detail from *2000AD* (1983). Art: Carlos Ezquerra. Below: Panels from *Judge Dredd: Lawman of the Future* (1995). Art: Jim Murray and Dondie Cox. Script: John Wagner. The latter was heavily influenced by the Dredd movie (1995), starring Sylvester Stallone.

It was left to the new strips to make the running, which they did with great success. This was largely because of the quality of their creators: by the early 1980s, *2000AD* was featuring a roster of excellent writers (notably Pat Mills, Alan Moore, John Wagner and Alan Grant), and equally superb artists (including Brian Bolland, Dave Gibbons, Mike McMahon, Ian Gibson, and Kevin O'Neill).[9] Many of these had previously worked on underground comics, and all were intimate with American styles: although it is hard to generalize, they brought with them a sense not only of the potential for the medium to reach an adult audience, but also an ethic that shunned pandering to the lowest common denominator. As a result, *2000AD* never talked down to its readership, and in the process the strips garnered a following aged anywhere between eight years old to the mid-twenties.

The best example of such a crossover story was the lead strip, the extraordinary 'Judge Dredd'. This was a character who struck a chord with a wide readership, and who was introduced in the comic thus: 'Life is harsh in twenty-second-century Mega City One. Atomic wars have devastated the planet, and left it a mean and lawless place. Out of this chaos a radical new system of justice has arisen. Here law and order is upheld by a new force: the Judges. They are judge, jury and executioner, and Judge Dredd is the toughest of them all. Judge Dredd is the Law!' Yes, Dredd was hard but fair – but mostly hard – and there was much to enjoy in his (ironic) near-fascist behaviour. The kids loved the excessive violence, and the ruthless way he dealt with street scum ('Ten years, creep!'), while adults could chuckle at the nicely observed satire. There were witty plotlines about the democracy movement in Mega City, with apartment blocks named after politicians and pop stars, while there was much black humour in Dredd's over-the-top methods – his punishments typically far outweighing the crime. The

strip's roots were certainly in the superhero genre, but Dredd was a more complex character than many of his American counterparts: there was a political ambiguity about him that made him fascinating. As one critical source has noted: 'Dredd is only Dredd because he is the opposite of the punks on the street – in whom we half-recognise ourselves ... The comic transposes us to "America" to play out the futuristic drama of the complete realisation of Thatcherite law and order politics. Dredd must be both hero and villain ...'[10]

Other strips were similarly layered, and also included healthy dollops of satire: 'Nemesis', about a war between vile humans and agreeable aliens, included metaphors for racial and religious intolerance, as well as some appalling puns; 'Slaine' was, on the surface, a sword-and-sorcery tale in the style of *Conan the Barbarian* (see below, p 150), but included detailed references to Celtic mythology and feminist plotlines – again laced with

humour; 'Halo Jones', about an ordinary woman conscripted into the army to fight in an intergalactic war, commented more seriously on feminism and militarism. Other strips that did particularly well included 'Skizz', 'ABC Warriors', 'Rogue Trooper' and 'Strontium Dog'. All of them would eventually be collected together in graphic novel form, and sold from bookshops and specialist comics shops (see p 157).

By the early 1980s, *2000AD* was selling around 120,000 an issue. This was not a remarkable figure compared to some of the adventure comics of the past (in the mid-1960s, the big publishers expected to sell treble that for their top titles), but in the context of the market conditions prevailing at the time, it was impressive.

The success of *2000AD* meant it soon spawned competitors. It had shown a possible way out of the industry's nosedive, and other comics followed in a similar science fiction vein. DC Thomson attempted to compete with *Starblazer* (1979), which featured present and future *2000AD* creators (Mike McMahon, Grant Morrison and Cam Kennedy), and which appealed to an early teen market. A much smaller publisher, Quality Comics, produced the more ambitious *Warrior* (1982),

a magazine-format title, which again used *2000AD* stars (Alan Moore, Alan Davis, Dave Gibbons and Jim Baikie): it is best remembered for two strips: 'Laser Eraser and Pressbutton', a lively romp about a partnership between a gun-wielding female and a psychotic cyborg, and 'V for Vendetta' by Alan Moore and David Lloyd, a technically brilliant dystopian adventure, with an anarchist hero ('V') who disguises himself as Guy Fawkes to carry out subversive activity.

Then there were the science fiction comics that originated from a more underground source (not really 'competitors' to *2000AD* because mainstream distribution was often a problem). They included *Graphixus* (Graphic Eye, 1977), which included work by Brian Bolland; *Near Myths* (Galaxy Media, 1978), which featured 'Gideon Stargrave' by Grant Morrison, plus the innovative 'Luther Arkwright' by Bryan Talbot, a complex, Michael Moorcock-inspired story about a war waged across parallel worlds; and *Pssst!* (Never-Artpool, 1982), a lavishly produced magazine much influenced by European comics, which continued the 'Luther Arkwright' story and featured colour painted artwork from artists such as Angus McKie. (Its tendency towards strips with a high quotient of naked female flesh landed it in hot water with feminists.)

None of these newcomers succeeded: *Starblazer* was never a big seller, while *Warrior* crashed after twenty-six episodes due to financial pressures; *Graphixus*, *Near Myths* and *Pssst!* lasted for six, five and ten issues respectively. In short, none was able to build up the same solid following that *2000AD* had achieved: the galaxy just was not ready for more than one science fiction hit.

Their failure left *2000AD* able to capitalize on its advantage into the late 1980s and 1990s. But first, a couple of pressing problems had to be addressed. The most difficult was that creators were consistently leaving the comic to go and work for American companies, where conditions and pay were better. Mills, Moore, Bolland, Gibbons and others had already taken this path.[11] Fleetway should have learned its lesson, but instead of adapting, it continued to offer substantially the same contracts as before, and to compensate for resignations by making extra efforts to find fresh blood. This worked in the short run, and *2000AD* had a second wind thanks

This page: Competition with *2000AD* hotted up over the years, but only one or two newcomers were worth a read. Left and above: Cover and pages from *Warrior* (Quality). Cover (1984), art: David Jackson. Top: 'V for Vendetta' (1982), a remarkable drama about a masked anarchist avenger. Art: David Lloyd. Script: Alan Moore. Centre: 'Twilight World' (1983), an *Alien*-influenced tale. Art: Jim Baikie. Script: Steve Moore. Right: Cover, *Graphixus* (Graphic Eye, 1978). Art: Gary Leach. A much more underground-flavoured magazine.

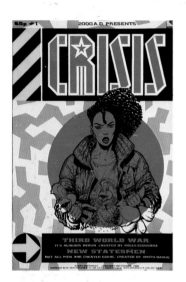

Right: Page from 'Slaine', *2000AD*, (Fleetway, 1989), featuring the majestic fantasy art of Simon Bisley. New artists like Bisley kept the comic alive, but eventually they would be lured to American companies. Below and below right: Examples from three of the late 1980s/early 1990s titles from the *2000AD* stable (all Fleetway). Top: Cover, *Crisis* (1988), a brave attempt at a right-on comic for right-wing times. Art: Carlos Ezquerra. Bottom: Cover, *Revolver* (1990), featuring yet another revival of Dan Dare. Art: Rian Hughes. Bottom right: 'The Angriest Dog in the World', *XPresso* (1991), an oddity with art/script by American filmmaker, David Lynch.

to the talents of relatively unknown names such as writers Grant Morrison, Peter Milligan and Garth Ennis, and artists like Simon Bisley, Glenn Fabry and Brendan McCarthy (many of whom had been avid readers of the comic as youngsters). Of course, as these creators became famous in their own right, they too would leave in the long run.[12]

The second problem was that American comics were continuing to steal a march on their British counterparts. As we shall see in Chapter 7, in the 1970s and 1980s a fan-scene based on superhero titles emerged, and this grew at a rate proportional to the decline of the news-stand market. So, in order to compete, *2000AD* took on more of the look and feel of an American product. Its first overtly superhero strip appeared in 1986, in the form of the very popular 'Zenith' (by Grant Morrison and Steve Yeowell), while in terms of presentation, the comic now became more of a magazine, with glossy paper and fully painted artwork.[13]

At the same time, the pop and rock references were beefed up to appeal to an audience that also read *NME* (*New Musical Express*) and *The Face*. This kind of quotation had always been an element in *2000AD* (arguably a hangover from the underground), but in

the late 1980s namedropping by pop stars of the comic, and vice versa, reached epidemic proportions: Anthrax advertised their 'I am the Law!' single with a Judge Dredd poster; two ex-members of Madness recorded under the name of the 'Fink Brothers' – a direct *2000AD* steal; and Run DMC, Ian Astbury, the Beastie Boys, Motorhead, the Ramones, Zodiac Mindwarp, Transvision Vamp and Gaye Bikers on Acid all claimed to be fanatical devotees. In 1987, the *NME* was able to comment: '*2000AD* in the 1980s is to rock what Brylcreem was in the '50s, what drugs were in the '60s, what hair gel was in the '70s.'[14]

But this policy of becoming 'hipper' and raising the age profile was only partially successful. Inevitably, the comic's traditional younger audience gradually drifted away, which proved more damaging in the long run than had been expected, because not enough older readers were recruited to bridge the deficit.[15] Also, although established strips like 'Slaine' and 'Dredd' were given a shot in the arm by the spectacular art styles of Bisley et al, newer strips like 'Big Dave' and 'Really and Truly' were not popular. The net result was that in the 1990s, sales dropped off quite substantially, as American comics continued to be the preferred option for most comic buyers.

Partly because of this decline in *2000AD*'s fortunes, the early 1990s were a lively time for British news-stand comics, as new titles were launched to try to take advantage of what was perceived as a gap in the market. Fleetway itself launched no less than four new titles, all aimed at readers aged sixteen and over, and which made the most of the existing stable of *2000AD* creators. Chronologically, the first was *Crisis* (1987), which capitalized on *2000AD*'s political edge with a mix of aware action adventure ('Third World War'), angsty domestic drama ('Straitgate') and science fiction superheroics ('New Statesmen'). Next up, *Revolver* (1990) similarly tried to broaden its range away from science fiction, but paid its dues to the genre by reviving Dan Dare – this time as a straight parody, deriding the original's imperialist sensibility. Other strips included 'Purple Daze', a biography of Jimi Hendrix, and 'Rogan Gosh', a druggy odyssey inspired by Indian comics art.

The third Fleetway title was *The Judge Dredd Megazine* (1990), a straightforward spinoff from *2000AD* starring its most popular character. It included inventive new Dredd storylines (plus new enemies), and a selection of unconnected strips, such as the splendidly bizarre 'Devlin Waugh: Swimming in Blood', about a homosexual exorcist and his battle with a swarm of vampires. The fourth and final Fleetway offering was *XPresso* (1991), an out-and-out 'adult' comic (strapline:

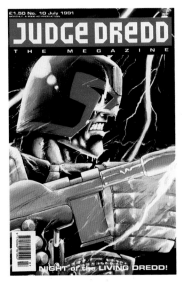

'For Sophisticated Coffeetables'), modelled on successful European anthologies, and showcasing continental creators such as Milo Manara and Max Cabanes.

At the same time, other publishers were similarly putting out new products. *Toxic!* (Apocalypse, 1991) was founded with the explicit intention of recreating the early energy of 2000AD, and was put together by some of that comic's leading lights (Pat Mills, Kevin O'Neill, John Wagner and Alan Grant among them). It was a sanguine mix of science fiction and black humour, with superhero satire 'Marshal Law' proving the most popular strip. *Blast!* (John Brown, 1991) was more rock literate, and along with reprints of hip American material featured a reworking of *Warrior*'s 'Laser Eraser and Pressbutton', and new work by 2000AD's then-biggest star Simon Bisley (notably, 'Mr Monster'). Even Marvel UK decided to test the waters. Their first two releases (*Strip*, 1990, and *Meltdown*, 1991) relied heavily on low-risk reprints of other Marvel products, but their third, *Overkill* (1992), was designed specifically as a rival to 2000AD and featured new science fiction stories by British creators which interlocked into a self-contained 'universe'.

For all the effort that these new titles represented, collectively they were a disaster. This fresh burst of publishing activity was no more successful than the early 1980s one had been. Britain's economy was deep

This page: More examples from the late 1980s/early 1990s flood of titles aimed at competing in the *2000AD* market. As ever, quality was variable. Above and above right: Cover and detail from *Judge Dredd: The Megazine* (Fleetway, 1991 and 1993). Cover art: Dean Ormston. Detail is from 'Devlin Waugh', a lively tale about a debonair homosexual exorcist. Art: Sean Phillips. Script: John Smith. Below: Covers, *Toxic!* (Apocalypse, 1991), art: Kevin O'Neill; *Overkill* (Marvel Comics, 1992), art: Dermot Power; *Blast!* (John Brown, 1991), art: Simon Bisley; and *Meltdown* (Marvel Comics, 1991), art: Cam Kennedy.

in recession by this time, and it was not a wise policy to launch new products (especially not at high 'adult' prices). Also, once again, publishers had failed to bargain for 2000AD's extraordinary staying power, and the fact that its fan base was loyal, even if it was declining. The numbers of issues the new comics survived for were as follows: *Crisis* 63; *Revolver* 9; *Xpresso* 2; *Blast!* 7; *Toxic!* 31; *Strip* 20; *Meltdown* 5; and *Overkill* 12.

It is revealing that the only real success from the crop – and for all that, a modest one – was *Judge Dredd: The Megazine*. This has survived to the present, boosted to some extent by the release of the Hollywood blockbuster *Judge Dredd* (with Sylvester Stallone) in 1995, and the huge merchandising campaign that surrounded the film. The movie succeeded in capturing some of the ironic humour of the original strip, and Stallone was perfect as the square-jawed hero, but it tended to eschew plot in favour of special effects, and thus appealed to a more limited (teenage) audience than was expected. It was panned by critics ('Dredd-ful' being the typical verdict),

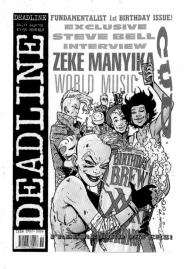

and fared disastrously at the box office.[16] The decision by Fleetway to launch yet another Dredd title to coincide with the film – *Judge Dredd: Lawman of the Future*, this time aimed at younger (pre-teen) readers – was a cash-in too far and was soon cancelled.[17]

For its part, *2000AD* continues on its way. It still relies on fan-favourite strips first created nearly twenty years ago, but has a smattering of new material each issue. Some of the original creators are still there (Pat Mills is as productive on the comic as ever, and his latest story, 'Finn', a bloody tale about a futuristic eco-warrior, looks like being one of the most popular additions for a long time); meanwhile up-and-coming creators continue to be keen to strut their stuff within its pages. The truth is, however, that the title now sells in the order of an unimpressive 70,000 per issue, and even this is dipping quite drastically. The failure of the Dredd movie has not helped, and it's hard not to be pessimistic about the future for this once-great comic.

The second of the three British successes, *Deadline* was linked to *2000AD* by its founders, Brett Ewins and Steve Dillon, both of whom had worked on various strips on the comic (including Dredd).[18] But *Deadline* was always of a very different nature. Above all, it emphasized humour over adventure, and added prose features about pop music. In effect, it was a cross between an adult humour comic, and a music/style magazine – the term 'style comic' soon became a common description.

The music connection was a central selling point. By focusing on what were becoming known as 'indie bands', the comic staked its claim as a (self-consciously) hip publication, with a definite punk attitude. Whereas in *2000AD* the music references had been oblique, here they were explicit: giveaways of records, tapes, and other band-related merchandising became a regular feature, rock-referencing in strips was typical, while articles were often penned by well-known journalists from *NME* and *Melody Maker*.

Deadline's other distinguishing feature was that it was published by a wealthy individual, Tom Astor, rather than by an established comics company.[19] This meant that the production values were not very lavish (at least to begin with), with no interior colour, and that the rates of pay for creators were low. But it also meant that the comic could be kept afloat financially even through periods of poor circulation figures – a situation that would see the cancellation of any other comic. This explained, above all else, its longevity: *Deadline* never sold in extraordinary numbers, and even at its peak only reached around 40,000 per issue.

The comic always had an experimental feel. In its early days, the strips were eclectic, and based around a clutch of strong characters. There was 'Beryl the Bitch' by Julie Hollings, a spiky gag strip about a stone-hearted man-eater; 'Hugo Tate', by Nick Abadzis, which developed into an alternately amusing and disturbing meditation on identity; 'Wired World' by Philip Bond, about a pair of post-punk female friends; and 'Johnny Nemo' by Peter Milligan and Brett Ewins, a witty tale about a rock and roll detective and his gun-toting adventures in 'New London' ('Not a place for the squeamish', says Johnny. 'It's ugly, violent, dangerous, filthy and decadent ... it suits my personality ... ').

But the strongest character of all, and a firm reader favourite from issue 1, was 'Tank Girl' by Alan Martin and Jamie Hewlett. Inspired by the tough females in films like *Alien*, Tank Girl was a shaven-headed outlaw

This page and opposite: Examples from *Deadline* (Tom Astor), the comic that brought the world 'Tank Girl'. Above and right: Covers, (1989 and 1993), showing the changing attire and hairstyle of the stroppy star, a sort of antipodean, science fictional skinhead. Art: Jamie Hewlett. Right: 'Beryl the Bitch' (1989), featuring the comic's second female-with-attitude, a predatory socialite. Art/script: Julie Hollings. Opposite: Page from 'Tank Girl', (1989), relating a typically pointless story. Art/script: Jamie Hewlett.

with a knack for gratuitous violence. She roams the Australian outback in a tank, getting drunk, bedding kangaroos and starting fights. Sexy and anarchic, she was 'the girl that makes Superman want to take off his pants'. The story lines were extremely fast-paced and amusing – lots of snappy one-liners – while the art was clean and vivid: it was clear from day one that a cult had arrived.

It may be stretching things to search for deeper meanings in Tank Girl, but there were a few. For example, she reflected successive fashion 'looks' that were popular in the London club scene (to begin with, the cropped hair and boots; later the 1970s retro clothes), and would have appealed to a certain kind of readership on that (hip) level. Also, she interested women readers. Even though she was drawn in a way that might be attractive to men, it was still unusual to see a female comic character who was not a stereotype: this was definitely not the pointy breasted sex goddess of so many Marvel comics. Unsurprisingly, she soon became a mascot for various feminist groups, and later for 'riot grrl' bands.

With a success like Tank Girl to sell the comic, *Deadline*'s other strips could afford to be more exploratory. Over time, it increasingly acquired a reputation for publishing new talent, and in particular for raiding the best material from the so-called 'small press'. This was a network of low- or no-budget comics that were home-produced (often on a photocopier), and generally sold through the post or in specialist comics shops. Because the small press was not tied to

commercial imperatives, it became synonymous with self-expression and unorthodox material. In a sense, *Deadline* fed from this source in the same way that 2000AD had once fed from the underground and fan scene – the important difference being that creators at *Deadline* kept copyright over their work.

One by-product of this was that *Deadline* featured a higher proportion of female creators than other contemporary newsstand comics. This was because women had traditionally been less intimidated by the small press than by the (male-dominated) mainstream. Three names in particular stood out: the aforementioned Julie Hollings; Carol Swain, whose dark, charcoal-rendered stories dealt in a heightened reality; and Rachael Ball, whose humour strips relied on a finely tuned ear for dialogue, and whose 'Box City' stories developed a cult following. The fact that women characters and creators generally had such a high profile meant that the comic attracted a higher proportion of female readers than any other on the shelves (estimated at around twenty-five per cent by the publishers in 1989).

For all *Deadline*'s merits, sales continued to be unspectacular, and a decision was taken in the early 1990s to make it more of a magazine. A number of steps were taken: the number of articles was upped, and the proportion of strips cut; more colour was added, along with glossy paper throughout; and finally, a presentation makeover was undertaken by noted designer/cartoonist Rian Hughes. Under a new editor, *Deadline* would be sharper than before, with a spiky

Above and above right: Pages from *Deadline* (Tom Astor). Above: 'Tank Girl' (1989) as she will be remembered, in battered but pouty pose. Art: Jamie Hewlett. Script: Alan Martin. Unfortunately, the character was killed off by an appalling film adaptation in 1995. Right: 'Milk and Cheese' (1993) a none-too-sensible strip about two calcium-fuelled heroes. Art/script: Evan Dorkin. Below: Covers to two other British 'style comics': *Sphinx* (Bold, 1990), Art: Paul Peart, aimed at black youth; and *Heartbreak Hotel* (Willyprods, 1988), Art: Groc.

letters page, and straplines like: 'The Style Mag for Underachievers' and 'Wrong Headed Notions For Right Minded People'.

In terms of the strips, Tank Girl was still the favourite (though running decidedly short of ideas by the mid-1990s), now backed by reprinted stories from the hit American title *Love and Rockets*, about music and romance in post-punk Los Angeles (see pp 203–4), and newer indigenous material like 'Cheeky Wee Budgie Boy', a bizarre tale of a lino-laying giant budgie, 'Milk and Cheese', about some stroppy animated dairy products, and 'Bugs and Drugs', an in-your-face punk collage. Again, links with the small press were as important as ever.

Beyond these additions and improvements, hopes for a sales boost were pinned on the 1995 release of the movie of *Tank Girl*. This was another big budget Hollywood affair, directed by Rachel Talalay and starring Lori Petty in the lead role, with plenty of appropriate indie rock on the soundtrack. Unfortunately, however, none of the anarchic humour of the original strip survived its transition into celluloid, and the movie

bombed spectacularly amid some of the worst reviews seen in cinema journalism. The consequences for *Deadline* itself were entirely negative. There was no way to reason the situation, and Tom Astor eventually decided to pull the plug on the comic later in the year.

The film did, however, have further knock-on effects. By the time of its release, various other comic spinoffs had already been put into production. These saw publication later in the same year. DC Comics produced the official adaptation of the film, plus a four issue Tank Girl series *The Odyssey*, with a story by Peter Milligan and art by the original co-creator Jamie Hewlett, concerning the heroine's efforts to save the soul of her boyfriend, Booga the kangaroo. This was followed by a monthly *Tank Girl* comic (Manga Publishing/Deadline), which reprinted the 'Odyssey' story and added new strips by other creators. Once again, it did not survive in the wake of the film's eventual fate.

Deadline's influence outside of these Tank Girl-related products is hard to quantify. Certainly there have been competitors and imitators. For example, *Heartbreak Hotel* (Willyprods, 1988) was also a 'style comic' and featured the strapline: 'Where Music and Comics Meet'. Again, it was aimed at an adult audience, and was mostly humorous – though with a more political, left-wing tone. Contributors were encouraged to interpret a song lyric or musical theme each issue, and included notable 2000AD names, such as Alan Moore, Dave Gibbons, Kevin O'Neill and Grant Morrison. Even these talents, however, could not keep it afloat for more than a year. More originally, *Sphinx* (Bold, 1990) styled itself 'The

Above: Cover, *Viz* (Viz/John Brown, 1989).
Art/script: the *Viz* team. One of the great
moments in British comics history. Part
throwback to British children's comics,
part pastiche of the tabloid press, *Viz*
bucked the slump like no other title.
Underneath all its vulgarity, there was a
vein of trenchant satire, and it ended up
saying more about modern Britain than
any number of social commentators.

Magazine of Black Music, Culture and Comics', and
featured articles on rap and hip hop, plus strips about
black experience and history (including, notably, a
biography of Malcolm X). It too was short-lived.[20]

The third and final of the British triumvirate of titles,
and the one which most resoundingly confounded the
falling trajectory of comics sales, was the remarkable
Viz. This was an adult humour title like no other –
violent, brutal, offensive, and a complete stranger to
notions of taste and decency. There had never been
anything like it, even in the days of the underground: in
no other comic was the sensibility of punk so authentically
replicated. Undoubtedly, it represents one of British
comics' finest, and funniest, moments.

In fact, *Viz* started life as a small press comic: a poorly-
produced, photocopier job, with a print run of 150, and a
retail price of 20p (its similarities to punk fanzines were

unmistakeable). The creators were three Newcastle
youths: brothers Chris Donald, a DHSS clerk, and Simon
Donald, a schoolboy, assisted by their friend Jim
Brownlow. In true small press fashion, they sold the
comic themselves: their market for early issues mainly
consisted of students, because they found that wider
newsagent distribution was impossible (both on the
grounds of low print runs and 'difficult' content).

At first, *Viz* was satisfied to concentrate on pastiching
past and present British children's comics: strips appeared savaging everything from *The Beano* and *The Dandy*,
to boys' war comics, to girls' titles like *Jackie* and *Bunty*.
It was not so much the characters that were parodied, but
the archly innocent formulas. Thus, early favourites
included 'Johnny Fartpants', a *Beano*-esque tale of a 'boy
with a windy bottom'; 'Billy the Fish', a Roy of the Rovers
homage about a semi-piscine goalkeeper; 'Sid the Sexist',
about a Newcastle macho man who never gets the girl,
but maintains a relentless line in appalling banter ('tits
oot for the lads!'); and 'Roger Mellie, the Man on the
Telly', ever unable to contain his expletives, even on air
('Good evening, and bollocks.')

As the comic found its feet, so more attention was
given to spoofs of tabloid newspapers. A mock letters
page was included, and a list of 'Readers' Top Tips'
('an elastic band with a dab of toothpaste makes an
economical substitute for chewing gum, and is better for
your teeth'). Also, there were full prose features, often
involving celebrities and the royal family. For example,
the special investigative report 'Mutant Horror at the
Palace' was a touching story about Prince Derek, the lost
son of Edward VII, who was born a rhino and tragically
received no royal visitors in his time at Whipsnade.

Pop stars were especially popular targets: Shakin'
Stevens, Paul McCartney and a number of others came
in for particular attention. Eventually, a fake pop chart
was instituted whereby a band's chart positioning was
a function of how much they had 'bribed the editors'.
However, unlike *2000AD* and *Deadline*, pop culture was
only included in order to be sent up: because *Viz* had
no pretensions, it remained more 'credible' than either
of them (one mark of counterculture respect was the
fact that strips were reproduced in the respected punk
magazine *Vague*).

By the mid-1980s, *Viz* was selling around 4,000
copies per issue in Newcastle, but virtually none
anywhere else. It was at this point, however, that the
creative team was expanded by hiring two new staffers,
Graham Dury, who would draw and write 'Buster Gonad
and his Unfeasibly Large Testicles' (so unwieldy that they
are constantly being bruised – 'Yow! Me Plums!'), and
Simon Thorp, responsible for 'Finbarr Saunders and his
Double Entendres' (consisting of a stream of crashingly
obvious, but constantly amusing nudge-nudge
misunderstandings). Even though the comic was
probably at its creative peak during this period, it still
lacked a proper marketing strategy, and distribution in
the south remained elusive.

This difficulty was overcome in 1987 when John
Brown, the former managing director of Virgin Books,

This page: Excerpts from *Viz* (Viz/John Brown), featuring some of the comic's best-loved characters. More 'Carry On' than 'right on', they were sometimes controversial. Above left: 'Sid the Sexist' (1989). Art: Graham Dury. Script: *Viz* team. Above right: 'Buster Gonad' (1987). Art: Graham Dury. Script: *Viz* team. Far left: 'Billy the Fish' (1986). Art: Chris Donald. Script: *Viz* team. Left: 'Johnny Fartpants' (1989). Art: Chris Donald. Script: *Viz* team.

Orson Cart
He comes a-p-a-r-t!

SINCE HE WAS STRUCK BY A RADIOACTIVE LAWNMOWER YOUNG ORSON HAS THE ABILITY TO REMOVE ANY PART OF HIS BODY.... NOW READ ON

IT'S HUGH PHARISM (FPM)

HE'LL ALWAYS CALL A SPADE A YOU-KNOW-WHAT

(OH MY)

DESPERATELY UNFUNNY DAN

NORMAN'S KNOB

ONE RUB AND YOUNG NORMAN'S MAGIC BRASS DOOR-KNOB WILL OPEN ANYTHING HE WISHES!

TERRY FUCKWITT

THE UNINTELLIGENT CARTOON CHARACTER

This page: More Viz (Viz/John Brown). Left: A selection of minor characters and one-offs from the post-1985 period. Art/script: Viz team. Pathetically juvenile, they still manage to raise a titter. Below: 'The Fat Slags' (1989), a strip that started out as a characteristically unapologetic response to charges of sexism. Art: Chris Donald. Script: Viz team. Bottom: Fake advert, 'Learn to Swear' (1991), the likes of which were increasingly popular. Art/script: Viz team.

OH, DEAR, I DON'T FANCY YOURS MUCH... IT'S THE FAT SLAGS

47

LEARN TO SWEAR
with SWEAR-AID
IN JUST 3 WEEKS

Have you ever wanted to Swear at People you don't like?
Use dialogue that would put a Football Hooligan to shame?

Now, you can do all this, and more with Swear-Aid, in just 3 weeks you can be competing amongst leading Swearers such as Mr Bollocks from Hartlepool or Mr Foreskin from Bolton, just two of hundreds more statisfied customers.

Just send us a subscription for £300, and we will send you our Easy-to-follow, step-by-step manual and accompanying cassette, "Swear-Aid" Every Week!

Never has Swearing been made so easy. But don't only take our word for it, it speaks for itself!

Normal Person's Dialogue.	
"Kindly leave, you are, annoying me."	
After just 3 weeks with 'Swear-Aid'	"Piss Off or Ah'll brek yuh fuckin legs."

And remember, if you're going to swear, do it like a professional, with Swear-Aid!

"Ah was a reet posh bastard afore ah larnt aboot Swear-Aid."
- Mr Bollocks, Hartlepool

"Ah've lost all me posh mates wi Swear-Aid an' ah divvent give a shite."
- Mr P Foreskin, Bolton.

SWEAR-AID
69 Bollocks Road, SHITTINGTON, Yorkshire.

Please send me the Bloody course.
I enclose a cheque/P.O For £300.
NAME.............
ADDRESS.............
Post Code.............

148

---

formed his own company, and began marketing *Viz* independently. The sales curve took off exponentially: by 1987 it was selling 47,000, and by 1990 it had broken the one million barrier. The final sign that the comic had arrived was when the big retail chains, Smiths and Menzies, set up separate 'adult humour' shelves. *Viz* was now established as a kind of modern *Ally Sloper's Half Holiday*: it was cheap, irreverent, working class, male and hugely successful.

The big time brought its own pressures. *Viz* was now in the media eye as never before, and the reaction of the press took two forms. The first was broadly positive, and involved praising the comic for its earthy style. Newspapers keen to prove their liberal credentials ran pieces comparing the humour to Rabelais, Swift, Chaucer, and anybody else from the high culture canon who could be roped in. At the same time, it was fashionable for celebrity interviewees to sing the comic's praises.

The second kind of reaction was not quite so affirmative, though the kind of critique depended on the particular political orientation of the paper. The right-wing press, for instance, took the view that *Viz* was simply beyond the pale, and even a threat to the moral stability of the country: smut was bad enough, it was argued, but this was smut which could easily land in the hands of children, who would mistake the drawing style for *The Beano*.[21] Certain Tory MPs became regular contributors of frothing soundbites. Left-wing objections were more focused, and tended to centre on the question of sexism.

The misogynous attitudes expressed in *Viz* were bound to be a problem sooner or later. The comic had always had a 'laddish' reputation, and traditionally only fifteen per cent of readers were female.[22] Certain strips were potentially more offensive than others. 'Sid the Sexist' had stirred things up, but now there was a new addition that was becoming even more popular: 'The Fat Slags', concerning two overweight friends whose hobbies were sex, fags and as much junk food as they could eat. Unsurprisingly, both strips were excoriated on a number of levels, though it should be said that the creators produced them with a sense of knowing ambiguity. Even today, sexism remains an accusation that the comic has never quite been able to dispel.[23]

In this way, *Viz* was categorized as a focus for controversy (at least in some quarters). How far it was politically or culturally 'subversive' in reality is a moot point: it can be argued that it had much in common with the reactionary 'anti-culture culture' of the Thatcher years. Certainly, despite the outraged headlines, there was never any question that the police would mount a clampdown in the same way as they had against the underground. It just was not 'dangerous' enough.

The *Viz* team's response to the various complaints was to ignore them (indeed, critical articles were cut out and used to decorate the office). Instead, they concentrated on consolidating their success by initiating television crossovers – Sid the Sexist, Roger Mellie, Billy the Fish and The Fat Slags all became animated series – and by getting organized on the merchandising front.

As well as videos of the TV shows, there were *Viz* calendars, T-shirts, mugs and books, to name but a few of the items available.

Unfortunately, this diversification was coupled with a concomitant decline in the quality of the comic (it was as if one heralded the other). The spoofs were less inventive, while the satire became more focused on particular 'types'. The best of the new strips were: 'The Modern Parents', about a pair of New Agers who insist on feeding their son wholefood produce when he would rather eat chips, and make him watch them 'having intercourse' when he would rather play nintendo; and 'Student Grant', a merciless satire of students who have too much money and too little taste. Despite these, perhaps the main sign that the team were running out of ideas was that the comic now relied more and more on contributions from the general public.[24]

As *Viz* became less punky with time, so sales began to decline. In the mid-1990s, they had dropped to around 700,000 – still a very respectable figure, but sliding fast. Whether the comic will last for much longer is questionable: certainly, the creators are rich enough not to have any financial incentive for keeping it going. Even so, qualitatively speaking, *Viz* past its best is still infinitely funnier than any other comic on the racks: long may it offend.

The *Viz* story does not end there, however, because inevitably by the mid-1990s, it was not on its own, and had inspired a plethora of copyists. In fact, there were so many that it is pointless to list them thoroughly. Suffice to say that the majority were published by small companies, only lasted a few issues, and were content to cash in on the 'adult humour' retail network that *Viz* had pioneered. In terms of quality, most were lamentably dull

– titles like *Blag, Poot, Smut, UT* and *Gutter* were more gross than funny, and lacked any sense of their progenitor's originality or style. Some were more inventive. *Brain Damage* (political satire), *Talking Turkey* (a mix of underground and European strips) and *Electric Soup* (Scottish vulgarity) were more honourable additions to the roster.

As well as these, *Viz* inspired comics and magazines that were genuinely new in some senses. Titles for a black readership, for example, became visible for the first time (the most notable were *Skank*, the humour of which is best described as 'Brixton wide boy', and *Africaman*, a sort of African *Private Eye*). Furthermore, there was a significant crossover with the football fanzine scene, with titles like *Sweet FA* and *Red Card* developing a new kind of readership. In most cases, these titles were read by people who would not normally pick up a comic at all (something that also applied to a significant degree to *Viz*) and although their sales remain very small, they are a definite indication that new British comics publishing – such as it is – continues to be orientated towards adults rather than children.

In the United States, the crisis in the comics industry was felt, if anything, more keenly than in Britain. As we have seen, the decline in sales after the Code was never halted, and publishers continued to go out of business at an alarming rate. The narrowing of competition meant that after the 1960s, Marvel and DC Comics inherited a greater share of a rapidly shrinking market. Both companies now devoted themselves to what they called 'a period of research and development' – in other words, a desperate hunt for new ideas to keep them afloat. It is not without some justification that historians of American comics refer to the period between the end of

Below: Covers to just a few of the *Viz* copyists. They tried to step into the distribution network that *Viz* had spent years building up, but most found that it helped to be funny. Left to right: *UT* (Sport Newspapers, 1991), art: Anon; *Electric Soup* (Electric Soup/John Brown, 1991), art: Frank Quitely; *Talking Turkey* (Galaxy, 1991), art: Hunt Emerson; *Gutted* (Humour Publications, 1992), art: Anon; *Zit* (Humour Publications, 1991), art: Anon.

the 'Marvel Age' and the start of the specialist fan movement as a 'dark age'.

However, it would be wrong to see this phase as entirely devoid of interest. There were significant moments, and these in many ways heralded the reshaping of the market in the 1980s. Unsurprisingly, it was the superhero genre that was initially the focus of activity, since by 1970, the wave of interest sparked by the Marvel superheroes was seriously on the wane, and stories were tending either to get bogged down in endless fight scenes (the Kirby formula minus imagination), or to go 'camp': the 1960s Batman TV series had started a trend for tongue-in-cheek stories, and the period thereafter was notorious for un-thrilling plots about heroes getting married, being transformed (shrunk, enlarged), battling ridiculous monsters (rather than criminals), travelling through time warps and meeting pop stars.

Marvel was first to come up with a solution. Ever the opportunists, they realized that there was a revival of interest in the novels of Robert E Howard, and especially in one of his characters, Conan the Barbarian, and that this was something they could capitalize upon. The Conan stories were set in a mythological, prehistoric past, and involved the incredibly gory adventures of a none-too-bright hero – impossibly muscular, and armed to the teeth with broadswords and axes – and his quests to save comely princesses and do battle with evil magicians and fanciful monsters. They had originally appeared in pulp magazines in the 1930s, but were republished in paperback form in the mid-1960s, and were garnering a new and enthusiastic readership – thus signalling the start of the rise of modern 'sword and sorcery'.

Conan the Barbarian, the comic, hit the stands in 1970, written by a longtime Howard fan, Roy Thomas, and drawn by a young Englishman, Barry Windsor-Smith. The title was a gamble in some ways because it did not fit into the established 'Marvel universe'. On the other hand, Conan looked like a superhero, and it was not difficult to market the title to the same audience. To all intents and purposes, he was one more superhero to add to the roster. Plus, Thomas and Windsor-Smith

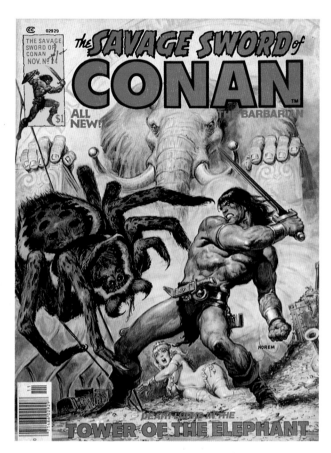

This page: American comics were similarly in crisis, post-1960s. Superhero comics in particular became increasingly desperate. Right: Cover, *Action Comics* (DC Comics, 1961), an example featuring 'super-pets' in a tug-of-war. Art: Curt Swan. Above right: Cover, *The Savage Sword of Conan* (Marvel Comics, 1977). Art: Earl Norman. One way forward for the publishers was to think laterally: Conan the Barbarian looked like a superhero, and found a new audience.

made a fine team: the stories kept to the spirit of the original tales, and the artwork was a mix of Kirbyesque dynamism and almost Art Nouveau decoration.

The one restriction was the amount of violence that could be shown in a Code-approved comic. So, to get around this, Marvel launched a black-and-white magazine starring Conan, entitled *Savage Tales*, in 1971, to be followed by *The Savage Sword of Conan* in 1974 – Marvel's most successful magazine title. Now the blood could flow freely, as Conan battled an ever-more brutal array of enemies, including 'death wizards', elephant gods and giant spiders. These more adult magazines also allowed for a certain level of naked female flesh to be shown – another attraction for their mainly teen readership. They are credited with providing the inspiration for the series of Conan movies, starring Arnold Schwarzenegger, which appeared in the 1980s.

Conan was followed by various other 'barbarian' comics in the 1970s. *Kull the Conqueror* (1971) and *Red Sonja* (1977) were adapted by Marvel from Howard stories, and the latter became a movie in 1986 starring Bridget Nielsen. DC Comics hit back with *Sword of Sorcery* (1973), an innovative anthology which only lasted a year, while other companies cashed in with less high-profile superhero-cum-barbarian titles.

But there were other developments on the superhero front, albeit of a more traditional nature. DC Comics' top creators now included Neal Adams, who took responsibility for steering Batman back to his sinister roots, and ex-Marvel stalwart Jack Kirby, who created a completely new line of superheroes, who inhabited a universe which he called 'the Fourth World'. Marvel, meanwhile, experimented with magazine-format superhero stories, and were briefly controversial for three issues of *Spider-Man* which dealt with the dangers of drugs; they also scored a remarkable hit with a revamped *X-Men* under writer Chris Claremont (more about which on p 159).[25]

Finally, towards the end of the decade, there came the release of the eagerly awaited *Superman* movie (1978), which gave a temporary boost to comics sales. This was not the first attempt to bring the 'Man of Steel' to the silver screen, but it was by far the most successful: Christopher Reeve made a charismatic lead, and the special effects were indeed special for their time ('You'll Believe a Man Can Fly!' ran the advertising blurb). It led to a number of follow-ups, which proved beyond any doubt that Hollywood could make a profitable job of translating superheroes to the screen for a modern audience. It would be a lesson well learned for the 1980s, when Batman was given the big-budget celluloid treatment. (See Chapter 7 for more about this film.)[26]

Other genres also saw developments. Humour, for example, entered a new phase, partly inspired by the success of the underground, and partly by the continuing popularity of *Mad*, which in the early 1970s reached the peak of its success, selling an impressive two-and-a-half million per issue. Marvel sought to mix these two influences by bringing out magazine-format comics with more satirical, adult themes.

Their main success was *Howard the Duck*, a regular comic from 1976, and a magazine from 1979. The witty scripts by Steve Gerber, about a cigar-chewing fowl from another dimension, 'trapped in a world he never made!', did not go as far as, say, Robert Crumb's *Fritz the Cat*, but were socially relevant in a way that was rare in a Marvel title. They caught something of the spirit of the

time, and the comic became a cult, especially among students. Howard eventually became the star of a misguided live-action movie in 1986 (executively produced, but later disowned, by George Lucas).[27]

More obviously designed as an underground cash-in was Marvel's *Comix Book* (1974), an anthology featuring many of the movement's biggest names – including Robert Crumb, Skip Williamson, S Clay Wilson, Art Spiegelman and Trina Robbins (see also p 118). It appeared with the somewhat un-comixy strapline 'America's Craziest Contemporary Cartoonists!', which served to make a link with *Mad*, and indeed it went on to include contributions from *Mad* luminaries such as Harvey Kurtzman and Basil Wolverton. Despite some hilarious moments, it fell between two stools, neither appealing to the counterculture nor to fans of mainstream funny comics, and lasted for five issues.

Horror went through a more robust revival. As we have seen, the fashion for the genre had restarted after the Code in the 1960s with the key Warren titles (*Creepy*, *Eerie* and *Vampirella*) and had been continued into the early 1970s by companies like Skywald (*Psycho*, *Nightmare*, etc). Now Marvel took its cue, and launched a range of magazines aimed at different age groups. The first wave, in 1973, were pretty juvenile, and included *Tales of the Zombie, Dracula Lives!, Monsters Unleashed* and *Vampire Tales*, which featured the enjoyably derivative 'Morbius the Vampire' and 'Satana – Queen of Evil'. Later, titles experimented with more adult references, such as the story in *Haunt of Horror* (1974) about a unit in Vietnam that is cannibalized by one of its own members ('Nam breeds a different kind of man than what you'd find back home. A person has to make adjustments ... he has to learn to accept, and then like the horrors he has to live with ...').[28]

Warren itself returned to the horror fray with two titles: *Comix International* (1974), which, as the title suggested, was closer in sensibility to the underground horror titles, like *Skull*, than any of the Marvel line, and which featured some tongue-in-cheek, but still disturbing, stories by Richard Corben and Reed Crandall (an ex-EC contributor); and *Dracula* (1979), a 120-page solo outing by top Spanish creator Esteban Maroto. Smaller publishers also tried to compete. They included Seaboard with *Weird Tales of the Macabre* and *Devilina* (both 1975), and Modern Day Periodicals with *Weird Vampire Tales* (1981). None, however, were successful.

It was in the field of science fiction that the biggest advances were seen. The key title here was *Heavy Metal* (Heavy Metal, 1977), a glossy science fiction anthology – and nothing to do with the headbanging musical genre. In its first incarnation, the comic was a version of the French title *Métal Hurlant* (Les Humanoides Associés, 1975), which was part of the new wave of adult comics on the Continent: the latter was influenced both by the American underground and the French student revolts of the late 1960s (and their accompanying cultural expression), and took its science fiction very seriously. *Métal Hurlant*'s stories were a mix of psychedelic, and often very pretentious, future odysseys and heavy satires,

This page: Magazine formats opened up new avenues especially in humour. The implication of a more adult readership meant that influences from the underground were prevalent. Below: Cover, *Comix Book* (Marvel Comics, 1974). Art: Peter Poplaski. Marvel's ill-fated 'subterranean' anthology. Below right: Cover, *Howard the Duck* (Marvel Comics, 1976). Art: probably John Costanza. Ostensibly a funny animal comic about 'Marvel's wildest waterfowl', but also a political satire: Howard stood for President against Jimmy Carter in 1976.

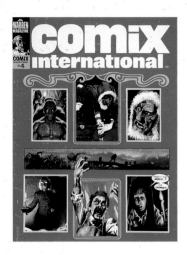

and typically included a great deal of female nudity. The production standards were unprecedented, and many strips featured fully painted art, where creators made the most of the magazine-quality paper by utilising airbrush techniques, which gave a smooth finish to the colour work.[29]

Heavy Metal followed this formula, and translated *Métal Hurlant*'s best fantasy creators (the satire strips were generally ignored on the grounds that they would not travel). The foremost of these creators was 'Moebius', the 'grand fromage' of French science fiction, many of whose strips became readers' favourites over the years (including 'Arzach', 'The Airtight Garage' and 'The Incal' – see also p 221). His art style was influenced by Robert Crumb, but was much more realistic, and introduced a new sophistication into comics: his were science fiction worlds you could really believe in, and it was no surprise that Hollywood would borrow his ideas for movies such as *Blade Runner* and *The Empire Strikes Back*.

Other creators came from all over Europe. Notables included: Enki Bilal, Yves Chaland and Phillippe Druillet from France; Stefano Tamburini and Milo Manara from Italy; Francois Schuiten from Belgium; and Matthias Schultheiss from Germany. These were joined by two Americans, both ex-undergrounders, who had also proved popular in Europe – Richard Corben, whose art for 'Den' and 'Sinbad' was luminously colourful (not to mention overtly sexual), and Vaughn Bodé, whose cartoony style provided a humorous contrast.

As *Heavy Metal* found its feet, so the mix of American and European contributors became more even (with indigenous names like Arthur Suydam, Peter Kuper, George Pratt and Rick Geary joining the roster). At the same time, the comic was playing more of a role in youth culture, with the airbrush art style taking over from the old underground look as an inspiration for album and book covers, as well as for posters, motorbike art, T-shirts, and so on. The publishers eventually cashed in on this craze themselves by initiating a variety of merchandising (*Heavy Metal* calendars, posters and collected stories).

The culmination of this trend was the release in 1981 of the *Heavy Metal* movie, a big-budget animation epic that adapted five of the most popular strips from the comic. At the time, this was the most ambitious project of its kind ever attempted, and employed 5000 animators in five countries. It also went for a youth audience, and included a soundtrack with music by Devo and Cheap Trick, among other mainstream rock acts. The film, however, ended up as a mish-mash of styles and influences, and was the subject of some controversy for its sexism: it was killed at birth by poor reviews.

Since the film, *Heavy Metal* itself has never reached the same level of public awareness, but has continued to thrive thanks to a progressive policy of trying out new talent. In the 1980s and 1990s, it showcased work that would usually be considered 'avant garde', by creators such as the Dutchman Joost Swarte, the Spaniard Daniel Torres, and the Americans Drew Friedman and Charles Burns. But even if the comic is leaving the legacy of the underground behind, it still regularly features 'cheese-cake' depictions of women: this obviously serves to retain its traditional readership, but also has the twin disadvantages of attracting criticism from feminists, and of encouraging newspaper vendors to rack the comic on the top shelf, next to the soft porn.

NO PROBLEM?! WHAT ABOUT THE REVOLUTION?!

I THOUGHT THE PEOPLE HAD TAKEN TO THE STREETS TO GET RID OF YOU LOT!

YOU LOT?! MY DEAR EDWARD — THE AFFAIRS OF STATE ARE OBVIOUSLY A TOTAL MYSTERY TO YOU

CRINGE

I GUESS SO!

THE PEOPLE RIOTED IN ORDER TO REMOVE THE GOVERNMENT... THAT IS... THE LEGISLATURE..WE HOWEVER ARE THE EXECUTIVE!

SHIT! WOTS THE FUCKIN DIFFRINCE

THE FUCKIN DIFFRINCE!

CLUTCH

MY DEAR EDWARD!

THE FUCKING DIFFERENCE IS...

THE LEGISLATURE MAKES THE LAW. WE, THE CIVIL SERVANTS CARRY THE LAW INTO EFFECT!

WE ARE NON POLITICAL...

THOSE PART-TIME PARTY HACKS COME AND GO AT THE WHIM OF THE UNEDUCATED ELECTORATE !..

...WHILST WE ARE FIRST DIVISION CAREER PROFESSIONALS!

THATS THE FUCKIN DIFF'RINCE OK!

I GET IT! JUST DOIN' YOUR JOB EH?!

YES! AND YOU WILL JUST DO YOURS !... AN' WOTS THAT?

TO USE COMICS THE PEOPLE'S ARTFORM TO TELL THE WORLD ABOUT OUR NEW REPUBLIC

SCREW OUR NEW REPUBLIC

I SPEAK ONLY FOR MYSELF! AND IN THE WORLD OF MY NEW REPUBLIC NOBODY WILL EVER BE ABLE TO SAY I WAS ONLY DOING MY JOB

I CAN SEE HE'S GOING TO BE A PROBLEM

IT IS ONLY TO BE EXPECTED, HE IS AN ARTIST. HE IS INSECURE. HE DESPERATELY WANTS TO BE AN INDIVIDUAL

WE CAN'T ALL BE INDIVIDUALS

WHY ARE INDIVIDUALS ALWAYS SO AWKWARD

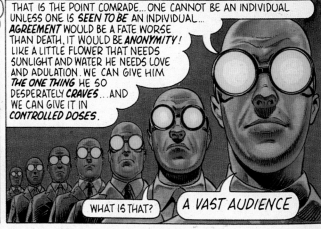

THAT IS THE POINT COMRADE... ONE CANNOT BE AN INDIVIDUAL UNLESS ONE IS SEEN TO BE AN INDIVIDUAL... AGREEMENT WOULD BE A FATE WORSE THAN DEATH, IT WOULD BE ANONYMITY ! LIKE A LITTLE FLOWER THAT NEEDS SUNLIGHT AND WATER HE NEEDS LOVE AND ADULATION. WE CAN GIVE HIM THE ONE THING HE SO DESPERATELY CRAVES ...AND WE CAN GIVE IT IN CONTROLLED DOSES.

WHAT IS THAT?

A VAST AUDIENCE

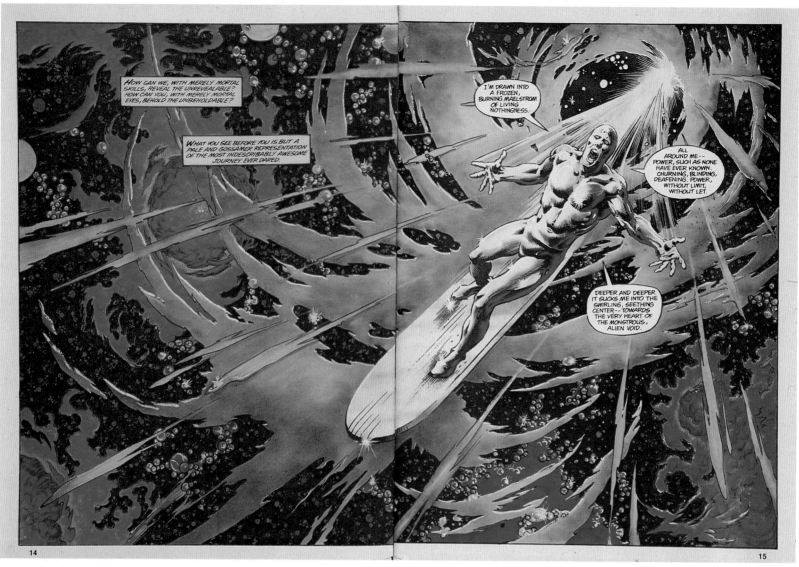

Above: Cover and pages from *Epic* (Marvel Comics), the main rival to *Heavy Metal*. Cover (1980), by Richard Corben, featuring a typical 'fantasy art' scene. Pages (1980), depicting 'The Silver Surfer', originally a 1960s Lee/Kirby creation. Art: John Buscema. Script: Stan Lee.

The success of *Heavy Metal* led to a variety of imitations, none of which were of the same quality. Marvel got in on the act with *Epic Illustrated* (1980), which privileged American creators over foreign ones, and which tried to tone down the sexual content in order to appeal to a wider readership. The glossy production values, coupled with a creative brief to 'express yourself', led to some startling work by Neal Adams, Howard Chaykin and Jon Muth, as well as some memorable sword and sorcery covers from Frank Frazetta and Richard Corben, but also a fair share of self-indulgent tosh. If anything, the storytelling was better than in *Heavy Metal*, drawing from contemporary American science fiction prose fiction (for example, Samuel Delany stories were adapted), but the comic never developed the same kind of 'personality', and was eventually cancelled in 1986.[30]

Far inferior to *Epic Illustrated* in terms of quality, but nearly as long-lasting, was *1984*, launched by Warren in 1978, and which survived until 1983 (after a name-change to *1994*). This tacky black-and-white effort made no pretence at seriousness, and featured as much sex as it could possibly fit into its pages (viz its suggestive strapline: 'Provocative Illustrated Adult Fantasy'). Some of the strips have since been re-evaluated as 'erotic classics' (such as Frank Thorne's 'Ghita of Alizarr'), but in general, comics fans prefer to forget the title ever existed.

In the 1990s, *Heavy Metal*'s influence was still being felt, as mainstream magazines embarked on a policy of bringing out comics supplements. *Penthouse Comix* (Penthouse, 1993) has included erotic science fiction strips, while *Omni Comix* (Omni 1995) was an offshoot of the respected science fiction journal. Both are glossy productions in the established style, with much emphasis on the trusty airbrush. How long they will last still remains to be seen.

In conclusion, this phase of American publishing initiated in the 1970s was important for a number of reasons, not least because it showed that there was a readership for mainstream comics among an older age range than had previously been catered for. The underground had shown the potential for more mature subject matter, and by cannibalizing some of that movement's ideas (typically the sex and violence rather than the politics), publishers like Marvel and DC Comics began to find a new teenage market. This was something that would develop over the next decade into a completely new system of comics marketing based on comics 'fandom' – the subject for our next chapter.

1. Accurate figures for the uptake of television are most easily available in the case of the USA: see R Pearson and W Uricchio (eds), *Many Lives of the Batman*, (London, BFI Publishing/Routledge, 1991), p 72.

2. Figures for the decline in British comics generally are notoriously hard to come by, not least because many publishers did not release statistics. As a rule of thumb, we can say that in the mid-1960s, a first-division boy's adventure comic was expected to sell 350,000 (some regularly achieved the half-million mark). By early 1980s, top sellers were around 100,000 (*2000AD* included). Today, in the mid-1990s, successful comics sell around 40,000 (though there are exceptions: *Viz* sells roughly fifteen times as many; *The Beano* probably three times; *2000AD* roughly double). For a population of 56 million, this figure is not terribly impressive.

3. *Star Wars* had been published by Marvel in the US since 1977.

4. DC Comics did not set up a subsidiary company like Marvel. Instead, they came to licensing and republishing arrangements with a variety of British companies – among them, London Editions and Fleetway.

5. Andrew Moreton, *FA*, no 98, August 1986, p 37.

6. There was one other significant title on the news-stands in this period, *Escape*. However, since it started out by being sold from the specialist fan shops, it has been covered in Chapter 8.

7. See Martin Barker's *Action: The Story of a Violent Comic* (London, Titan Books, 1990).

8. *The Eagle* was cancelled in 1969, but revived in 1982, finally to expire in 1994. So far as Dan Dare was concerned, *Lion* continued to run reprints in the 1970s, while the character was revamped by first *2000AD* and then *Revolver* (see below, p 140).

9. As well as these now-famous names, it should be noted that *2000AD* also used European and South American artists in its early days (a policy that was very much in the IPC tradition – see p 51).

10. Martin Barker and Kate Brooks, 'Waiting for Dredd', *Sight and Sound*, vol 5, issue 8, August 1995, pp 16–9.

11. Some of these creators would later return to the comic to work on individual strips (the main exception was Alan Moore, who stayed true to his pledge never again to work for Fleetway).

12. The 'creators' rights' issue was slightly complicated in the case of *2000AD* because the comic had always included creator-credits – the first mainstream British title to do so since *The Eagle*. However, it was slow to offer a royalty deal, and only began to do so in the early 1990s. In terms of copyright, the situation remained the same as it had always been. To give one instance, in 1994, the strip 'Zippy Couriers' became the subject for dispute when creator Hilary Robinson tried to establish control over it. After a campaign by the Comic Creators Guild, the strip was eventually relinquished by Fleetway, who emphasized that this move was definitely not a precedent.

13. In one sense, it is possible to see the fully painted style of people like Bisley as a revival of a British tradition begun by comics such as *TV Century 21* (see pp 52–3).

14. The Legend! and S Wells, 'Inks, Oinks, Love and Rockets!' *NME*, 18 July, 1987.

15. Fleetway had been worried about the fact that *2000AD* was losing its juvenile audience for some time, and had planned to release a new children's science-fiction title called *Alternity* in the mid 1990s. However, in 1992 the company was bought by Belgian publishers Guten Berghus, who insisted that any new product should be re-sellable in Europe. Therefore, the *Alternity* project was subsequently scrapped. See Martin Barker 'Very nearly in Front of the Children: the story of *Alternity*' in C Bazalgette and D Buckingham (eds) *In Front of the Children* (London, BFI, 1995).

16. Dredd was not the first *2000AD* strip to get the movie treatment. In 1990, the 18-rated science fiction film *Hardware* lifted a story without crediting its creators: this was later rectified in an out-of-court settlement.

17. The fact that characters in both *Lawman of the Future* and *The Megazine* were re-designed to look like the actors in the film did not bode well.

18. Steve Dillon had also been the artist on the aforementioned *Warrior* strip 'Laser Eraser and Pressbutton'.

19. Astor was a member of the famous family of British aristocrats.

20. One other title that was undoubtedly influenced by *Deadline*'s style was *Purr* (Blue Eyed Dog, 1993), a squarebound music and comics anthology aimed at a youth audience. However, it was never sold through newsagents, and instead was marketed through record shops and specialist comics outlets.

21. There is no question that many children did read *Viz*, despite the 'Adults Only' label. There was no 'mistake' involved, however, and playground banter was influenced by this comedy hit in exactly the same way as a previous generation had picked up on 'Monty Python', and the one before that on 'The Goons'.

22. *Viz* readership survey, 1988 (House of Viz/ John Brown Publishing Ltd).

23. How far *Viz* has ever been 'feminist' is debatable. For example, 'Sid' could be interpreted in a positive light because it is, after all, a satire about sexism (even though the language is highly sexist); similarly 'The Fat Slags' has been hailed as pro-feminist because its central characters are assertive women with healthy sexual appetites. Indeed, some leading feminists have championed these characters as an acceptable counter to 'political correctness'.

24. This idea of soliciting contributions from the public was not one invented by *Viz*, and indeed has been a time-honoured scam for many a humour comic. *Ally Sloper's Half Holiday* took exactly the same route a century before.

25. The *Spider-Man* anti-drugs stories, which appeared in 1971, are widely believed to have inspired a review of standards by the Comics Code Authority. (The Code forbade any reference to drugs, and therefore the comic had to be put out without the Code stamp.) However, it is equally likely that the review was a result of the Authority being increasingly ignored by publishers: magazine-format comics did not have to be submitted, and the underground had deliberately circumvented the system.

26. There were also some notable TV movies and series based on comics in the 1970s, including *Wonder Woman* and *The Hulk*, which similarly boosted comics sales to some extent.

27. *Howard the Duck* is another example of a dispute over creators' rights. In 1979, Steve Gerber left the comic after an argument over copyright.

28. 'The Nightmare Patrol' in *Haunt of Horror*, no 1 (1974).

29. An airbrush is essentially a paint spray-gun, which can produce a fine jet of paint and thus give a controlled, graded finish. It is especially effective in the depiction of flesh and certain kinds of metals.

30. *Epic Illustrated* was also notable for the fact that the strips were creator-owned, in contrast to Marvel's previous policy of work-for-hire. This was an obvious sop to underground sensibilities, and was welcomed at the time: an entire line of creator-owned titles followed, under the banner of 'Epic'. (In terms of the comic's subject matter, it is also worth noting that Marvel had earlier attempted to produce a science-fiction magazine, *Unknown Worlds*, in 1975, but were unsuccessful, possibly because the time was not yet right.)

Below: Cover and pages from *1994* (Warren, 1981), one of the less illustrious *Heavy Metal* competitors. Cover art: Nestor Redondo. Strip art: Alex Nino. Script: Will Richardson.

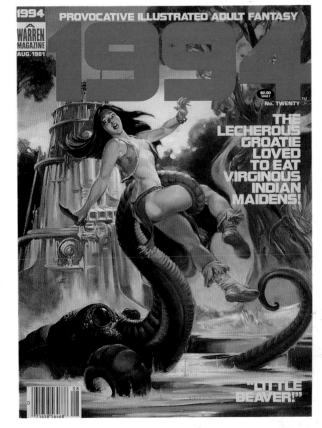

A new mainstream

The late 1970s and 1980s saw huge changes in the way comics were marketed, designed and, eventually, in the way they were perceived. The old newsagent market was declining at an alarming rate, but at the same time a more specialized network based on specialist 'fan' shops (selling solely comics) began to take off. Inevitably this had an effect on where publishers saw their future, and by the mid-1990s, over ninety per cent of all comics were being sold through this channel. In the space of a few short years, the fan market had gone from being a parallel outlet of little commercial importance, to becoming the new mainstream.

The shift originated with the small band of hardcore fans of titles by Marvel and DC Comics in the 1960s. Marvel was the most important of the two companies because their titles were designed to be collected. Fans would accumulate every issue of their favourite series, and religiously follow the careers of certain artists, especially Steve Ditko, Jim Steranko, Neal Adams and, of course, Jack 'King' Kirby. As they got older, some of the more committed enthusiasts set up mail-order businesses, and joined together to organize regular markets ('marts') and conventions ('cons') and to publish their own fan-magazines ('fanzines'). This was the beginning of comics fandom, which in its early days owed a large debt to the long-established rituals of the science fiction fan-world: indeed, because the two subcultures shared an interest in the fantastical, they remained closely linked.

The shops were a natural next step. Fandom grew steadily in the United States and the United Kingdom from the mid-1960s, and the hippie headshops were contemporaneously demonstrating the potential of a comics market separate to the newsagents. The first fan shops appeared by the end of the decade, typically evolving out of mail-order businesses, and usually selling science fiction literature as well as comics. The growth in the number of shops was slow but steady in the 1970s, while in the 1980s things began to boom: by the end of that decade, there were estimated to be roughly 400 in Britain and 4,000 in America. Enough, in other words, to constitute a 'network', and to sustain a viable comics subculture.

This subculture turned out to be somewhat obsessive ('fan' is an abbreviation of 'fanatic', after all). The shops sold an endless array of superhero comics, which to an outsider seemed like pointless riffing on the same theme, but which to a fan were continually fascinating, and hence limited their clientele to males between the ages of about twelve and twenty-five. Women were certainly not welcome: the comics were in the traditional mould of power fantasies about macho muscle men, and commercially speaking there was very little incentive for publishers to think about any other kind of subject matter.

Fans were often also speculators, and this inevitably added to the sense of 'geekishness'. Collecting had always been a major part of the hobby, but increasingly fans would buy comics purely in order to resell them at a profit at a later date. Thus, hefty 'price guides' were produced, while the practice of keeping comics 'mint'

Above: Cover to *X-Men* (Marvel Comics, 1975). Art: John Buscema. An engagingly complex tale about a group of 'mutant' superheroes whose powers are as much a curse as a blessing, and who exist in a morally ambiguous world. Originally a Lee/Kirby title from the 1960s, it was revamped in the mid 1970s and became the biggest-selling comic of all time: at one point Marvel estimated that *X-Men* and related titles alone outsold the combined output of any other comics publisher.

by storing them unopened in plastic bags became common practice. (In this way, first issues became especially prized, while subsequent numbers were sometimes completely ignored.) Curiously, speculators did not seem to appreciate the paradox that if everybody was collecting the same comics, they could no longer be considered rare.

It would be easy to be excessively negative about fans – too easy, in fact. It should also be borne in mind that fandom has the potential to be a creative force. It offers opportunities to form friendships, and to express opinions about aspects of comics as an artform. It is also true that some fanzines have been used to speculate on the relationships between characters, to rework stories and to comment on them satirically. Fanzines have also solicited artwork, giving many professional artists their first break. In this sense, then, there is no point in complaining that fans should 'get a life', because they already have one. Also, so far as collecting is concerned, some speculators had the last laugh when auction houses like Sotheby's and Christie's began to realize astronomical sums for comics in good condition.

More than this, after the slump of the 1970s, the fan shops offered unique commercial advantages for publishers, and this presented a way for comics to move forward. Distributors found that by supplying the shops directly, they could cut costs, because unlike the newsagent network, there would be no returns. Publishers would send flyers to shops promoting their forthcoming comics, which would then be ordered in specific numbers on a sale-or-keep basis. This 'direct sales' system thus stabilized print runs, reduced waste and increased efficiency for everyone. It also completely bypassed the newsagents.

As this market reorientation happened, so new publishers were founded, eager to take advantage. Companies like Pacific, First and Eclipse conceded that they could not compete with the might of Marvel and DC Comics on the newsstands, but recognized that they could still make profits by concentrating solely on the fan shops. So, they began to put out their own superhero comics, and to carve out their own piece of pie. Indeed, by offering to pay royalties to creators, they were able to attract some major names away from the big two: this was a major step forward for creators' rights, and eventually the entire industry had to follow suit.[2] In this way the shops became the main focus for comics publishing activity, with a majority of the premier companies, American and British, producing titles that sold solely through this market.

In spite of the new competition, it was Marvel that scored the biggest early hit. They published what was to become the ultimate fan comic in the form of a revamped *X-Men*. The new direction for the title had been initiated in 1975, before the shop network had properly been established, but through the 1980s the fans were the ones who ensured its market dominance. The revamp involved adding new mutants to the X-roster, with 'Wolverine', 'Nightcrawler', 'Storm', and others replacing three of the five originals ('Angel',

'Iceman', and 'Marvel Girl'). The new team garnered a fresh following, and added zip to an old formula: 'Wolverine' became especially popular, a werewolf-type character who enjoyed killing with the huge metal claws that issued from his wrists, and was eventually given his own title.

The new *X-Men* established the 'fan comic' style. The writing, by Chris Claremont, who was fourteen years at the helm, had an engaging level of psychological depth, as well as a complexity that ensured that readers would have to buy every issue to know what was going on: the story lines could sometimes last years. This continuity allowed for the title to 'speak' to its readership. The X-Men were complete personalities whose mutancy could be viewed on as a metaphor for adolescence, race or sexuality. The fact that they fell in love, fell out, got married, gave birth, died and, above all, experienced discrimination from prejudiced humans only added to their appeal.[3] The art, too, was fan-orientated, and names like John Byrne, Marc Silvestri, John Romita Jnr and Jim Lee quickly became new favourites.

In this period, the *X-Men* became the most successful Marvel series ever, and would be much imitated – not least by Marvel themselves. Numerous other teams of Marvel teenage superheroes followed through the 1980s, notably *The New Mutants* (1983), *Alpha Flight* (1983) and *X-Factor* (1986). All were suitably 'fannish', and sold in large quantities, with the first issues becoming 'must-have, double-bag items'.

In the face of the Marvel onslaught, other companies were temporarily left standing. Historical rivals DC Comics responded by reviving two teams that had their origins in the 1950s and 1960s. *The Legion of Superheroes* was resuscitated in 1980, while in the same year the *Teen Titans* went through an *X-Men*-style revamp to become *The New Teen Titans*, as 'Robin', 'Wonder Girl' and 'Kid Flash' were joined by 'Starfire', 'the Changeling', 'the Raven' and 'Cyborg'. This latter title was the main competition to the Marvel line thanks to some outstanding artwork by George Perez.

As for the independent companies, they did not have the wherewithal to compete at the same level, and so instead responded with satire. The 'teenage mutant' boom was mercilessly parodied throughout the 1980s by a string of titles inspired by the success of *Teenage Mutant Ninja Turtles* (Mirage, 1984). We have seen in Chapter 6 how this comic became the basis for a huge kids' craze (spawning movies, TV shows and endless toys). In its original form it was a fan-orientated, adult, satire, in black and white, with a print run of a few thousand. This 'teen team' was played purely for laughs, and the more involved the reader was in the comics subculture, the more gags they understood. Other satires in a very similar vein included the more obscure *Naive Interdimensional Commando Koalas* and *Adolescent Radioactive Blackbelt Hamsters*.[4]

This first wave of fan-orientated publishing was so successful that publishers began to think in terms of new strategies to keep up the momentum. They speculated that there might be more to the fan market

Right: Pages from *X-Men* (Marvel Comics, 1980). Art: John Byrne. Script: Chris Claremont. An excerpt from one of the most popular story-arcs in the continuity, about the death of 'The Phoenix'.

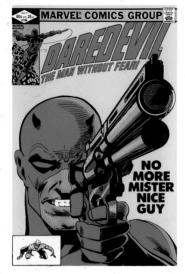

than X-style heroes, and as they became more confident, so new comics were launched, which included more adult content and better production values. (After all, the fans were generally older than traditional comics buyers, with more disposable income.) This was the start of what became the boom in 'adult comics' – arguably the most artistically interesting phase in mainstream comics history.

The resulting titles featured more politics, social parody and moral ambiguity, as well as liberal helpings of cinematic sex and violence. In this, they brushed aside the strictures of the Comics Code (within the confines of fandom, these could be ignored without fear of retribution).[5] Yet the comics were still essentially superhero-orientated. For the publishers also recognized that it would be commercially unwise to stray too far from established formulas. Thus, the new genre was an odd hybrid – essentially consisting of a childish form (superhero comics) given adult overtones.

Artistically, the comics were more ambitious than ever before, with artists given the freedom to experiment. Fully painted art, collages and multi-media work became common, sometimes published on photographic quality paper to show them at their best. At the same time, the design boom of the 1980s was in full swing, and this had a marked effect on the look of typography, panel compositions and, especially, covers.

This split between the sophistication of the product and the essentially childish nature of the content only exacerbated old fan/non-fan tensions (such as they were). For outsiders, the very existence of comics about characters in brightly coloured tights which also featured a label on the cover proclaiming 'For Mature Readers', merely confirmed suspicions that fans were not capable of growing up (those few articles that appeared in the mainstream press about comics in this period are notable for their scornful tone). For the fans themselves, this was the most exciting direction in comics for years – possibly

This page: The drive for 'older readers' commences. **Above:** Cover, *Daredevil* (Marvel Comics, 1982). Art: Frank Miller. A relatively sophisticated yarn about a blind superhero who can still aim a magnum. **Right and opposite:** Cover and page from *Swamp Thing* (DC Comics). Cover (1984) art: Tom Yeates. Strip (1986) art: Rick Veitch, script: Alan Moore. Here, eco-hero 'Swampy' lectures mankind on its failings: 'You blight the soil, and poison the rivers, you raze the vegetation till you cannot even feed your own kind.' **Below:** Pages from *American Flagg!* (First, 1984). Art/script: Howard Chaykin. Starring future lawman Reuben Flagg, the stories were a satirical mix of Raymond Chandler and Philip K Dick.

since the advent of the Marvel Age.

The title that started the trend in earnest was *Daredevil*, a failing Marvel superhero series reconceptualized by rising fan favourite Frank Miller in the early 1980s. Originally a run-of-the-mill tale about a blind superhero who fights crime using his supersharp remaining senses, Miller started to add new features. These included breathtaking action sequences influenced by martial arts movies, and a new foe – Elektra, a female ninja assassin – who was to become the most popular female character in mainstream comics. Miller also made the most of cutting techniques pioneered by Jim Steranko, and introduced a new sense of 'edge' into storylines by setting them in a more lifelike, sordid reality. The fans loved it, and *Daredevil* was soon one of the bestselling Marvel titles behind the *X-Men*.

DC Comics countered by reviving an old character of their own, star of the eponymous *Swamp Thing*. This was, again, an already existing title with unimpressive sales, given a revisionist treatment, this time by British writer Alan Moore (ex-*2000AD*), who added new psychological depth to the original story of a sentient swamp monster. Moore was justly praised for his ability to incorporate into plots the political issues of the day: feminism, the pros and cons of drug-use, American gun laws and, above all, the Green movement (in some of the best storylines, only 'Swampy' can avert ecological catastrophe). Moore was aided by the atmospheric artwork of a number of artists, notably John Totleben

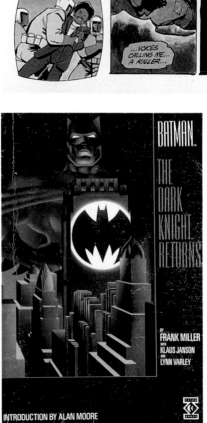

Left, above and right: Cover and pages from *The Dark Knight Returns* (DC Comics/Titan, 1986). Art/script: Frank Miller. Many found the level of violence shocking: above, The Joker breaks his own neck ('...KKRAAAKKK...') to put Batman in the frame. This was a very dark Dark Knight indeed. The use of TV screens to impart narrative information was effective, but had been used before by Howard Chaykin in *American Flagg!* (see p 160).

This page: Cover and pages from *Watchmen* (DC Comics/Titan, 1987). Art: Dave Gibbons. Script: Alan Moore. Another groundbreaking graphic novel: the story, about a group of superheroes who come out of retirement, was structured like a Chinese puzzle in order to work over a longer page-count. Right: the assembled Watchmen try to decide what to do ('Somebody's got to save the world...'). Below right: One of the team, looking a bit past it, tries on his old costume.

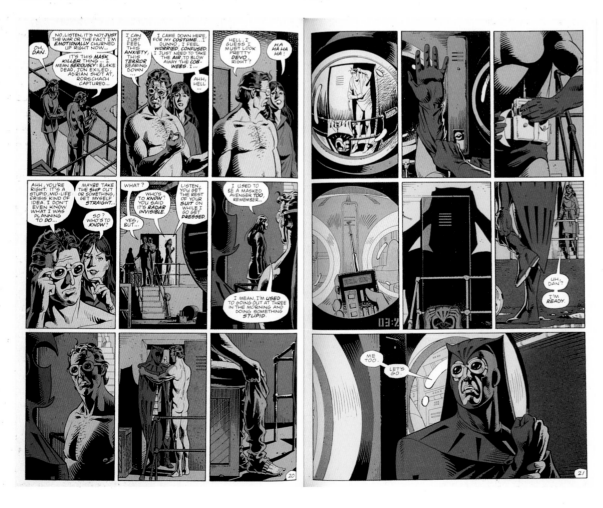

but which few of them believe in anymore. Their powers may be just as potent as when they first donned their costumes, but their spirits are broken, and amid the often horrific action, there is much soul-searching and psychological trauma – in true Alan Moore fashion. The complexity of the structure of the story, in twelve parts, with each episode redefining the one previous, made for a compelling read.

Although Moore has taken much credit for the story, the contribution of artist Dave Gibbons should not be underrated. His deceptively simple style was a testament to his unselfish attitude to his craft: for him, the narrative was everything, and there was no room for flashiness or for playing the old fan-game of 'artist-as-star'. His disciplined approach to panel layouts worked perfectly: 'What we wanted to do with *Watchmen*', he said in an interview, 'was to make the story the paramount thing, and it seemed to me that if all the pictures were the same size, you'd get the same effect that you'd get in the theatre or at the cinema, or even watching TV. Because the frame or the proscenium arch is always the same, you block it out, and get sucked into the picture that much more quickly.'[7]

The success of these comics can be attributed to three factors. Firstly, their quality: both were extremely interesting works in their own way, better by far than most other titles on the shelves. Secondly, Batman was a character that was extremely well known to the general public already (not least through the 1960s TV series), and could be sold on the basis of his 'product awareness rating'. Thirdly, the two titles were repackaged from their original bit-part form into square-bound books, and then marketed as 'graphic novels'.

This third point needs further elucidation. In a sense, the idea of the 'graphic novel' was hype – the invention of publishers' public relations departments. It meant that publishers could sell adult comics to a wider public by giving them another name: specifically, by associating them with novels, and disassociating them from comics. They hoped that, even though the actual stories were about superheroes, people would buy them on the grounds that they represented a 'new wave' in literature. With a bit of careful media orchestration, it was even speculated that a whole new market could be opened up away from the fan-shops.[8]

So it was that the industry began to solicit the mainstream press for reviews, and to advertise outside the fan market. (The hot comics creators were 'sold' like hot novelists.) As one DC Comics advert put it, placed in general interest magazines: 'You outgrew comics – now they've caught up with you!' In other words, the comics industry started operating like any other sector of the book publishing world.

In fact, there was more to the 'graphic novel' than hype. To begin with, they were not as new as the public relations people made out, and had a respectable history stretching back to the 1940s. In essence, they were what they said they were: novels in graphic form. More specifically, they could be defined as: 'lengthy comics in book form with a thematic unity'. As such, it was possible to locate examples from just about every phase in American comics development (the venerable Will Eisner, for example, had produced a well-known graphic novel *A Contract With God* in 1978). Meanwhile in Europe, album-form comics had been extremely popular for roughly the same span of time: few homes were without *Tintin* albums on the bookshelves, while adult albums had been extremely popular since the mid-1970s. (This will be expanded on in Chapter 9).

Why the graphic novel had lasted so long, albeit in a marginal capacity, and what made it appealing, both for readers and creators, was that it opened up fresh storytelling possibilities. Put simply, in a longer narrative there was more scope for building up tension, generating atmosphere, developing characters and so on. At the same time, the visuals could often be superior to the usual comics, because the status of the work was supposedly higher. Unsurprisingly perhaps, some creators actually preferred to work to graphic novel specifications than to those of ordinary comics.[9]

The effect of *Dark Knight* and *Watchmen* was thus not to revolutionize comics, as has often been supposed, but to introduce a new readership to these 'graphic novelistic' possibilities. Which is not to say that hype was not a crucial part of the process: as a result of the publicity given to the form in 1987, graphic novels were taken up in high-street bookshops and public libraries, where special shelves were devoted to them. At the same time, the many reviews in the literary sections of newspapers meant that the names of Alan Moore and Frank Miller became widely recognized.

This was a cue for mainstream book publishers to enter the fray. In time, Penguin, Gollancz, Mandarin, Boxtree and many others launched graphic novel lines. As well as using comics creators, some publishers tried to adapt the novels of popular authors into graphic form (as happened in the case of Clive Barker and James Herbert), while others even attempted to commission

Below: Pages from *When the Wind Blows* (Penguin, 1982). Art/script: Raymond Briggs. Mainstream book publishers entered the graphic novel field in the 1980s, with very limited success. Briggs's tale of two pensioners caught in a nuclear holocaust was an unexpected early hit, and chimed with the growth in Britain of CND (Campaign for Nuclear Disarmament). Here, our unfortunate protagonists survive the blast – just.

This page: Pages from *Arkham Asylum* (DC Comics, 1989). Art: Dave McKean. Script: Grant Morrison. Another grim take on the Batman myth, this time putting The Joker centre-stage (Arkham Asylum is where Batman's foes spend time between crimes). The comic appeared as a one-shot, hardback graphic novel, fully painted in a spectacular photo-realist style, and published on top quality paper.

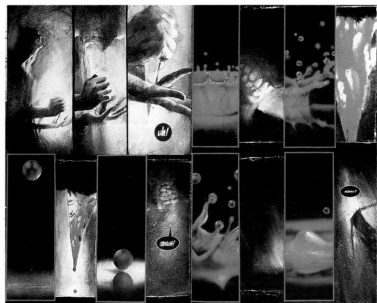

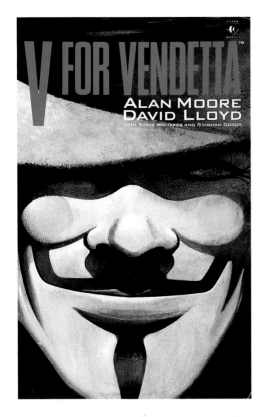

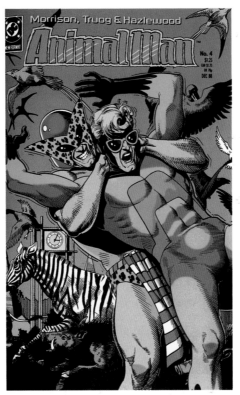

graphic novels from authors such as Doris Lessing. Naturally, such strategies attracted the attention of the literary press, and graphic novels became even more widely publicized. However, unfortunately, the publishers' choices of material were not always wise, and few new titles from this source lived up to expectations.

For the same reasons, the time was ripe for regular comics publishers to capitalize on the situation. Now just about every new comics series was commissioned on the basis that it would eventually be collected into a graphic novel, while at the same time there was a rush to repackage runs of four, six or eight comics into album form even if they had no thematic unity (thus perverting the meaning of 'graphic novel' into a marketing tool).[10] Moreover, the emphasis was now on adult material: it was believed that this was where the sales would be in the future, so long as the media continued to ply the 'comics grow up' line. Thus, with perhaps an inevitable lack of imagination, new projects were heaped onto the shoulders of Miller and Moore, while a search was initiated for their successors. Similarly, a flood of titles was commissioned about revisionist superheroes, usually grim psychological portraits of established characters, in the now-familiar mould.

DC Comics were the most anxious to plough ahead. They had published both *Dark Knight* and *Watchmen*, and had half-a-century's worth of much-loved characters that could be revamped in a similar way. Because these 'properties' had such potential, the company became the subject for a takeover by Warner Brothers, the multi-national media conglomerate. Now, with extra economic clout, DC Comics were in a position to exploit various characters' copyright from top to bottom, and in more than one medium.

This was especially true of Batman stories – now the

hippest hero in the world due to *Dark Knight*. Many more adult Batman comics were commissioned, partly to maintain the momentum of that title, and partly to capitalize on the publicity surrounding *Batman: The Movie* (eventually released in 1989). This was a Warner Brothers production partly inspired by the Miller comic, starring Michael Keaton as Batman and Jack Nicholson as The Joker. In terms of the story, the grim feel of *Dark Knight* was retained, but not much else, and even Nicholson's wildly over-the-top performance could not disguise the flimsy plotting. Nevertheless, it would become the fastest-grossing movie of all time, and the focus for a merchandising campaign of unprecedented success.

Some of the tie-in Bat-tales were better than others. For example, *Arkham Asylum* (1989) was a lavishly produced graphic novel with outstanding photorealist painted artwork by Dave McKean, and a cynically amusing story by Grant Morrison: it concerned the thin line that separates Batman's mental make-up from that of his foes. Similarly, *The Killing Joke* (1988), by Alan Moore and Brian Bolland, was a superior take on the origin-story of The Joker, again juxtaposing The Joker's psychosis with that of Batman. Both of these titles were also remarkable for their scenes of explicit violence.

Less distinguished Bat-products included: *Digital Justice* (1990), by Pepe Moreno, a computer-generated romp with cyberpunk references; and *Judgement on Gotham* (1991), written by John Wagner and Alan Grant, and illustrated with visceral gusto by Simon Bisley, about a punch-up cum team-up between Batman and Judge Dredd. Perhaps the nadir of Batmania came in 1988 when Robin was killed off in the four-part story 'A Death in the Family' in *Batman*. DC Comics achieved this by inviting a phone-in from fans, who voted on whether he should live or die. The vote went 5,343 to 5,271 in favour of killing him (which pleased the makers of the 1989 movie no end because they had no intention of featuring Robin in the first place): naturally, the character made a comeback soon afterwards.[11]

Batman was not the only DC Comics hero. Other newly revised titles included: *Green Arrow* (1988), *Black Orchid* (1988), and most impressively, *Animal Man* (1988), by Grant Morrison and various artists, which chronicled the adventures of a sort of costumed animal rights activist, who uses his animal-like powers to thwart their evil human exploiters. The company also scored a major hit with a graphic-novel version of an old Alan Moore story, now with an added conclusion and colour reproduction: (*V for Vendetta* 1990), about a more subtle kind of hero, driven by anarchist motivations (see p 139).

Marvel hit back with some revisions of their own. *The Punisher* had originally debuted in 1974, a story about a trigger-happy villainous ex-Marine. Now, he was revived by writer Mike Baron (ex-of *Nexus*) as a *Dark Knight*-style vigilante, and a 'one-man war on crime'. The character appeared in both a regular comic (1987), and a black-and-white magazine (1989): the level of violence in both was remarkable, as was their right-wing politics (The Punisher made Miller's Batman look like a social worker). Eventually, the comic became the

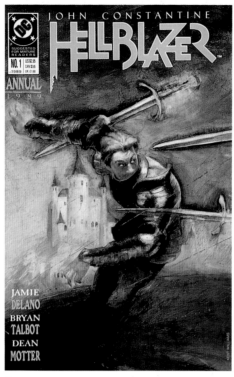

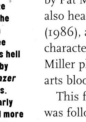

This page and opposite: Horror did particularly well during the 'adult comics' boom. Above, below and opposite: Covers and strip from *Sandman* (DC Comics). Covers (both 1989): art: Dave McKean. Strip (1989): art: Sam Keith and Mike Dringenberg, script: Neil Gaiman. The Sandman is the immortal ruler of a mystical realm that humans can see only in their dreams. Here, he visits hell to watch a nightclub performance by demons. Above right: Cover, *Hellblazer* (DC Comics, 1989). Art: Kent Williams. The horror in *Hellblazer* was similarly occult-driven, but less playful, and more British: this issue included a parallel story about Arthurian legend.

inspiration for an 18-certificate movie: a dire, straight-to-video effort, starring Dolph Lundgren.

Other notable Marvel titles included *Marshal Law* (1987), a black satire of the whole adult superhero fad, by Pat Mills and Kevin O'Neill (another British team, also headhunted from 2000AD), and *Elektra: Assassin* (1986), a limited series starring the popular supporting character from *Daredevil*, which allowed scripter Frank Miller plenty of space to indulge his passion for martial arts bloodshed.

This first flurry of post-*Dark Knight/Watchmen* activity was followed in the 1990s by further sparring between DC Comics and Marvel. While one concentrated on the adult market, the other orientated its efforts more towards teenagers. Both were prepared to use gimmicks to sell their products.

Most interestingly from a creative point of view, DC Comics capitalized on its innovations in the adult comics field by launching the 'Vertigo' line, a new imprint designed to encompass titles devoted to horror and fantasy. In the now-established fashion, comics would first appear as single-issues, with a 'Suggested For Mature Readers' label, and would later be collected as graphic novels. Two titles in particular became central to the line's success, *Sandman* and *Hellblazer*. Both were essentially horror stories, though both had links with DC Comics' superhero mythology.

Sandman, for example, had first appeared in 1941 as a member of 'The Justice Society of America', an early superhero team-up series. This rather bizarre character used sleeping gas to outwit criminals, and wore a gas-mask to protect himself. However, he was not a hit, and drifted into obscurity. That was until 1988, when he was revived in spectacular fashion by British writer Neil Gaiman. His 1980s incarnation was dramatically different: now the Sandman was cast as 'The Master of

Dreams', a pale-faced immortal who inhabits the realm of the unconscious, a mythical figure who is at once attractive and sinister.[12]

The popularity of this new *Sandman* series came down, chiefly, to the quality of the writing. Gaiman had been much influenced by Alan Moore, but developed his own, sometimes very literary, style. The stories would weave together elements from Greek mythology and European folklore, and were often designed to be read as complete graphic novels. This aspect was fortified by the gradual introduction of supporting characters over the years: for example, it transpires that the Sandman has a 'family', known as 'The Endless', who include Destiny, Desire, Despair, Destruction, Delirium, and most memorably, Death – a rather cheerful, sexy young woman. (Death was eventually given her own series, and has become something of a cult.)

More than this, *Sandman* was one of those comics that captured something of its time. In particular, it chimed with some of the preoccupations of the 'gothic punk' subculture, especially the romantic obsession with death (both Sandman and Death dress entirely in black and could be mistaken for 'goth' band-members). At the same time, it reflected many of the trends in contemporary horror novels and film: plotlines about demons and serial killers were often dealt with in an ironic, blackly humorous style, but could still be very shocking for their level of gore. Finally, there was some resonance with the not unconnected New Age interest in states of the unconscious. As Gaiman put it in an interview: 'One of the joys of *Sandman* is that what it basically says is that "yes, every single theory about dreaming is true". This is a world created by the fact that people personify dreams; and so the Sandman exists in the same way that, because people personify death, death exists. Personal realities are all valid because they're based on perception, and agreement is reality.'[13]

Hellblazer was also a revival of sorts, and similarly dated back to 1988. This much more sombre title starred a bit player from the Alan Moore-era *Swamp Thing* stories, namely John Constantine, an 'occult investigator'. In *Hellblazer*, Constantine is a complex character, a sort of tough Philip Marlowe, but also a haunted man whose meddling in the 'black arts' often ends up costing his friends their lives. His exposure of lurking supernatural horror could be truly frightening, both on a visceral and psychological level.

Again, *Hellblazer* was a writer-led title, scripted by Englishman Jamie Delano, and again it tapped into contemporary trends. Most interestingly, it included political subtexts. In one darkly amusing example, our working-class hero battles the 'demon yuppies from hell': other monstrous villains included mutant football hooligans, quaint English serial killers, sinister police units that attack peace convoys, ultra-militant Christians and supra-masonic plotters. The title may have lacked *Sandman*'s lyricism (and sales), but was nevertheless a superior horror series.

The Vertigo imprint also incorporated old hits like *Swamp Thing* and *Animal Man* (now both past their

This page: More *Sandman* (DC Comics), all scripted by Neil Gaiman. Right: Pages (1989). Art: Sam Keith and Mike Dringenberg. A scary but untypical early story. Below: Panel (1989). Art: Mike Dringenberg. Featuring the first appearance of 'Death', the Sandman's sunshiney sister who 'everybody meets in the end': she would later become a cult in her own right. Below left: Pages (1990). Art: Chris Bachalo. A witty story about Sandman meeting his 1941 incarnation (in gas mask). Below right: Pages (1991), in which Sandman visits an angel in crisis. Art: Kelley Jones.

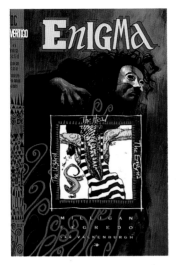

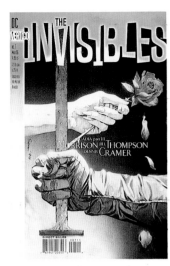

This page: Some 1990s titles from DC Comics' 'Vertigo' imprint (all DC Comics). Although labelled 'For Mature Readers', the line between sophistication and pretension could sometimes be a thin one. Above left: Cover, *Enigma* (1993). Art: Duncan Fegredo. About 'an existential superhero, looking for meaning in a meaningless world'. Above right: Cover, *The Invisibles* (1995). Art: Sean Phillips. Concerning a group of heroes who remain undetectable by operating in small cells. Below: Pages and cover from *Doom Patrol* (1990). Strip art: Richard Case. Script: Grant Morrison. Cover art: Simon Bisley. A self-consciously weird revamp of an early 1960s superhero team-up story, that took its surreal elements to the hilt.

peak), plus newer works such as *Shade the Changing Man*, *Enigma*, *The Invisibles* and *Doom Patrol*. What was remarkable about all these titles was their heavy reliance on British talent: 'the British invasion', as it became known in fanzines. Writers included not only the key threesome of Morrison, Gaiman and Delano, but also the up-and-coming Peter Milligan and Garth Ennis. Artists were also well represented, and included Duncan Fegredo, Sean Phillips, John Ridgway and Simon Bisley. Nearly all these names had learned their trade (and especially their feel for more 'adult' subject matter) on the venerable *2000AD*.[14]

The Vertigo line was undoubtedly successful – but not that successful. Sales were never on the scale of *Dark Knight* or *Watchmen*, and media exposure was miniscule in comparison. Similarly, the predicted expansion of the graphic novel market never happened, and indeed, the early enthusiasm for the form shown by high-street bookshops evaporated very quickly. As the 1990s progressed, therefore, adult comics increasingly

seemed like a false hope – at best, a cultish sideline.

Marvel, very shrewdly in retrospect, saw which way the wind was blowing and decided not to compete with Vertigo. Instead, they concentrated on more traditional material, aimed at a teenage market. The focus would be on established characters rather than new ones, 'continuing comics' rather than graphic novels, and, above all, artist-led rather than writer-led titles. As a corollary, every effort would be made to appeal to the fans in the specialist shops (by way of gimmicks, collectable covers, and so on), while the casual reader in the book-shops would be virtually ignored. It was a 'back to basics' approach that certainly made commercial sense.

There was another incentive for Marvel to take this path. In 1991, the company became a publicly owned corporation, and began trading on the New York Stock Exchange. What this meant was that there was now more pressure than ever to expand their market share, and to extend the market in general, in order to keep shareholders happy. As a result, there was a rush to launch new titles – not always with very much thought for quality. Many were unsuccessful, but the one or two really big hits more than made up for this.

The first of the big sellers pre-dated the flotation, and was a re-launch of *Spider-Man* (renumbered as 1 from 1990). Written and drawn by fan-favourite Todd McFarlane, it set the tone for future releases: the art style was impressively flashy, while the story line was virtually nonexistent. Also, it was released with various different

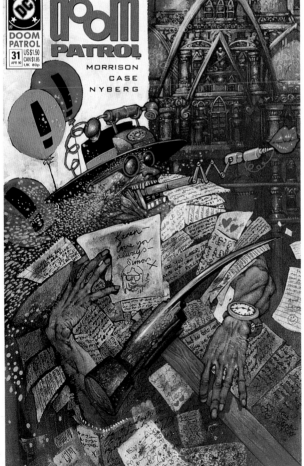

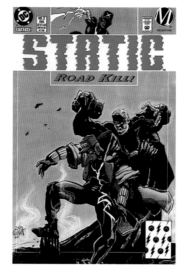

Above: Cover, *Static* (DC Comics, 1993). Art: John Paul Leon. An old-fashioned tale about a high-school hero with a superheroic alter-ego, different only in that it was part of an imprint (Milestone) consisting of comics designed for black youth and starring black characters. Below: The superheroes start to bite the dust (all DC Comics). Two of the more cynical marketing ploys of recent years were the killing of Robin and Superman: most tackily, Robin's fate was decided by a phone-vote from readers.

Above and right: Artwork prepared if Robin had been allowed to live (DC Comics, 1988), and page from *Batman: A Death in the Family* (DC Comics, 1988), showing how things really worked out. Art: Jim Aparo. Script: Jim Starlin. Far right: Cover to the graphic novel *The Death of Superman* (DC Comics, 1993). Art: Jon Bogdanove. Only a fool could have imagined that the greatest hero of them all was gone for good.

coloured covers – all of which were collected by completist fans. It became the biggest selling comic ever, at over 3 million copies. However, even this figure was trumped by a follow-up release, *X-Force* (1991), which sold an estimated 3.5 million. The comic was yet another *X-Men* related title, and boasted some dynamic art by Rob Liefeld. The real secret of its success was the fact that five *X-Force* cards were produced to be bagged with the first issue. In other words, one comic, five cards: again, completists could not resist. Other hits for Marvel included gimmick-laden versions of the *Silver Surfer* and *Wolverine*.

DC Comics were left sprawling once again, but could hardly be accused of ignoring the teen market. They also tried gimmicks and different covers, but with limited success. They also tried to compete by launching another imprint, this time aimed at black youth. Milestone was a collection of titles starring black superheroes. It was an attempt, in DC Comics' words, to 'make comics multicultural'.[15] In fact, comics had been multicultural for many years in the context of the underground, and there had been black superheroes before. Nevertheless, the line marked an important step forward, and introduced some exciting new creators and characters. Titles like *Static*, *Icon*, *Hardware* and *Blood Syndicate* (all 1993) displayed an intimate knowledge of superhero lore, mixed with a hip and often humorous veneer. In *Static*, the eponymous hero is a variant on the Spider-Man theme, an 'electrically-charged' avenger who wears a 'Malcolm X' cap and battles villains who are 'built like Riddick Bowe'.

His alter ego is a schoolboy who works nights in a fast-food chain not unlike McDonald's. Whether the Milestone titles will have the same impact on comics as the films of Spike Lee have had on Hollywood remains to be seen.

It was not until 1993, however, that DC Comics revealed its biggest master plan: to kill off their greatest hero, Superman. There were several reasons why, not least because the character had recently slumped in popularity. The Christopher Reeve movies had been very successful, and had continued into the late 1980s, and were matched by a revamp of the *Superman* comic by John Byrne, which had split fan opinion (this mid 1980s incarnation looked like Reeve, and was more 'human' than ever before). But in the late 1980s and 1990s, Superman had been well and truly eclipsed by the Batman movies and comics. His old rival had once more got one up on him.

In order to claw back sales, something drastic had to be done. Killing off a character was a time-honoured scam, and could be a major moneyspinner (as the 'Death of Robin' had shown), but to meddle with such a major figure as Superman was still a risk. The fan market could reasonably be relied upon, especially if the comic was launched with gimmicks (it was, including a memorial armband and a clipping from *The Daily Planet*). But to make sure of success, DC Comics went all-out to garner coverage in the mainstream media, which they achieved to a degree unequalled since the heady days of *Dark Knight* and *Watchmen*.

The actual 'Death of Superman' story line cleverly

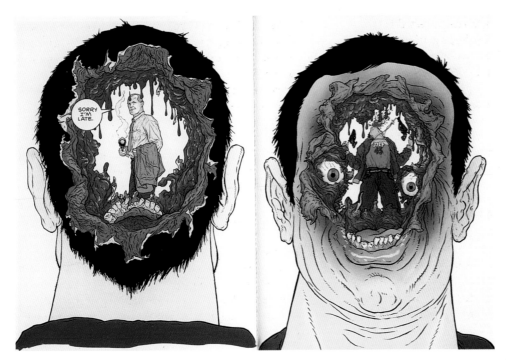

This page: Of the new independent publishers, Dark Horse was one of the most successful, thanks in part to its signing of Frank Miller. All the following examples are scripted by him. Above and above right: Pages and cover from *Hard Boiled* (Dark Horse, 1992). Art: Geof Darrow. This story of a cyborg with a big gun was indeed hard boiled: a balletically choreographed exercise in ultra-violence. Below left: Cover to the graphic novel *A Dame to Kill For* (Dark Horse, 1994). Art: Frank Miller. The second novel in the enormously popular 'Sin City' series of noir thrillers. Below right: Cover to *Give Me Liberty* (Dark Horse, 1990). Art: Dave Gibbons. A more politically aware tale, set in a science fictional future, with a black heroine.

reflected the religious metaphor of the character's origin (see p 61). In it, he attempts to stop the 'murderous blitzkrieg' of a monster called (appropriately) Doomsday, and gets killed in the process. Some time afterwards, people start to report seeing him. Eventually, some friends of his break into his tomb. They find it empty. It was a simple formula, but very effective. The entire saga was collected into a hugely successful graphic novel, while individual issues became some of the biggest selling DC Comics titles ever. Of course, Superman did not stay dead for long, and after a convoluted plotline about various imposters, he was soon whizzing around the skies in his usual fashion.

Yet for all the intense battling between Marvel and DC for market share, the truth that they both had to face was that in the 1990s, they were no longer alone. For by now, certain independent companies had grown to such a stature as to pose a real threat. Three companies in particular made an impact on the early years of the decade: Dark Horse, Voyager and Image. They proved beyond any doubt that significant

commercial success was by no means the preserve of the big two.

Dark Horse, founded in 1986, had always had a reputation for quality comics, but never really hit paydirt until the 1990s, when their movie tie-ins began to sell in large quantities. In particular, *Aliens* (1988), *Predator* (1989) and *Terminator* (1990) were popular, spinning out stories as if they were sequels to the original movies, and leading to various additional titles which used the characters in crossover plots (for example, *Aliens vs Predator*, 1990). The publisher also generated a movie hit of its own with *The Mask* (1991), originally a satirical superhero fantasy with horror overtones, which became a slapstick Hollywood movie in 1994, with Jim Carrey in the lead.

Dark Horse also kept one eye on the adult comics market, and introduced some new heroes into the field. In this they had one trump card because they now employed Frank Miller almost exclusively. He was responsible for writing *Give Me Liberty* (1990), with art by Dave Gibbons, about a gutsy black woman's attempt to gain spiritual freedom in a future America on the brink of civil war, and *Hard Boiled* (1990), with art by Geof Darrow, a darker, more visceral tale about a pitiless cyborg in search of his memory and his purpose, in which Darrow's obsessive but meticulous rendering lends the mayhem of the story a curiously designer quality. Miller also scripted and drew *Sin City* (1993), about an ex-con's search for a serial killer, which was simultaneously one of the best-looking comics of the 1990s, rendered in stunning black-and-white chiaroscuro, and also one of the most violent: the killer mounts his victim's heads on the wall, while the hero is not above a bit of torture to get his way.

The second independent publisher to make an impact, Voyager, was the least interesting, simply because their titles stuck to tried-and-trusted superhero formulas. Set up by an ex-Marvel editor, Jim Shooter, the company used its Valiant imprint to launch new titles. At first, these were revivals of little-known 1960s heroes (originally published by Gold Key) such as *Magnus, Robot Fighter* and *Solar, Man of the Atom* (both 1991). But in 1992, a clutch of original titles such as *X-O Manowar*, *Harbinger*, *Shadowman* and *Eternal Warrior* formed the basis for a successful 'Valiant Universe'. They were all drearily predictable teen fare, but made

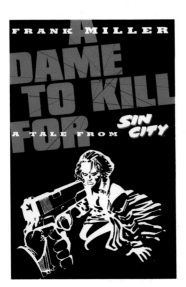

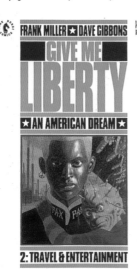

This page and opposite: Examples from the biggest independent publisher of them all: Image Comics, a company formed by renegades from Marvel. Top: Cover to *Wild CATS* (Image, 1993). Art: Jim Lee. A title that perpetuated the notion of superheroines with breasts larger than their heads. Above, below right, and opposite: Covers and pages from *Spawn* (all Image, 1993). Art/script: Todd McFarlane. The diabolic costumed hero was an instant hit: despite the absence of any detectable storyline, the comic was kept at the top of the sales charts by fluid artwork, good-looking monsters (and women), and inevitably extreme violence.

respectable amounts of money.[16]

The third indie publishing success was certainly the most significant in commercial terms – Image Comics. The company was formed as a 'creator-owned' concern by a group of disgruntled writers and artists from Marvel, who felt that they were not seeing enough of the profits of their work under the traditional Marvel system. These profits had been substantial indeed, since the names in question included Todd McFarlane, Jim Lee and Rob Liefeld, creators of some of the best-selling comics of all time. In some ways, their new venture was an enormous risk; but their optimism was justified by the success of their first three releases (all, inevitably, superhero comics). The first, Liefeld's *Youngblood* (1992) came complete with gimmicky trading cards, and broke the record for the best-selling independent comic; the second, McFarlane's *Spawn* (1992), again broke the record; and the third, Lee's *WildCATS* (1992) did the same again. It was not long before Image were beating DC Comics into third place in the sales charts.

Why the Image titles should have been such hits is not difficult to explain. They were essentially re-runs of Marvel formulas produced by the biggest names in the business. (Later, other top creators joined, such as Erik Larsen, Marc Silvestri and Whilce Portacio.) But they also had their own attractions. Many of the story lines, for example, tapped into fashionable horror and science fiction themes: the character Spawn is a kind of Mephisto figure, who is not above dismembering those who displease him, while some titles had definite cyberpunk references. Also, the artwork, as well as representing the peak of the fan aesthetic, was coloured by computer in an unusual and striking fashion. These factors all combined to make the imprint appear 'now' and happening.

So what are we to make of the new mainstream comics of the 1990s? In some ways, the Marvel/DC Comics/Image axis was merely perpetuating formulas that had been around since the beginning of the superhero genre. But in others, there was a new sensibility afoot. Violence was much more a part of the stories, and the essential innocence of the old-style superhero tales had been replaced by a kind of hip cynicism. An article in the fanzine *The Comics Journal*, from 1991, asked where it would all lead: 'At stake is the continued status of superheroes as bona fide American myth – they risk their essence by mythologizing the Reagan era's precepts..If publishers keep pandering to ... bloodlust, superheroes will lose the glamor and the glory readers associate with the red, white and blue ... and retain only the guilty thrill induced by the grisly, gory red.'[17]

The other thing that is striking about this period is the extent to which comics have become tied to other media. Film especially has become crucially important, as publishers have increasingly put their faith in the fact that comics characters can make even bigger bucks as celluloid heroes. This was always the case to a degree, of course, but in the late 1980s and 1990s, publishers have ruthlessly exploited their situation as part of (or as

sister companies of) larger multi-national media corporations which have the capacity for film-making. For example, DC Comics is owned by Time Warner, Marvel is owned by the same organization that owns New World Pictures, while Dark Horse has close links with 20th Century Fox.

The sheer number of recent movies based on comics and comic strips demonstrates the point. They include (as well as the aforementioned *Teenage Mutant Ninja Turtles*, *Batman*, *The Punisher* and *The Mask*): *Batman Returns*, *Batman Forever*, *The Crow*, *Dick Tracy*, *Richie Rich*, *Dennis the Menace*, *Caspar the Friendly Ghost*, *The Shadow*, *Judge Dredd* and *Tank Girl*. There are also an estimated seventy further comic-related movies in production or pre-production, including, if rumours are to be believed, *Spider-Man*, *Daredevil*, *Elektra*, *Sgt Rock* and *The Fantastic Four*. (This is not to mention the numerous recent TV series based on comics, notably the 'Batman', 'Mask' and 'X-Men' cartoons and the 'Lois and Clark' live action shows.)

All this activity can be taken as a comment on Hollywood, of course. On the one hand it shows how far special effects have come. It used to be true that comics had one-up on movies because their capacity for picturing spectacular settings and situations was unrivalled. Not any more. Now, film budgets of 30–50 million dollars are commonplace, and advances in computer modelling and animation mean that almost any comics effect can be replicated. It is no exaggeration to say that, finally, 2-D comics have entered the third dimension.

On the other hand, it shows how hard-up Hollywood is for new ideas. Rather than forge new myths, the movie moguls have decided that it's easier to deal with ready-

1. This essentially sexist atmosphere was reinforced by the way in which certain comics were deemed to be collectable for their 'Good Girl Art' (abbreviated in collectors' guides to 'GGA'). Thus, creators like the veteran Wally Wood, and the more contemporary Dave Stevens, became highly regarded for their flair for 'cheesecake'.

2. For example, Pacific's *Captain Victory and the Galactic Rangers* (1981) was by Jack Kirby, and thereby proved that the indies had the capacity to attact big names.

3. In the 1990s, the X-Men's greatest enemy was the Legacy Virus, a deadly disease which infected and killed mutants – a timely metaphor for AIDS.

4. Mention should be made here of another important independent satire title, *Cerebus the Aardvark*, a send-up of Conan the Barbarian. However, because of the comic's more 'alternative' nature, it has been covered in Chapter 8.

5. Although the Code could be ignored, publishers never-theless decided to label their comics. This was partly in response to the rise of right-wing pressure groups and led to a number of resignations by creators disgusted by what they saw as censorship. Marvel, DC Comics and most others used words such as 'suggested for mature readers' to cover sexual themes, religious themes and certain kinds of violence.

6. Frank Miller, in *The Comics Journal*, no 10, August 1985,

7. Dave Gibbons, in *The Comics Journal*, July 1987, p 100.

8. In Britain, this strategy was finely honed. In particular, Titan Books, who repackaged *Dark Knight* and *Watchmen* (among others) for the British market, went so far as to hire a PR specialist to push adult comics.

9. Creators particularly associated with graphic novels include Alan Moore, Art Spiegelman, the Hernandez Brothers, Will Eisner, Dave Sim, Neil Gaiman, Howard Chaykin and Bryan Talbot.

10. Although these books were routinely marketed as graphic novels, they were also more accurately known as 'trade paperbacks'.

11. Strictly speaking, the original Robin (aka Dick Grayson) never disappeared. The one who died was another Robin, Jason Todd, a newer addition to the 'Bat universe'.

12. Confusingly, DC Comics also put out a *Sandman Mystery Theater* (1993), by Matt Wagner and Guy Davis, which revived the 1941 character in more or less his original form.

13. Neil Gaiman, interviewed in *Speakeasy*, no 114, p 38.

14. The role of editor Karen Berger should be noted: she was responsible for British liaison at the company, and central to setting up Vertigo.

15. Technically speaking, Milestone was a separate company, owned and controlled by black Americans, which used DC Comics for distribution and publicity: many of the characters had been conceived before DC Comics became involved.

16. Jim Shooter left *Valiant* in 1992, and went on to form Defiant Comics, a less successful company again dominated by teen-orientated superhero titles.

17. Darcy Sullivan, 'The Politics of Superheroes', *The Comics Journal*, no 142, June 1991, p 88.

made visual material and characters which can be reduced to easily marketable soundbites. For them, comics characters are simply instantly recognizable brand names – a corporate logo, an icon embodying a neat tag-line. And if the back-catalogues of comics publishers can be exploited at no extra cost, and if, then, the film, comics and associated merchandising can be 'vertically integrated' into a coherent marketing campaign, so much the better.

But the new interdependency may also have important long-term consequences for the comics industry. Movies, of course, can be very lucrative; and who can blame the comics publishers for making hay while the sun shines? But they can also serve another function: as an escape route in times of crisis. To be specific, the current emphasis in the enclosed world of fandom on comics collectability, with its ridiculous associations with gimmicky covers and the like, is a very fragile basis on which to plan the future of the business. Sooner or later the bubble has to burst, as fans realize that they are being conned, and when that happens the consequences for the shop network could be dire. Under those circumstances, publishers would be very wise to have a life-raft at the ready, and their movie connections might prove to be the obvious answer.

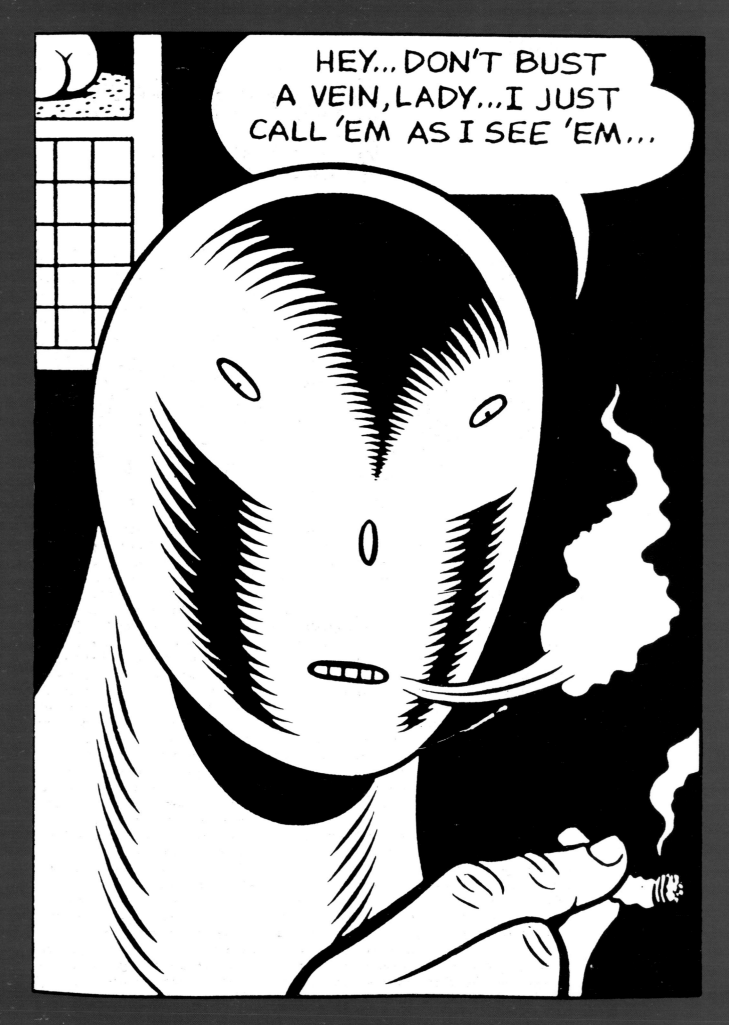

Eight

Alternative Visions

The new breed of alternative comics came in many forms, and showcased a brilliant array of oddball creators. Opposite: Panel from *Hardboiled Defective Stories* (Penguin, 1990). Art/script: Charles Burns. The decidedly strange sleuth was based loosely on Mexican wrestler El Santo. Right: Detail from *Neat Stuff* (Fantagraphics, 1985). Art: Peter Bagge. A comic dealing in less-than-mature comedy. Right centre: Cover, *Mister X* (Vortex, 1984). Art: Paul Rivoche. A moody science fiction tale. Far right: Panel from *Aargh!* (Mad Love, 1988). Art/script: Steven Appleby. A political anthology protesting against establishment homophobia.

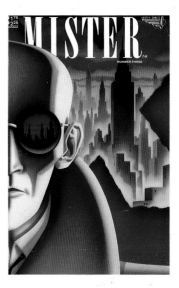

With the rise of a new mainstream came a new wave of alternative comics. The 1980s and 1990s were indeed a kind of golden age for nonconformist titles; among them were comics that tackled topics never covered before, and which pushed back artistic expectations. They were in many ways an extension of the old underground comix, but this time they were sold from the fan shops, like the majority of other titles. Overwhelmingly American in origin, and almost always orientated towards an adult readership, they were minute in number compared to the Marvel, DC Comics and Image titles that swamped the shelves. Yet creatively, they marked another step forward for the comics medium.

It is difficult to generalize about the new alternatives because they were so diverse. The best way to define them is by contrasting them to the mainstream. First, and most obviously, they were not about superheroes. Instead, they were concerned with a wide spectrum of mature subject matter: it was possible to find genre fiction (thriller, western, horror and science fiction), autobiography, politics, satire and many others. It was the same range that one might associate with prose fiction or cinema films. The mainstream comics had professed to be 'adult', but as we have seen, this was more often than not a marketing ploy: the new alternatives were the real item.

Indeed, purely in terms of genre, the alternatives could stretch into areas that the mainstream would not touch. Often this was because the big publishers could see no money in publishing things like autobiography. But also, topics like radical politics, sex and hardcore horror were viable for the alternatives because the mainstream could not, or were not inclined to, cope with them. For this reason, alternative comics tended to be more extreme than their mainstream counterparts, and much more prone to censorship by the establishment.

Similarly, the alternatives were in a position to capitalize on countercultural trends. Punk, in particular, was an influence. As we have seen, this was a relatively short-lived phenomenon (lasting from about 1976 to 1979), but its impact was long-term, and directed attention away from the old underground hippie obsessions. Thus, the first wave of alternative comics would often exhibit a more confrontational and aggressive writing style, and commonly starred characters who were punks or post-punks rather than hippies, and would sometimes reflect a punk-art aesthetic, as opposed to a psychedelic or fantasy art one: this could mean anything from 'spontaneous' drawing styles to art influenced by punk-inspired 'neo expressionism'. Later comics built on this, and reflected the concerns of more recent subcultures, such as the rave, 'indie' and travelling scenes.

This kind of content inevitably meant that the alternatives drew from an entirely different well of creators than the mainstream, and appealed to a different audience. As well as being a 'hipper ' crowd, the most striking contrast was the number of women involved. As we have seen, women first began to create their own comics during the underground era, and this tradition was continued and strengthened in the 1980s and 1990s, with women making a bigger contribution to the medium than ever before. Superheroes may have been a turn-off, but the opportunity to explore other kinds of subject matter was clearly one that many women relished. By the same token, audiences for the new comics tended to be of both sexes; though not, it has to be said, anywhere near equally split.

The comics were anti mainstream in other ways. For example, their output was not necessarily dominated by commerce. The tradition started by the underground of paying creators a royalty, and allowing them copyright control, was continued here. The comics similarly tended to be small scale, and issued by small publishers. Often this could mean an emphasis on self-motivated work, rather than profit-driven escapism: it was typical for alternative comics to be produced by one or two people rather than by a team. Production values were rarely up to mainstream standards, though collected graphic novels of alternative material were an increasingly common part of the scene.

The alternative publishers were thus very different to the Marvel/DC Comics/Image nexus. We have seen how the explosion of independent companies in the 1980s led to many that tried to compete in the arena of superhero titles. The other independents, broadly in the alternative camp, took three forms. First, there were those that were uncompromisingly different to the mainstream, the foremost among them being the Seattle-based Fantagraphics, responsible for publishing some of the most remarkable comics of the modern period (others included America's Raw Books and Graphics, Canada's Drawn and Quarterly and Britain's Escape Publishing). Second, there were publishers that decided to keep a foot

in both camps: examples included Dark Horse and Eclipse, whose lists included an often incongruous mix of mainstream and alternative creators. Third, there were companies that had their origins in the underground, but which continued to do business, often putting out new alternative work as well as familiar underground material: these included Kitchen Sink and Last Gasp in America and Knockabout in Britain.

If it is hard to generalize about the comics themselves, it is even harder to get a handle on who bought them. Certainly, the readership was vastly different to that of something like the *X-Men*, and the two audiences, although frequenting the same shops, would rarely buy the same comics. As we might expect, readers of alternative fare would generally be 'alternative' to a degree themselves. They were not part of a 'grand political project' like the hippies before them, but they were commonly countercultural within the context of the 1980s and 1990s. To be more specific than this involves looking at the wider cultural context. As one alternative creator explained: 'There is a real crossover between the people who are buying alternative comics, and these alternative rock music records that come out on small labels and books published by small publishing companies like REsearch, Amok, Farrow House and Loompanics. They never go to a Spielberg movie [laughs]. They read *Film Threat*. It's like the medium is beside the point. I don't know what to call it. [It's] "Anti-corporate culture." These people are willing to buy into anything that isn't part of a corporation where they sense material has been watered down and made to be inoffensive.'[1]

As such, the alternatives carved out a niche for themselves on the shelves of the comics shops. Anthology titles were especially important, because these were the titles that were chiefly responsible for introducing new creators to the field, much in the way as their underground ancestors *Zap* and *Bijou Funnies* had a generation before. Containing anywhere between four and forty stories, they were typically cheaply produced, in black-and-white, but sported eye-frazzling colour covers.

In the 1980s, one anthology in particular made a huge impact: *Raw* (Raw Books and Graphics, 1980). The title was the brainchild of a New York based couple, Art Spiegelman, a veteran of the underground, and Françoise Mouly, a fine artist interested in European comics. The first thing they did was to set up a publishing company, Raw Books and Graphics, with the idea of putting out material that would not be undertaken anywhere else. In this way, the company would become a mecca for quirky and visionary illustrators, artists and comics creators.

The origins of *Raw* itself were rooted in Spiegelman's desire to provide a platform for avant-garde comic work. In order to emphasize this, an unusual format was adopted – 11 x 14 inches – in order to show off the artwork better. This was at a time when other New York art-scene tabloids were also appearing in a large size – magazines like *Interview* and *Skyline* – and it was hoped that *Raw*, as well as being sold from specialist comics shops, would be also be shelved in newsagents next to them. As such, it was pointedly not intended to be 'mass

This page: The alternative boom was anthology-driven, and no title was more important than *Raw*. Committed to self-expression, this outsize magazine from New York set new standards in comics art, and although labelled 'avant garde', included a wide range of non-mainstream material. Above and right: Cover and strip from the first issue (Raw Books and Graphics, 1980). Cover art: Art Spiegelman. 'Jack Survives', art/script: Jerry Moriarty.

THE GRAPHIX MAGAZINE THAT LOST ITS FAITH IN NIHILISM

This page: More from *Raw*: these wonderful covers measured 11 by 14 inches. (All examples Raw Books and Graphics.) Left: Cover (1981), art: Gary Panter. Bottom left: Cover (1985), art: Art Spiegelman. (The notorious 'torn' issue.) Bottom right: Cover (1984), art: Mark Beyer. Below: Pages from 'Mister Wilcox, Mister Conrad', *Raw* (1981). Art: Jose Munoz. Script: Carlos Sampayo. An atmospheric strip about life in New York, by two South Americans who had never been there.

THE TORN-AGAIN GRAPHIX MAG

THE GRAPHIX MAGAZINE THAT OVERESTIMATES THE TASTE OF THE AMERICAN PUBLIC

179

Left: 'Dead Things', *Raw* (Raw Books and Graphics, 1980). Art/script: Mark Beyer. Distinctive cartoony abstraction from a new American talent, with a somewhat thin story about rag-doll characters in bizarre situations. It is difficult not to agree with critics that Beyer's work represented a victory of style over content, but then in many ways *Raw* was all about style.

market', and had a modest initial print run of 5000.

In terms of content, *Raw* had certain connections with Spiegelman's last big comics project, *Arcade*, in that it featured new work by many of the old stars of the underground, including: Robert Crumb, Bill Griffith, Kim Deitch, Justin Green and Lynda Barry. Like *Arcade*, it featured jokey cover straplines that were very comix-esque, such as 'The Graphix Magazine that Lost its Faith in Nihilism' and 'The Graphix Magazine That Overestimates the Taste of the American Public'.

The centrepiece was Spiegelman's own 'Maus', a story which had previously appeared in prototype form in an underground.[2] It related the tale of his father's life in Poland before and during the Second World War, and in particular his harrowing experiences of the Holocaust. It was serialized a chapter at a time in each issue of *Raw*, and showed Spiegelman at his most daring: most remarkably, it recast events in 'funny animal' form, with the Jews as mice, the Nazis as cats and the Poles as pigs. Of course, the history being related was far from funny, and Spiegelman's intentions were as serious as George Orwell's was in *Animal Farm*. It was a very delicate operation to carry off, but somehow it worked, thanks to Spiegelman's attention to historical detail, and understated art. In fact, by anthropomophizing events, the horror was personalized in a way that it could not have been if the characters had been depicted in human form.

Maus was later collected as a graphic novel, and published by the mainstream book publishers Pantheon in America and Penguin in Britain in 1986–7. This opened the way to distribution in high-street bookshops,

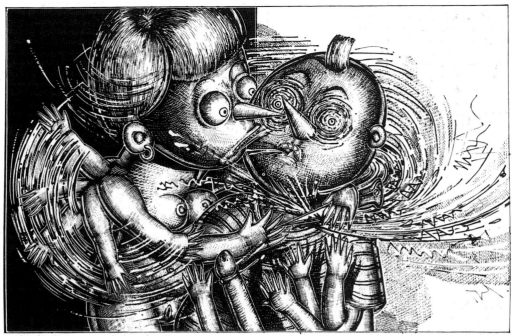

Paul prefers his Mommy to the love of a girl.

This page: *Raw*'s manifesto also encompassed bringing unusual European creators to a wider audience. (All Raw Books and Graphics.) Above right: Page from 'Paul' (1989). Art/script: Pascal Doury (from France). Above: Page from 'The Clock Strikes' (1981). Art/script: Joost Swarte (from The Netherlands). Right: Pages from 'Crash' (1981). Art/script: Javier Mariscal (from Spain).

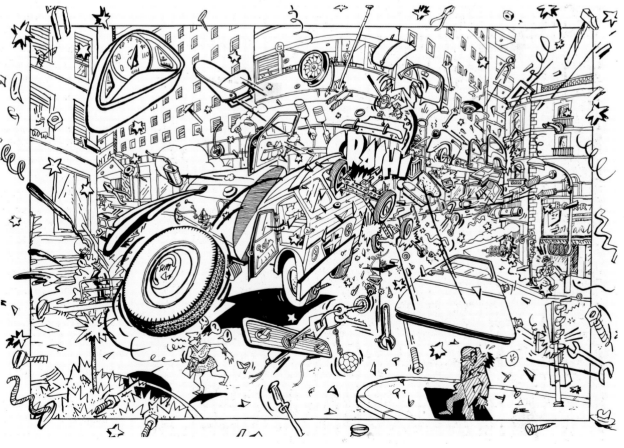

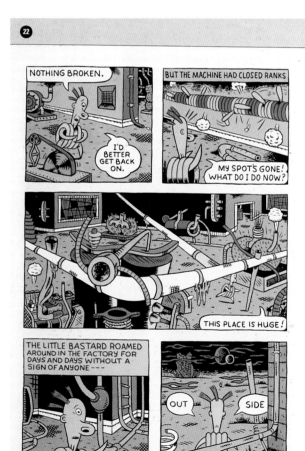

This page: *Raw* again (all Raw Books and Graphics). Above: Pages from 'The Basket Case' (1990). Art/script: Jacques Tardi. A haunting story by Frenchman Tardi about a madman's encounter with a prostitute and her dribbling, bowler-hatted charge. Below: Pages from 'Little Bastard' (1991). Art/script: Kaz. Dazzlingly colourful work, but another contributor whose work was better looked at than read.

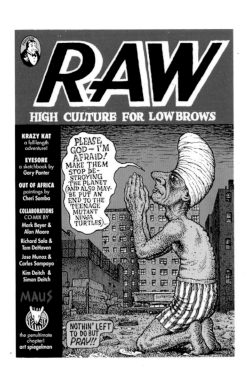
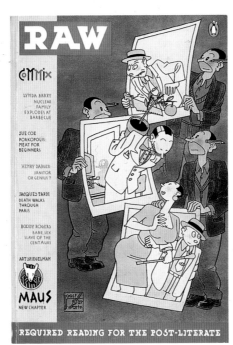

This page and opposite: Covers and pages from the graphic novels *Maus* and *Maus II* (Penguin, 1987 and 1992). Art/script: Art Spiegelman. The epic story of one individual's experience of the Nazi Holocaust, as told in anthropomorphic terms, with Jews as mice, and Nazis as cats (a sort of deadly serious Tom and Jerry), and a milestone in the history of comics. Originally serialized in *Raw*, it was in the form of the twin graphic novels pictured here that it received widespread attention in the mainstream media, and Spiegelman was awarded a Pulitzer Prize for Literature in 1992: the first cartoonist ever to be so honoured.

ALL NIGHT I HEARD SHOOTING HE WHO GOT TIRED, WHO CAN'T WALK SO FAST, THEY SHOT.

THE MORE WE WALKED, THE MORE I HEARD SHOOTING...

AND IN THE DAYLIGHT, FAR AHEAD, I SAW IT.

SOMEBODY IS JUMPING, TURNING, ROLLING 25 OR 35 TIMES AROUND. AND STOPS.

"OH," I SAID. "THEY MAYBE KILLED THERE A DOG."

WHEN I WAS A BOY OUR NEIGHBOR HAD A DOG WHAT GOT MAD AND WAS BITING.

THE NEIGHBOR CAME OUT WITH A RIFLE AND SHOT.

THE DOG WAS ROLLING SO, AROUND AND AROUND, KICKING, BEFORE HE LAY QUIET.

AND NOW I THOUGHT: "HOW AMAZING IT IS THAT A HUMAN BEING REACTS THE SAME LIKE THIS NEIGHBOR'S DOG."

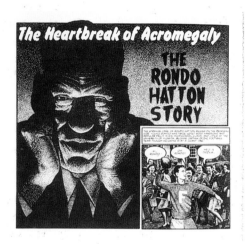

This page: A selection of 'Raw One-shots', which is to say, comics published under the Raw imprint. (All Raw Books and Graphics.) Left and below: Cover and strip 'The Rondo Hatton Story' from *Warts and All* (1990). Art/script: Drew and Josh Friedman. The lives of B-movie stars often formed the subject matter for the parodies of the Friedman brothers, whose meticulous pointillist technique gave the impression of photographic veracity. Below right: Cover to *Skin Deep* (Penguin, 1995). Art: Charles Burns. These were 'tales of doomed romance' with typically horrific undercurrents.

This art-punk attitude was underlined by the inclusion of new creators. Gary Panter contributed strips staring 'Jimbo' (already a cult character from a punk fanzine called *Slash*), about an indestructible, post-nuclear anti-hero; they featured unpolished, scratchy artwork and plenty of 'so what?' humour. Charles Burns was a master of meticulous 1950s-style horror and science fiction stories, resonant with noir references and sexual undercurrents, which managed to be both horrifying and hilariously funny. Jerry Moriarty's 'Jack Survives' was an oddly engaging view of the banal; it was a 'real time melodrama' about a man who survives everyday mundane menaces, including aggressive dogs and faulty plumbing. Also included were Mark Beyer's 'art brut' stories featuring rag-doll figures that became involved in horrendous and often fatal situations, and Drew Friedman's satires, which had a mission to expose 'the dark underbelly of show-biz glitz' (and which included some savage, and barely legal, pointillist caricatures of media personalities). Other American-based discoveries included Ben Katchor, Mark Newgarden and Kaz.

The final ingredient in the *Raw* mix was foreign material – mainly from Europe, but also occasionally from South America and Japan. The Euro-strips were largely down to Françoise Mouly's influence, though Spiegelman was enthusiastic. Often, the European creators themselves had been influenced by punk, and represented the post-*Heavy Metal* generation. They included: from Belgium, Ever Meulen, whose work was characterized by a precisely rendered expressionism; from France, Pascal Doury who specialized in bizarre fantasies, and Jacques Tardi who produced strips best described as noir realism; and from Spain, Javier Mariscal

and before long it had become caught up in the 'Comics Grow Up' story in the press (see p 165). The response from reviewers was generally very positive, and despite some dissenting opinions (*The Guardian*, for instance, thought the stereotyping of nationalities was essentially fascistic), it sold very well.[3] Spiegelman followed the book with *Maus II: And Here My Troubles Began* (1992), which followed its protagonist through 'Mauswitz' and the Liberation. If anything, this instalment was even better than the first, and mainstream recognition was sealed when Spiegelman became the first comics creator ever to receive a Pulitzer Prize for Literature in 1992.

Yet beyond this underground connection, the design of *Raw* spoke of other influences, notably punk. We have seen how punk was a pervasive influence on the alternatives in general, but in *Raw*'s case, punk was referred to selectively, and commonly interpreted though an ironic, neo-expressionist filter. Each contents page, for example, featured design ideas such as 'overprints' and 'drop outs' that were associated with the punk aesthetic. Similarly, the 'ripped and torn' fashion was reflected in issue 7, which had the right-hand corner of the cover torn off (a torn piece randomly selected from another cover was taped to the corner of page 1). These quirks gave *Raw* a reputation for novelty and for never standing still. They also lent it a sense of energy despite its artiness.

TALES OF DOOMED ROMANCE BY CHARLES BURNS

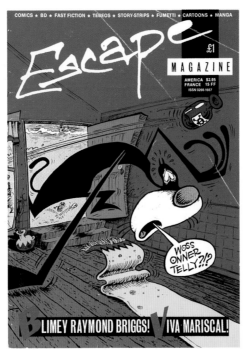

protest, and *X* (1993), a paean to Malcolm X.

Later One-Shots were taken over by Pantheon and Penguin, in the same way as they had contracted *Maus*, and sold from bookshops. These included Mark Beyer's *Agony* (1987); Panters' *Jimbo* (1988) – basically the same as the first edition, but with new material – and Burns' *Hardboiled Defective Stories* (1990). Finally, Pantheon/Penguin put out an anthology of the first three issues of *Raw* entitled *Read Yourself Raw* (1987). But unfortunately, by this time the novelty of the 'adult comics' hype was wearing thin, and sales of these titles were disappointing.

Spiegelman continued to court mainstream publishers, however, and eventually decided to publish *Raw* itself through Penguin. The trade-off was that the comic would now have to appear in a smaller size: Spiegelman justified this by saying that he now wanted to emphasise the writing, and wanted the look of a literary magazine rather than a graphic arts one. Penguin pushed the print run up to 30,000, and went on to publish further *Raw* One-Shots – Friedman's *Warts and All* (1990), Ben Katchor's *Cheap Novelties* (1991), and Burns' *Skin Deep* (1995). But the publisher had not learned from past mistakes: these may have been great comics, but they didn't sell. *Raw* itself has been on hold since 1994.

But in terms of its effect on 1980s comics, *Raw* had shown a possible road to take. It had not only demonstrated that the old undergrounders had more to offer, but it also revealed a wealth of new talent both in America and in Europe. Despite its later cooption into mainstream publishing, it had reinvigorated the tradition of alternative anthologies, and in so doing given a much needed boost to alternative comics generally. In the words of *Comics Journal*: '*Raw*'s appearance offered a corrective. In the face of so much that is contemptible in our popular culture, *Raw* was and remains, a fortnight declaration that comics are a sophisticated, adult medium.'[4]

In Britain, the most important *Raw*-imitator was *Escape*, which was also part of a larger publishing house (Escape Books and Graphics) which published one-shot comics. *Escape* was started by Paul Gravett and Peter

who injected into the comic an avant-garde whimsy. Above all, there was the Dutchman Joost Swarte, whose elegant linework and sophisticated designs spoke of cool irony, and did much to give early issues of the magazine their character.

'*Raw* One-Shots' developed as a separate line of titles by individual contributors, published by Raw Books. Highly designed, they were intended as a means to showcase a body of work or tell stories longer than could be handled in *Raw* itself. The first was a collection of Panter's strips, *Jimbo* (1983), printed on newsprint and bound between cardboard covers with gaffer tape. It was followed by another Panter outing, *Invasion of the Elvis Zombies* (1985) and Charles Burns's *Big Baby* (1986) about an odd-looking suburban child who lives in fear of monsters and Jerry Moriarty's *Jack Survives* (1985), which had an acetate cover in which the colour slid out. There were also two books by illustrator Sue Coe: *How to Commit Suicide in South Africa* (1983), an anti-apartheid

This page and over: Britain's answer to *Raw* was *Escape*, another groundbreaking anthology. (All Escape Books and Graphics.) Above left: Cover to the first issue (1983). Art: Phil Elliott. Above right: Cover (1984). Art: Hunt Emerson. Right: Panels from 'Big Ideas' (1985). Art/script: Lynda Barry. *Escape* leant more towards home-grown cartoonists, but included a significant quantity of outlandish strips from America and Europe. Over: Pages from 'Calculus Cat' (1984). Art/script: Hunt Emerson. Like *Raw*, *Escape* always found room for ex-underground creators. Which was just as well, because Emerson was currently producing some of his best work.

Stanbury in 1983, and although certain aspects were very similar to *Raw*, there were important differences. The designer aesthetic was still a feature, though *Escape* was far less gimmicky (for one thing, it did not have *Raw*'s budget); it too mixed old underground creators with new home-grown talent, and with European work – though with more emphasis on the latter than *Raw* was prepared to give. Finally, there was a 'fanzine' aspect to *Escape* that was absent in *Raw*: reviews and interviews were a feature from the start.

Thus, the self-styled 'Comics Magazine of Style and Vision' made no apologies for publishing many of the same names as *Raw* (Mark Beyer, Gary Panter, Charles Burns, Lynda Barry, Ben Katchor, Javier Mariscal, Jacques Tardi and Joost Swarte), but the real interest was in the material that was unique. The main star from the former underground was Hunt Emerson, whose 'Calculus Cat' strips were as wild as anything he had produced before; Brian Bolland was another creator who had started his career in that period, and here returned to his roots with the Crumbesque 'Mr Mamoulian', about an ageing introvert and his troubles with women (about as different from 'Judge Dredd', with whom Bolland was then associated, as could be imagined).

The new British names kept pace quite admirably, and included: Ed Pinsent, responsible for the mesmerizing 'Primitif', about a tribal warrior and his battles with nature and the gods, drawn in an 'avant-primitive' style with narrative captions; Tim Budden, who produced claustrophobic tales about a group of weary badgers, and their problems with humankind (including, ultimately,

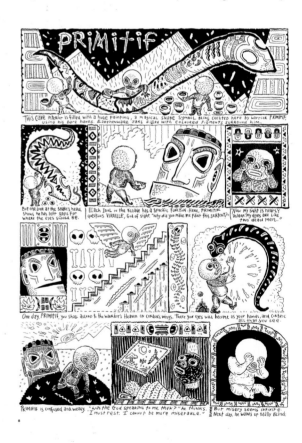

their fate during a nuclear war); Carol Swain, whose charcoal-rendered slice-of-life stories were as vivid as they were affecting; and Savage Pencil, whose jagged, spontaneous style perfectly captured the punk spirit. Other names included the Pleece Brothers, Phil Elliott, Chris Reynolds, John Bagnall, Bob Lynch and Julie Hollings.

Finally, the foreign strips included less familiar names, and drew especially from avant-garde work in France. Creators included: Serge Clerc, a humorist in the 'clear-line' tradition of Hergé; Jean-Claude Götting, master of atmospheric romantic psychodramas; Alex Varenne, who used delicately-rendered cityscapes as a background to rather obvious gags; and the pairing of Edmond Baudoin and Claude Gendrot, responsible for a strip about the dark side to sexual obsession.

The *Escape* one-shots were every bit as interesting as their *Raw* counterparts, although were rarely as expensively produced. The early ones especially were rough-and-ready, but made up for it with charm and energy. They included Phil Laskey's *Night of the Busted Nose* (1984), about love and punch-ups in a northern town, and *Alec* (1984), a brilliant semi-autobiographical account of bedsit life by Eddie Campbell. Later, Gravett and Stanbury followed Spiegelman and Mouly's example by courting more mainstream publishers, and subsequent one-shots were published by Titan Books. These were much more professional-looking productions, and included *Violent Cases* (1988) by Neil Gaiman and Dave McKean, who were soon to make big names for themselves in mainstream American comics; *Joe's Bar* (1988) by the South American pairing of José Munoz and Carlos Sampayo and *London's Dark* (1989) by James Robinson.

During the course of its existence, *Escape* went from a small A5 size to a larger square-bound magazine format, and eventually obtained a measure of news-stand

Above: Cover to the 'Escape one-shot' Violent Cases (Escape/Titan, 1987). Art: Dave McKean. Script: Neil Gaiman. A graphic novella about, among other things, the unreliability of memory and Al Capone's osteopath, that launched the careers of its creators. Above right and below: Cover and panels from Weirdo, the second great American anthology, which developed a personality that was more punky and free-spirited than Raw. (Both Last Gasp, 1986). Cover art: Robert Crumb, depicting disapproving yuppie 'Mode. O'Day'. 'The Schlep Set', art/script: Aline Kominsky, featuring husband Bob (Crumb) and daughter Sophie.

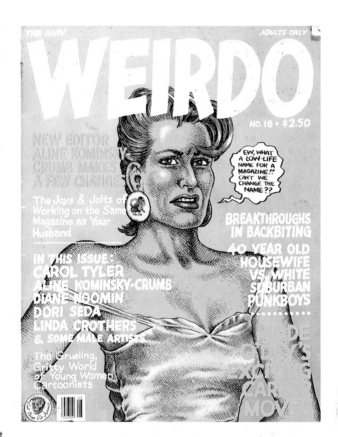

distribution. It would be as influential in Britain as *Raw* was in the US, though sales were never impressive: it was eventually cancelled in 1990. Nevertheless it succeeded in being the most progressive British comic to be seen since the underground.

If *Raw* and *Escape* were the 'cool and sophisticated' end of the anthology market in the 1980s, *Weirdo* (Last Gasp, 1981) was the complete opposite. Another American title, it was heir to the more spontaneous 'do what thou wilt' tradition of the underground, which segued perfectly with new punk attitudes. (Indeed, perhaps no comic of the period better reflected the punk worldview.) Originated by the great Robert Crumb, it too had room for veteran underground creators. They included Spain Rodriguez and Aline Kominsky (or rather, Aline Kominsky-Crumb, as she was by now the wife of the editor). The main emphasis, however, was on showcasing fledgling new creators. Thus, the world was introduced to the side-splittingly bitter comedy of JD King and Peter Bagge, and to a roster of new female creators, most notably Dori Seda and Phoebe Gluckner.

As for the contribution of Crumb himself, this was truly remarkable. He seemed to feed off the energy of the younger cartoonists, and went through something of a creative renaissance. He was no longer taking LSD, and was drawing in a much more realistic style: among his best *Weirdo* strips were 'Trash: What Do We Throw Away?', an ecological protest about the amount of unnecessary garbage produced by American economy, which ended with a pointedly disgusting depiction of a ravaged Mother Earth; 'Mode O'Day', an acid comment on the advent of the 1980s yuppie; and 'Uncle Bob's Midlife Crisis', an autobiographical piece about 'growing up' and having children, told in typically self-loathing fashion.

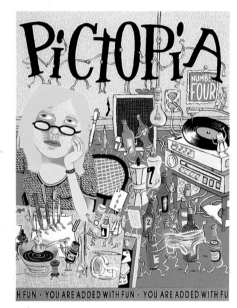

These three magazines (*Raw*, *Escape* and *Weirdo*) in particular heralded a golden age of new anthologies which blossomed into the 1990s. In America, Fantagraphics took up the torch with a number of exciting titles: *Prime Cuts* (1987), *Graphic Story Monthly* (1970), *Honk* (1987), *Snake Eyes* (1991) and *Pictopia* (1991), to name but a few. Other publishers too were important: Drawn and Quarterly's *Drawn and Quarterly* (1992), from Montreal, and Kitchen Sink's *Blab!* (1986), a digest-sized annual, were especially good; and so too was Dark Horse's *Dark Horse Presents (1986)*, which ambitiously mixed work by alternative folk like Eddie Campbell with that of mainstream creators like Frank Miller. In Britain, the anthology tradition tended to be taken up on the news-stands with publications like *Deadline* and *Heartbreak Hotel* (already dealt with on pp 142–5), though some, like *Inkling* (Inkling Inc, 1989) and *Purr* (Blue Eyed Dog, 1993), made an impact in the fan shops. Speaking in overall terms about the quality of these anthologies, it is fair to say that individual issues stand with the great undergrounds as some of the finest adult comics ever published.

On the shelves alongside them, the genres of alternative comics were split into fiction and non-fiction. There were five basic sub-categories in the former: humour (by far the biggest), soap opera, science fiction fantasy, horror and sex. The humour comics were extremely varied, and, in general, built on the formulas developed by the underground. But beyond being satirical to varying degrees, there was no 'party line'. Creators took their own path, and this commonly meant a style of humour that was unprecedentedly bitter, angry and offbeat: 'alienated comedy' would probably be a good description. Three prime examples of such creators were the Canadian Chester Brown and the Americans Peter Bagge and Dan Clowes.

Chester Brown's *Yummy Fur* (Vortex, 1986) was a consistently innovative title. The lead story in the early issues was 'Ed the Happy Clown', about a passive

Above: Two more notable anthologies from the 1990s, heirs to the *Raw/Weirdo* tradition. Top and above right: Pages and cover from *Pictopia* (Fantagraphics, 1993). Art/script for both: Julie Doucet. Above left: Cover to *Drawn and Quarterly* (Drawn and Quarterly, 1990). Art: Anne Bernstein. Right: Humour comics were the biggest single genre in the alternative world. Here, two examples with art/script by Chester Brown: panel from the graphic novel *Ed the Happy Clown* (Vortex, 1989) and cover from *Yummy Fur* (Vortex, 1989). The hero of both comics, the eponymous Ed, was not actually very happy at all, and prone to appalling misfortunes.

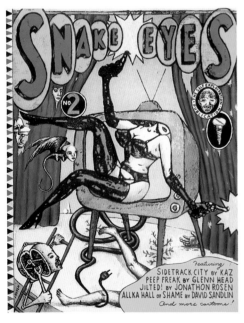

ingénue who suffers the most appalling humiliations and injuries. In various surrealistic episodes, he breaks his legs, is chased by cannibalistic pygmies, is beaten up and is sexually mutilated. He ends up an emotional and physical husk. Appalling though this may sound, it is also utterly hilarious: the more excruciating poor Ed's predicament, the funnier it is. The word 'schadenfreude' could have been invented for this strip, and the reader's response is a mix of belly laughs and cringing guilt. Brown manipulates this contradiction with knowing skill, and his artwork adds to the unsettling tone: the characters have thin bodies and big heads, and panels are spread out over pitch-black backgrounds. The result is a uniquely amusing and disturbing read.

Brown had appeared in various anthologies as well as *Yummy Fur*, most memorably in *Escape*, and had increasingly experimented with drawing on the darker areas of his subconscious, basing his comedy on free-form association. He explained later that, 'the Ed story came automatically, without any thought'.[5] This is undoubtedly what gives his work a nightmare-like quality, emphasized by the unworldly art. In Brown's world, however insane the turn of events, everything seems sinisterly normal. This tone could be perfect for bizarre comedy, but later, as we shall see, he would take *Yummy Fur* in more serious directions.

Peter Bagge was the second of the comedy masters,

This page: Examples by Peter Bagge. Above: Covers to *Neat Stuff* (both Fantagraphics, 1985). Bagge's first hit solo comic. Right: Advert for videos by 'grunge' bands on the Sub-Pop label (1993). Punk's influence was always evident in the artist's work, and he was often asked to produce illustrations like this. Below: Pages from 'The Bradleys', *Neat Stuff* (Fantagraphics, 1989). About a suburban family who spend their time finding out each other's psychic pressure points, and poking at them with a metaphorical sharp stick.

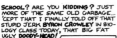

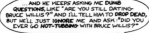

Detail from *Neat Stuff* (Fantagraphics, 1985). Art: Peter Bagge. The distortion of characters into wild shapes became a Bagge trademark.

and was responsible for two outstanding titles. The first was *Neat Stuff* (Fantagraphics, 1985), which featured a lead story about a dysfunctional family, the Bradleys, and their efforts to get along with each other in small-town suburbia. The satire was based on close observation of family dynamics and interpersonal relationships: when tensions erupt to the surface, faces become distorted into spike-toothed demons, while the air turns blue with the vilest of expletives. The publisher's blurb had more than a grain of truth: 'The only people who don't like *Neat Stuff* are those who are afraid they might recognise themselves in its pages.'

Bagge's second comic, *Hate* (Fantagraphics, 1990), was a bigger hit commercially, and followed the story of one member of the Bradley family, twenty-something slob Buddy. The humour was more brutal if anything, gleefully un-politically correct, with more emphasis on sex, drugs and rock 'n' roll. Buddy is most at home with his old records and comics, but has more trouble relating to his friend Stinky (another slob, and a member of a terrible punk band), and to the various women he hitches up with. The tenor of the comedy in the early issues can be gauged from an episode in which Buddy is accused of sodomizing a girlfriend while shoving her head down the toilet: all he can say is, 'Must have been one of those nights when I was on a bender ... the greatest moment of my life, and I don't even remember it!!!'

Bagge too had appeared in various anthologies, and pre-*Neat Stuff* had done a stint editing *Weirdo*. His love of underground comics and affinity with punk were the main influences on his work , and critics have traced his studied nihilism to these roots.[6] *Neat Stuff* and *Hate* were an expression of this, and because they happened to be set in Seattle, came to be seen as part of the post-punk 'grunge' movement. (On one cover to a *Hate* collection, Buddy is pictured with a Nirvana sleeve under his arm, while Bagge also produced various record covers for local bands such as Tad.) The creator later explained his attitude thus: 'I felt if I tried to be more idealistic as opposed to being nihilistic, I'd be a phony. So I figured there were bound to be people like me who are going to be shocked and disgusted by whatever it is that the people who are going to save society are going to shove down our throats. I'm getting on what I perceive to be an alternative bandwagon. There's always plenty to hate.'[7]

Dan Clowes completed the triumvirate of alternative comic comedians, and produced a brace of titles that were worthy of note. *Lloyd Llewellyn* (Fantagraphics, 1986) featured the adventures of a perpetually bemused sleuth, who navigates through a hyper-real version of the early 1960s (a sort of *Dragnet* on acid), and was a minor hit. *Eightball* (Fantagraphics, 1990) had more widespread success, and was an anthology in which 'Lloyd Llewellyn' appeared as one strip. Other, much funnier, additions included 'Young Dan Pussey', a bitter, hilarious satire of the comics industry; 'Like a Velvet Glove Cast in Iron', a bizarre mystery serial, crackling with sexual terror; and 'Duplex Planet', a semi-documentary strip based on the

This page: Examples from Bagge's more recent title, *Hate* (Fantagraphics). Above: Cover (1991). Right: Pages (1990). Here, the appalling Buddy Bradley (a leftover from *Neat Stuff*) and his even more appalling friend Stinky have one of their frequent 'physical discussions'. No comic better captured the absurdities of twenty-something slacker existence.

200

This page: Examples from *Eightball* (Fantagraphics) by Dan Clowes, one of the most successful alternative comics. Appealingly drawn in a 'retro' style, it is part freak-show, part nightmare, and part conventional comedy. Above: Panel from 'The Death of Dan Pussey' (1994), a savage satire of the comics industry. Above right, right, and far right: Covers (1989, 1991 and 1993).

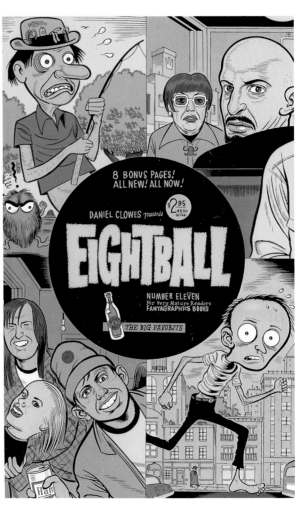

This page: More *Eightball* (all Fantagraphics). Top and left: Pages and panel from 'Like a Velvet Glove Cast in Iron' (1990, 1993), a bizarre, sexually intense, fever dream. Above: Panel from 'Duplex Planet' (1989), with dialogue recorded at an old folks home: the question posed was 'What is the most important invention of the 20th century?'. Opposite: Page from 'Mechanix', *Love and Rockets* (Fantagraphics, 1982). Art/script: Jaime Hernandez. This early example from the hippest comic of the 1980s features a typical moment in the relationship between Maggie and Hopey, plus the appearance of a hover-bike at the end (the SF elements were soon dropped).

utterances of senile occupants of an old folks home. All these were rendered in a meticulously 'clean' fashion; the artwork was detached, but never cold, and the cumulative effect was something analogous to the early movies of David Lynch.

Clowes was clearly another creator for whom anger was an energy: in one of his best *Eightball* strips, 'I Hate You Deeply', he simply lists everyone and everything that annoys him. However, unlike Bagge, he was prepared to explore more abstract territory. He has summed up his approach by saying: 'On the one hand, I'm trying to step into my own subconscious and trying to see what images and ideas excite me and scare me and affect me emotionally ... And I'm also trying to write an honest narrative, a narrative that works by its own rules ... I'm just trying to let the characters be themselves and do whatever they would do, and not really control them. Just let them act according to their own humanity – or lack thereof. And then, on some level, it's kind of a social satire, a comment on the way I see the world in my bleakest moments.'[8]

Finally, it's impossible to talk about humour comics without mentioning the titles being put out by the 'first wave' of underground creators who had continued to keep working when that movement had died down. Foremost among them, as ever, was Robert Crumb, who used his new comics to delve ever deeper into his psyche. They included *Hup* (Last Gasp, 1987), *ID* (Fantagraphics, 1990) and *Self-Loathing Comics* (Fantagraphics, 1995). More successfully from a sales point of view, Gilbert Shelton continued to produce stories starring the Freak Brothers, who after twenty years of social change did not look a day older, and who remained obsessed with drugs. In the extended 1985 story *Idiots Abroad* (Rip Off), the brothers go to Colombia to score an entire bale of top-quality weed: even in the 1980s, it seemed (to adapt their catchphrase) dope could get them through times of no money better than money could get them through times of no dope. Finally, British madman Hunt Emerson experimented with a number of comedy graphic novels based loosely on works of literature: they included a slapstick version of the banned DH Lawrence novel, *Lady Chatterley's Lover*; *The Rime of the Ancient Mariner*, a full-colour homage-cum-send-up of the Coleridge poem; and *Casanova's Last Stand*, based on the great lover's diaries (all Knockabout, 1986, 1990 and 1993 respectively).

The soap-opera genre was also a lively area, and produced one stone-cold classic: *Love and Rockets* (Fantagraphics, 1982). Produced by two brothers, Jaime and Gilbert Hernandez, it featured two continuing main stories, one set in post-punk Los Angeles (by Jaime) and one in a mythical village called 'Palomar' in Mexico (by Gilbert). Although their drawing styles were very different (Jaime's economic outlines were a world away from Gilbert's curvy kinetics), the brothers' work had much in common, and they certainly borrowed ideas from each other. For example, both stories featured a large cast of characters, and both featured women in central roles: similarly, the depth of characterization in both was

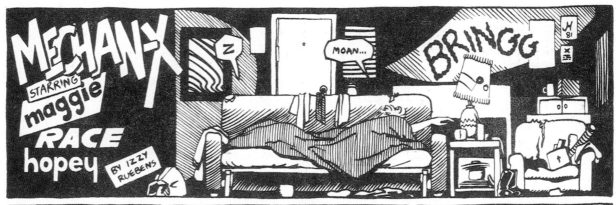

GOODY... TIME FOR WORK... I'LL PROBABLY BE LATE AGAIN... MR. GHOUL WILL YELL THE EYES OFF ME... EMBARRASS ME IN FRONT OF THE OTHER WORKERS... BUT, WHO CARES? HA HA... OHH...

MAGGIE! WHAT ARE YOU DOING?

GOING TO WORK, HOPEY...

WORK? NOW? SHIT, YOU JUST GOT TO BED TWO FUCKING HOURS AGO! YOU CAN'T GO TO WORK LIKE THIS!

BUT, I GOTTA GO TO WORK...

HOPEY! LEGGO! I GOTTA GO TO WORK! THEY NEED ME... THEY... MY HEAD... I THINK I DRANK TOO MUCH LAST NIGHT! OHH...

LOOK AT YOURSELF, MAGGOT! I'LL BET YOU WOULDN'T EVEN MAKE IT TO THE BUS STOP! C'MON! SLEEP SOME...

BUT, I JUST GOTTA GO TO WORK! I DON'T WANNA GET FIRED! THIS IS MY THIRD JOB THIS MONTH! OOH... LOOK AT THE BAGS UNDER MY EYES... I'M FAT AGAIN... AND MY HAIR... ICK!

COULDN'T YOU SKIP AT LEAST ONE DAY?

I'VE ALREADY SKIPPED TOO MANY DAYS! OOH, I CAN'T STAND THIS SHITTY JOB! I CAN'T STAND ANY OF MY STALE JOBS! I HATE DOING STUFF I CAN'T DO!

MAGGIE! SOMETIMES YOU'RE SO DAMN STUPID IT'S PITIFUL! WHY DON'T YOU GO BACK TO YOUR MECHANIX JOB? THAT'S WHAT YOU'RE BEST AT!

YOU CAN FIX ANYTHING! WHO KNOWS, MAYBE ONE DAY YOU'LL EVEN BECOME A PROSOLAR MECHANIC! JUST LIKE RAND RACE, YOU'LL GET A MILLION BONES FOR ONLY FIXING THE KING OF ZHATO'S HEARING AID! THEN, YOU COULD BECOME A RICH, FAT SLOB!

I NEED A HAIRCUT! WILL YOU CUT MY HAIR, HOPEY? I NEED ONE AWFUL BAD!

FRAM DAMN IT! OK! IF I CUT YOUR FUCKIN' HAIR, WILL YOU QUIT PLAYING YOUR SILLY-ASS GAMES AND GO BACK TO BEING A MECHANIC? HUH? TODAY? OKAY?!!

OK! OK! I'LL DO IT! JUST GET OFF! YEOW!

HOPEY, THAT SLUT! I TOLD HER, OVER AND OVER, "DON'T CUT IT TOO SHORT IN THE BACK! BUT NO, WHAT DOES SHE DO? NOW I LOOK MORE LIKE DEREK CINEMA THAN A FOTO MATE! OH WELL... NOW, AT LEAST I HAVE AN IMPORTANT JOB...

FIXING BROKEN EQUIPMENT ON THIS MILITARY BASE! ALAS, WE ALL GOTTA START ON THE BOTTOM! RIGHT NOW I HAVE TO WORK ON TAKYO WIRES! THAT'LL BE A CINCH!

COPYRIGHT © BY JAIME HERNANDEZ /'81

203

Right: Cover to the first issue of *Love and Rockets*. Art: Jaime Hernandez. Jaime's stories tended to be heavily punk-influenced. Far right: Panel from 'Farewell, My Palomar'. Art/script: Gilbert Hernandez. Gilbert's contributions were more serious in tone, and often set in the mythical Mexican village of Palomar. Below: Cover to the graphic novel of *Love and Rockets* (Fantagraphics, 1987). Bottom: Panel from *Downside* (Joint Productions, 1990). Art/script: Dave McNamara and Peter Ketley. A hard-hitting British variant on the political soap-opera theme, which ironically quoted Margaret Thatcher on the cover every issue ('Where there is discord, may we bring harmony').

outstanding, with constant shifts in perspective and time-frame (flashbacks and fast-forwards) adding believability. Although early plot lines had fantasy elements (hence the 'rockets' in the title), these gradually evaporated in favour of a more naturalistic approach, and subject matter tended to focus increasingly on the minutiae of love affairs. Like all good soaps, the effect was that the comic became unmissable, and it developed a healthy cult following.

Both the Hernandez brothers had punk connections, and had been involved with the scene in Southern California. In true punk spirit, they had taught themselves to draw, and then started to experiment with different kinds of storytelling. Jaime stuck with his roots, and populated his tales with struggling bands and cute punkettes; Gilbert, who went on to become by far the better writer, preferred to process his family history for his Palomar strips. As he said later: 'Sometimes my mother would be ironing or something, and she'd suddenly tell us a story about a jilted aunt or a drunk uncle or something. Things like that fascinated me. "Heartbreak Soup" [a Palomar strip] is in part a vehicle for those stories. Its cartooning style tries to make them closer to how they felt to me as a kid.'[9]

Britain also produced its share of soaps, and honourable mention should go to *Downside* (Macnamara and Ketley, 1988), which had more bite than most. Set in a future London denuded by years of uncaring govern-ment, a small group of squatters create their own culture in the last of the subsidized housing estates. Among them are single mothers, political activists, punks and people who just want to be left alone. The authorities, however, have other plans, and try to sell off the estate to developers. This is cue for much political heart-searching,

and violent confrontations with police. The story was hardly subtle in terms of characterization (the goodies are angels, and the baddies the spawn of the devil), but its class consciousness captured something of the spirit of the times.

Science fiction or fantasy was a more familiar comics genre, and in its alternative incarnation produced some remarkable offerings. It was particularly important in the early days of direct sales, because as well as appealing to comics fans, it succeeded in crossing over to those fans of prose fiction who also frequented the shops. Perhaps the biggest early hit was *Cerebus the Aardvark* (Aardvark-Vanaheim, 1977) by Dave Sim, which told the story of the adventures of a three-foot-tall aardvark, in a pseudo-medieval land populated by humans. It started out as a parody of Conan the Barbarian, but soon developed into something much more sophisticated. As Cerebus went from being a barbarian to kitchen-staff supervisor, to Prime Minister, to Pope, so the satire in the stories became ever more pointed, taking in some witty observations on politics and organized religion. The Cerebus saga has been subdivided into a number of graphic novels the size of telephone directories, and had been a pioneering work in terms of extended narratives.

Other kinds of science fiction fantasy were also popular. Three titles were particularly notable: *Elfquest* (Warp, 1979) by Wendy and Richard Pini, a Tolkienesque epic about magic and misdeeds among a community of elves; *Luther Arkwright* (Never Ltd, 1982) by Bryan Talbot, which appeared as a series of graphic novels developing the story initiated in British news-stand title *Near Myths* (see p. 137) and starring a Moorcock-style adventurer trying to avoid an English civil war in a parallel universe; and *Mr X* (Vortex, 1984) by the Hernandez brothers, the strange tale of a mysterious, speed-addicted architect and his visits to a futuristic city. In the 1990s, more contemporary themes took over, such as cyberpunk and dystopian eco-fiction.

The horror genre too had its place. The most outstanding title was *Taboo* (Spiderbaby Graphics, 1988), edited by Stephen Bissette, an anthology which promised to return horror comics to the 'forbidden' status they enjoyed in the 1950s. As such, its contents were gory and

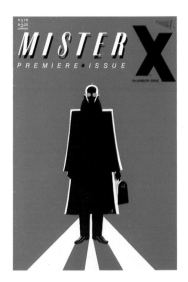

This page: Science fiction also had an alternative side. Above: Cover, *Mister X* (Vortex, 1984). Art: Dean Motter. In this first issue, the sinister bald hero returns to 'Somnopolis', the future city he has designed. Right: Pages from the graphic novel *Luther Arkwright* (Valkyrie, 1987). Art/script: Bryan Talbot. A tale postulating a future Britain in which the 'Puritan vs. Romanist' Civil War still rages. Below: Pages and panel from *Cerebus: Jaka's Story* (Aardvark-Vanaheim, both 1989). Art/script: Dave Sim. Cerebus the Aardvark (on the right) took a secondary role to the dancing Jaka in this richly-textured fantasy.

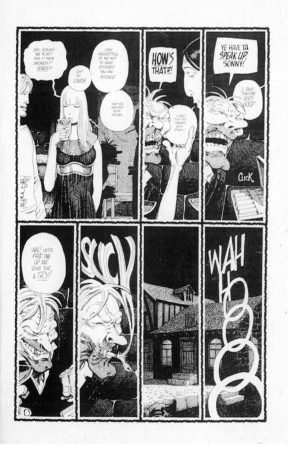

205

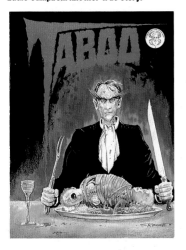

She wasn't at the hotel. But they said she may be with a fellow
reporter who lives in the area.
I found the house.
"Where is Sandy?" I asked. "She was here, had a few drinks
and left hours ago," replied her reporter friend.
And then I knew it was hopeless. People are what they are.
Nothing really changes. That old feeling was back.

Suddenly
I was a wild animal.
Chaotic pandemonium everywhere. The room exploded...
tables, chairs, everything was in orbit, CRASH BANG! I was dragging her across the floor...my blade seemed to be sucking
blood...slashing new orifices...in her eye...ribs...head...
Her inside was coming outside all over the floor...the walls...
the ceiling...

shocking, and in fact much closer to underground predecessors such as *Skull*. Contributors included a range of established alternative stars, such as Charles Burns and Eddie Campbell (whose 'Pyjama Girl' strip was a disturbing highlight), plus newer names on the alternative scene, such as Jeff Nicholson (whose 'Through the Habitrails', a Kafkaesque nightmare, became a reader favourite). These were complemented by work from old underground creators such as S Clay Wilson, Melinda Gebbie and the late Greg Irons, plus contributions from 'overground' names such as Clive Barker, Alan Moore and Neil Gaiman (whose 'Sweeney Todd' was a direct reference to the nineteenth-century British penny dreadful). Put together, this mix of styles and influences made for a substantial, and sometimes genuinely scary read.

Like the more conventional anthologies, *Taboo* spawned its own spin-off comics. The best was undoubtedly *From Hell* (Tundra, 1991), by Alan Moore and Eddie Campbell, which retold the story of the Jack the Ripper murders in London in the 1880s. Described by the author in its introduction as 'a post-mortem of an historical event, using fiction as a scalpel', it appeared as a series of graphic novels, and put the emphasis on characterization. 'Jack' himself is a mad medic obsessed with ancient ritual, who is wont to hold up handfuls of innards and say things like: 'Look! She's full of light!' More interestingly, the reader gets to know his victims – Mary Kelly, Liz Stride, et al. These are not just 'women in peril', but real people, with husbands, children and jobs to do. Which makes their ultimate fate all the more sickening.

The horror market also had its 'transgressive' end. That is to say, there were comics which were produced partly in the belief that being as extreme as possible had an aesthetic and creative value. They tapped into the vogue

Above: Cover to *Superfly* (self-published, 1993). Art: Mike Diana. One of many comics at the 'transgressive' end of the horror spectrum: the creator later became the first ever cartoonist to be jailed in America for their work. Below: Covers to two of the pioneering sex comics. Left: *Omaha the Cat Dancer* (Kitchen Sink, 1994). Art: Reed Waller. An anthropomorphic saga that included explicit scenes as a matter of course. Right: *Black Kiss* (Vortex, 1988). Art: Howard Chaykin. A porn title that set new standards in misogyny. These relatively restrained examples were followed by a 'smut glut' in the mid-1990s – and by an increasingly orchestrated censorship backlash.

for culture which 'transgressed a moral boundary'.[10] One such title was the collected work of *Taboo* contributor Joe Coleman, entitled *Cosmic Retribution* (Fantagraphics, 1993), which came complete with a cover-recommendation from Charles Manson. In it, intense, obsessive drawings complemented biblical quotations and densely-wrought prose yarns about murder, torture and horrendous retribution – with every wound, every degradation, lovingly depicted. The book established Coleman as an S Clay Wilson for the 1990s. Other transgressive material ranged from splatter-influenced superhero tales (*Faust*, Northstar, 1988) to extremist satire (*Lord Horror*, Savoy, 1989) to the self-published comics of Mike Diana (*Boiled Angel*, 1991; *Superfly*, 1994), which included meditations on child abuse and satanic sacrifice.

Finally, sex comics emerged as a recognizable genre, though they had no mainstream equivalents in the way that science fiction and horror did. They again traced their origins to the underground, and came to occupy a position in modern comics culture analogous to under-the-counter videos: they were usually sold pre-bagged and sometimes shrink-wrapped. The genre started to grow in the 1980s, but boomed in the early 1990s, as publishers initiated sex lines as a profitable way of supporting their other comics: such was the path taken by Fantagraphics and the 'Eros' imprint, Apple Press with 'Forbidden Fruit', and Slave Labor with their title *One Fisted Tales* (1992).

In terms of content, the sex titles ranged from risqué comedy to more serious porn: stories could be sophisticated, where the sex was simply part of a broader narrative, or calculating drivel, designed to get as many appendages into as many orifices as possible. Early hits included *Cherry Poptart* (Last Gasp, 1982) by Larry Welz, about a sparky blonde bimbo, and her humorous sexual encounters (the characters and settings were based on *Archie* comics, contrasting *Archie*-style innuendo with 'real' sex, and attracted numerous 'lawyer's letters' from the publisher of that title); and *Omaha the Cat Dancer* (Kitchen Sink, 1986), by Reed Waller and Kate Worley, an intelligently-plotted tale of a feline stripper – a sort of *Fritz the Cat* for the 1980s.

Later, the sex comics got uglier, a trend arguably started by the appearance of *Black Kiss* (Vortex) by Howard Chaykin, in 1988. Described by its creator in the introduction as 'carefree polymorphous promiscuity', with a mandate for 'sex, satanism and snappy repartee', it was in fact deeply misogynist. It was followed by other titles which featured violence against women as a matter of course: *Leather and Lace* (Aircel, 1989), featured rape for titillation, while *Scimidar* (Eternity, 1989), was described by one hardened reviewer as 'one of the nastiest comics I've ever seen'.[11] The 1990s saw less of this extreme material, but a parallel descent into pure smut: most notoriously, the Eros line featured such titles as *Wendy Whitebread, Undercover Slut* (1991), and *Time Wankers* (1990) – which, frankly, need no further explanation.

The non-fiction genres in alternative comics can be

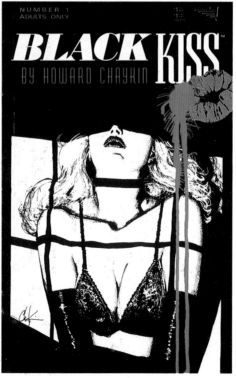

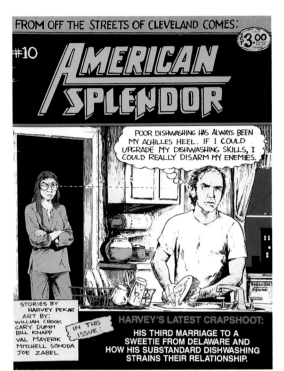

FROM OFF THE STREETS OF CLEVELAND COMES:

#10 $3.00

AMERICAN SPLENDOR

"POOR DISHWASHING HAS ALWAYS BEEN MY ACHILLES HEEL. IF I COULD UPGRADE MY DISHWASHING SKILLS, I COULD REALLY DISARM MY ENEMIES."

STORIES BY HARVEY PEKAR
ART BY:
WILLIAM CROOK
GARY DUMM
BILL KNAPP
VAL MAYERIK
MITCHELL SONODA
JOE ZABEL

IN THIS ISSUE!

HARVEY'S LATEST CRAPSHOOT:
HIS THIRD MARRIAGE TO A SWEETIE FROM DELAWARE AND HOW HIS SUBSTANDARD DISHWASHING STRAINS THEIR RELATIONSHIP.

This page: Autobiographical comics were unique to the alternatives, and grew to become a thriving sub-genre. Left: Cover, *American Splendor* (self-published, 1985). Art: Val Mayerik. Script: Harvey Pekar. A surprisingly riveting excursion into the minutiae of Pekar's life: this issue, 'His third marriage... and how his substandard dishwashing strains their relationship'. Below left: Page from 'Sexaholics Anonymous', *Drawn and Quarterly* (Drawn and Quarterly, 1990). Art: Joe Matt. Most autobiographical titles consisted of cringe-inducing admissions about their creators' sex lives – or lack of them: at least Matt had a sense of humour. Below right: Page from the graphic novel *The Playboy* (Drawn and Quarterly, 1992). Art/script: Chester Brown. A story less about sex than about guilt.

divided into autobiography, biography and political documentary. Taking autobiography first, we can say that the form was closely linked to the humour comics because stories tended to be told in an amusing way: the roots of the genre can be traced to underground 'confessionals' by the likes of Robert Crumb and Justin Green. Beyond this, however, titles were as idiosyncratic as their creators. Readers either loved them for being revealing, or reviled them for being navel-gazing and self-obsessed. As ever, certain creators were outstanding, and along with the previously discussed Art Spiegelman (*Maus*) and Eddie Campbell (*Alec*), four are worth singling out.

Harvey Pekar was perhaps the king of the autobiographers. In his comic *American Splendor* (self-published, 1976) he collaborated with different artists on stories recreating incidents from his life – the more mundane the better. These often involved episodes from work (he had a day-job as a clerk and porter in a Cleveland hospital), and relied for their effect on a sense of pacing and an ear for speech patterns – though Pekar often contrived to give them a left-wing political spin. The results ranged from the enlightening, to the hilarious, to the regrettably superfluous. The uneven tone was rendered more erratic by the changing roster of artists, who ranged from the excellent (Robert Crumb) to the appalling. Nevertheless, when Pekar was on song, there was nobody to touch him, and he could fulfil his own estimation of himself as an authentic 'voice of the common man'.

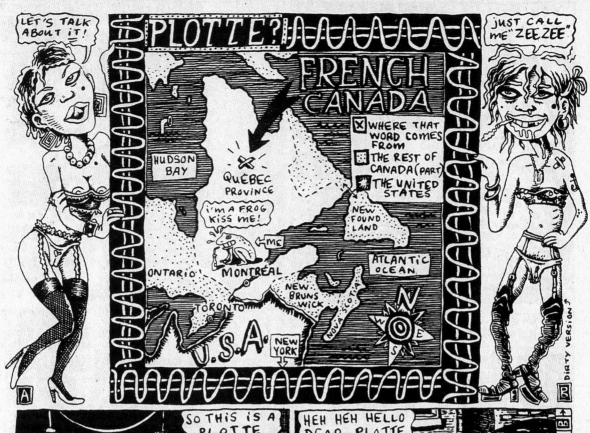

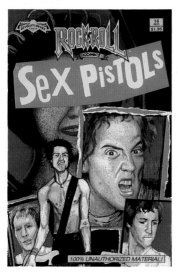

Although *American Splendor* had technically been going since 1976, Pekar only became widely known in the 1980s when his stories were collected into trade paperbacks and graphic novels. Indeed, for a while, he became a minor celebrity, with appearances on the David Letterman TV chat show. (These in turn became source material for subsequent comics.) In the 1990s, his life was blighted by cancer: his struggle back to health, aided by his wife, was related in the graphic novel *Our Cancer Year* (Four Walls, Eight Windows, 1995), drawn by Frank Stack, a moving and typically unsentimental account.

Chester Brown has already been mentioned in the context of comedy comics, but was also a fine autobiographer. In the 1990s editions of *Yummy Fur*, he experimented with highly structured narratives about his childhood and teen years, focusing especially on the legacy of a religious upbringing. In one story, he recounted with disarming frankness the relationship he developed with *Playboy* magazine, and the enormous guilt this caused him. In another, he recreated aspects of his angst-ridden school days, picturing himself as a painfully shy youth who cannot deal with girls, not least because his home life was so difficult (his mother was simultaneously suffering from mental illness). These tales were eventually collected as the graphic novels, *The Playboy* (Drawn and Quarterly, 1992) and *I Never Liked You* (Drawn and Quarterly, 1994), and worked magnificently in this form.

Joe Matt's work was similarly unflinching. In his

Peepshow (Drawn and Quarterly, 1992), he presented himself in an almost wilfully unflattering light: self-obsessed, hyperactive, paranoid and addicted to masturbation. ('Life isn't a fairy tale', the Matt character says at one point, 'and I'm not some two-dimensional Prince Charming!') He also claimed to be a 'sexaholic' with violent tendencies, and in one story admits to giving his girlfriend a black eye. This dark self-analysis was complemented by the obsessively detailed artwork, which sometimes packed a large number of panels on to one page. Whether *Peepshow* could be counted as an enjoyable reading experience or not (and often it was – some strips were very funny), Matt should be credited for challenging the conventions of autobiographical comics, and their tendency to self-aggrandise: by forcing readers to come to their own conclusions, he has carved himself a unique niche in the market.

Finally, Julie Doucet took the kind of women's autobiography pioneered by undergrounds like *Wimmin's Comix* into uncharted waters. Her *Dirty Plotte* (Drawn and Quarterly, 1991) was a hilarious, melancholic and disturbing odyssey through her everyday life, and took in the boredom of living alone, troubles with men, misadventures with tampons, and thoughts on breast cancer. There were also a number of stories about violent sex, and sexual mutilation: indeed, Doucet's fondness for knives, scissors and razors was guaranteed to provoke recessed testicles in male readers. These vignettes were illustrated in a dark, but somehow innocent rendering style, which was much influenced by Chester Brown, while the dialogue was in an appealing form of broken English – a reflection of her French Canadian background. Altogether, it made for a wittily original comic.

Biographical titles were less evident on the alternative racks, but nevertheless produced some impressive entries, ranging from historical studies to contemporary hagiographies. The best examples of the former were Jack Jackson's *Comanche Moon* (Last Gasp, 1978), about Comanche leader Quanah Parker and *Los Tejanos* (Fantagraphics, 1982), about Texan freedom fighter Juan Seguin. Both comics were remarkable works of realism, presented in a quasi-photographic style, and were accompanied by documentary evidence and full bibliographies. As one commentator wrote of them: 'An alternative writing of American history demands an alternative narrative medium, and the suppressed stories of minority figures such as Quanah Parker and Juan Seguin find an appropriate home in the culturally marginalised form of comic books.'[12] The latter kind of biography was probably best exemplified by the series of unauthorized profiles of rock bands and rock stars put out by Revolutionary Comics, entitled Rock N' Roll Comics (1989), which included *Jimi Hendrix, Prince, Alice Cooper* and others.

The new political titles only differed from the old 'committed' undergrounds such as *Slow Death* and *Anarchy* insofar as the causes they espoused had moved on. Vietnam had ended, but there were new wars to protest against – particularly the Falklands and the Gulf.

Similarly, the fear of atomic war decreased with the collapse of Eastern bloc communism: now, the destruction of the planet's resources came more to the fore. Finally, the movements for women's, black and gay rights moved into new areas of debate, and were fortified by having to face the challenge of a post-1980 backlash against the advances they had made in the 1960s and 1970s.

The contribution of one-shot comics was particularly significant, acting as concentrated bursts of agit-prop. Of the many examples, some were outstanding: *Strip AIDS* (Last Gasp/Willyprods, 1987) was the best of many titles protesting against government apathy towards the AIDS epidemic, while at the same time seeking to raise awareness; *Aargh!* (Mad Love, 1988) was an acronym for Artists Against Rampant Government Homophobia, and was brought out to protest new anti-gay legislation in Britain; *El Salvador: a House Divided* (Eclipse, 1989) chronicled the savage conflict in that country, and exposed American backing of the military regime there; *Brought to Light* (Eclipse, 1989) focused on the Irangate scandal, and featured some powerful graphics from Bill Sienkiewicz.

Continuing titles, too, made an impact. The best included *World War 3 Illustrated* (self-published, 1980), which lived up to its subtitle of 'Confrontational Comics' with some hard-hitting punk-influenced work by unknown names such as Peter Kuper, Seth Tobocman and others; *Real War Stories* (Eclipse, 1987), which looked deceptively like conventional adventure comics but which in fact carried anti-war messages in the form of documentary-style 'real' accounts; and *Palestine* (Fantagraphics, 1993), a frightening, moving and even-

handed piece of reportage by Joe Sacco from the troubles in the Arab Israeli Occupied Territories. Finally, there were a number of feminist examples, including *Girlfrenzy* (self-published, 1992), which amusingly reflected the angry attitude of the British 'riot grrl' scene; and the 'Fanny' line, an imprint of Knockabout Comics, which included individual angry rants against women's place

in organized religion (*Immaculate Deception*, 1992), and issues of sexism surrounding sex (*Voyeuse*, 1991).

That wraps things up in terms of the different genres encompassed by the alternative comics. However, there was one more final dimension to the scene that remains worthy of mention: the small press. This was a thriving do-it-yourself industry comprising of comics with very small print-runs: anything from tens to thousands, but usually in the low hundreds. Appearing in the wake of the punk fanzine explosion of the late 1970s, early small press comics tended to be photocopied and very rough-and-ready (the more ambitious stretched to using inked-roller duplicators). Completely non-commercial, they were generally produced with little investment, and mostly lost money (the parallels with the early history of the underground are clear): selling was a problem, and although some kindly comic shop owners allowed them shelf-space, many small press publishers were forced to trade by post.

In the later 1980s and 1990s, the small press became more sophisticated. The key to this was better organization, with special conventions and fanzines devoted to the scene. There were even small press 'star' creators. Also, with improvements in Desk Top Publishing, and a decrease in the price of printing, small scale comics took on a more professional appearance: now, square-bound titles with glossy covers became common. By 1995, the press even had a manifesto: 'Why self-publish?
• If no one else will publish your work, you can do it yourself.
• Free yourself from commercial constraints.
• You can justify your empty existence with a creative hobby.
• You have 100% control.
• You can say what you want when you want.
• It's the ultimate freedom of speech, for now, anyway.'[13]

Despite the small press' ephemeral nature, it proved a superb training ground for future professional comics creators. In Britain, perhaps the most famous of these were Eddie Campbell and the Donald brothers (*Viz*). In America and Canada, Chester Brown, Julie Doucet, Joe Matt, the Hernandezes, Peter Laird and Kevin Eastman (*Teenage Mutant Ninja Turtles*) and many more started from these roots. Which is not to say, of course, that the small press is simply a 'feed farm' for bigger publishers. It has retained its own integrity (as expressed in the manifesto), and there have always been small pressers who insist that they would not work professionally even if they had the chance.

So, taking the alternative sector as a whole, there was thus a remarkable diversity of subject matter, and an equally remarkable level of creative liberty. Yet there was a price to pay. Just as the underground had provoked the ire of the establishment, so too did the alternatives, and censorship became ever more intense. The backlash was sustained by the fact that politically both the USA and Britain were in the grip of a swing to the right. In the 1980s and 1990s, the policies of Reagan and Bush were echoed by those of Thatcher and Major, all supported by an overwhelmingly right-wing media. At the same time, the hardline evangelist Christian right was exerting ever more influence, and in America, the so-called 'moral majority' initiated a 'crusade' against popular culture, which took in records, videos, books, and, crucially, comics.

Mainstream and alternative titles were attacked, but it was the alternative comics that caught the brunt. They were vilified in a fashion that had not been seen since the height of the underground: their sexual and violent content was sensationalised, while their creators were portrayed as 'barbarians at the gates'. Newspapers and magazines reproduced panels out of context, Wertham-

This page: More political titles. Above and right: Cover and page from *Palestine* (Fantagraphics, 1993). Art/script: Joe Sacco. A remarkable piece of comics journalism, taking the reader to the front line of the Arab-Israeli conflict in East Jerusalem; its verite style was in some ways a return to pre-camera eye-witness illustrations in Victorian news magazines. Far right: Pages from 'Siege', *World War 3 Illustrated* (self-published, 1990). Art/script: Seth Tobocman. A 'historical fiction' about a squatters' revolt.

style, and went to town on shock headlines. Once again, the old Mcguffin that the comics were 'dangerous' because children might get hold of them was wheeled out.[14]

The outcry was followed by the inevitable busts on both sides of the Atlantic. In Britain, Knockabout Comics became the subject of the attentions of police and customs on numerous occasions. In 1982, they were cleared at the Old Bailey after police seized drugs-related titles; in 1996, they were again cleared in court, this time of an obscenity charge relating to comics by Robert Crumb. Similarly, Savoy Comics were subject to continual harrassment, and had various of their horror titles declared obcene and destroyed.[15] Additionally, numerous British shops and importers were raided. In America, the pattern was replicated, sometimes with even more serious consequences. In 1995, Mike Diana had the dubious distinction of becoming the first cartoonist ever to be imprisoned for obscenity, when his comics were confiscated in Florida.[16]

How could the producers of alternative comics cope? The short answer was, they couldn't. Legal defence funds were set up, and angry articles were published in the fan press. But ultimately, it was a losing battle, and as the underground had discovered twenty years before, the costs of defiance were simply too great. Therefore, self-censorship became an inevitable necessity. Publishers increasingly refrained from putting out strong material, while distributors and shop owners cancelled their orders of comics which might offend. One publisher summed up the situation when he said: 'I think it's always a good idea, when you have right-wingers on a roll, to cover your backside'.[17]

The backlash was further proof, if it were needed, that comics were still not accepted by society at large as an artform with the same rights to freedom of expression as other artforms. Almost all of the material objected to would have gone unremarked if it had appeared in a novel, and while much of it might arguably have been indefensible on aesthetic grounds, it was clear that the official limits of creative endeavour did not stretch as far for comics as they did for other media. The fact that the complaints were of the same nature as those made against comics at earlier points in history, showed how little had changed. Further, the fact that the clampdown should have arrived at the same time when comics were reaching a pinnacle of artistic and literary achievement was the ultimate irony.

Crumb cartoons cleared after 'preposterous' obscenity case

Duncan Campbell
Crime Correspondent

THE work of Robert Crumb, one of America's most celebrated cartoonists, was yesterday cleared of all charges of obscenity and passed for sale in the United Kingdom.

In a decision welcomed by comic booksellers and lawyers, Uxbridge magistrates in west London ruled that two frames from an 80-page comic book, My Troubles with Women, were not obscene and the book could therefore be sold in this country. Three other adult comic books were also cleared for importation.

Costs of £6,000, seen as remarkably high for a one-day hearing, were awarded to the distributors and importers of the books, Knockabout Comics of west London.

"This is a very good day for underground comics," said Tony Bennett of Knockabout after the verdict. "I'm absolutely delighted."

The decision came after a day-long hearing before three lay magistrates, two male and one female, after an action brought by Customs and Excise under the 1876 Customs Consolidation Act.

Customs had claimed that the book, and two Zap Comics and the Twisted Sisters, should not be sold here. Knockabout argued that the books were neither pornographic nor obscene, and were widely regarded as works of art.

Crumb — the creator of cartoon characters Fritz the Cat and Mr Natural — was the subject of a well-received eponymous documentary film, directed by Terry Zwigoff, which came out last year. He has enjoyed cult status in the United States and Europe since the 1960s and now lives in France with his wife and fellow cartoonist Aline Kominsky. Some stories in My Troubles with Women feature both Crumbs, each drawing themselves.

Paul Gravett, administrator of the Cartoon Art Trust, whose president is the Duke of Edinburgh, told the court that Crumb's work was in the tradition of Hogarth and Rowlandson and that he was one of the most important cartoonists of the last 25 years.

William Thompson, of the criminology department of Reading university, and an expert in obscenity laws, defended Crumb's work, saying he used it in his lectures.

Counsel for Knockabout, Geoffrey Robertson QC, a veteran of obscenity trials involving underground literature, said the action had been "preposterous".

After the verdict, Knock-about's solicitor, Bill Nash, said: "It amazes me that, in this day and age, art books like this are being seized. It's a very good result."

Mr Bennett said the seizure of the books had cost his firm £35,000 to £40,000 in lost profits. He would not be suing Customs, he said, but hoped that the "climate can now return to normal. It is a very important decision."

My Troubles with Women had previously been sold without any problems in Britain after it was first published here in 1990. A fresh importation of the book in 1995 was seized.

Previously Customs officers had accepted that the comics should not be classified as obscene, but last year this policy suddenly changed.

Customs and Excise had no comment last night.

A Crumb cartoon from his book My Troubles With Women

Left: Press cutting from *The Guardian* (1996) reporting the favourable outcome of the 'Crumb trial', and the judge's comment that the case was 'preposterous'. Nevertheless, the fact that it had been brought at all was evidence of a mounting establishment counter-offensive against alternative comics.

1. Peter Bagge, interview in *The Comics Journal*, no 159, May 1993, p 88.

2. *Funny Aminal* (sic), published in 1972 (Apex Novelties).

3. Richard Haynes, 'Caught in the Maus Trap' (*The Guardian*, 29 August 1987).

4 Dale Luciano, review of *Raw*, *The Comics Journal*, no 119, Jan 1988, p 40.

5. Chester Brown, quoted in an interview with Jay Torres, *Comics Interview*, no 93, June 1991, p 31.

6. Bagge had submitted strips to John Holmstrom's seminal *Punk* magazine, but it had gone out of business before they appeared. He then joined with Holmstrom to publish *Comical Funnies*, a small-scale comic-cum-fanzine with a punk orientation, in 1980.

7. Peter Bagge, quoted in 'Bagge to the Future: an Interview with America's Funniest Cartoonist.', *Amazing Heroes*, no 178, April 1990, p 56.

8. Dan Clowes, interviewed by Gary Groth, *The Comics Journal*, no 154, November 1992, p 76.

9. Gilbert Hernandez, quoted in 'Los Bros Locos', by Steve Beard and Jim McLellan, *The Face*, vol 2, no 1, 1988.

10. 'Transgressive culture' is a loose term that came to prominence in the early 1990s. It has its roots in the 'cinema of transgression', an art-punk film movement based in New York. Later, it became associated with magazines that dealt with the extremes of human experience. Examples of such publications in Britain included *Headpress* and *Divinity*.

11. Martin Skidmore, review of *Scimidar* 1, in *FA* magazine, no 111, May 1989, p 15.

12. Joseph Witek, *Comic Books as History: The Narrative Art of Jack Jackson, Art Spiegelman, and Harvey Pekar* (University Press of Mississippi, 1989), p 92.

13. *Small Press Manifesto*, displayed as part of the exhibition 'Cartoon Stripped', UK Comic Art Convention, 1995.

14. Examples of negative articles are too numerous to list. For a snapshot of the crisis at its height, see *The Comics Journal*, no 139, December 1990, which had a subtitle 'Adult Comics Under Siege' and which contained reports on busts of comic shops, and on the publication of a book entitled *Seduction of the Innocent Revisited*, published by a radical Christian press, which catalogued instances of sex and violence in contemporary comics.

15. The Savoy case is especially interesting because *Lord Horror* was published both as a comic and as a novel, and both were prosecuted at the same time. However, whereas the book was cleared the comic was ordered to be destroyed because, in the words of the judge, it 'might appeal to persons of a lesser intellect'.

16. Diana was released on appeal after serving a few days.

17. Ron Turner (of Last Gasp), interviewed by Julian Berger and Mark Borax, *Comics Interview*, no 43, June 1987, p 37.

International influences

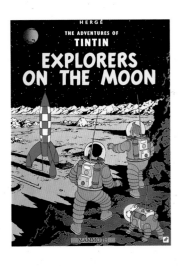

Comics constitute a large part of the cultural diet of many countries in the world. They are in some ways a 'universal language', and because of this there has been a measure of international traffic: British and American comics have influenced different parts of the globe, and, more germanely to us here, vice versa. Although it would be impossible to trace in detail a pattern of influence, we can narrow things down by looking at the impact on the anglophone industry of comics from the two most important areas in this respect: Europe and Japan.

The particular cultural significance of comics in these regions is due to the fact that they have never been subjected to the same kind of prejudice as in Britain and America. In fact, today, they are accepted as an artform on a par with novels, movies and television, and this difference in status has led to a situation where children form only part of the comics market. Unsurprisingly, therefore, Europe and Japan have become increasingly influential on the ever-more age-conscious British and American industries. On one level, this has meant the raiding of ideas – art styles, formats and working practices – to be imitated in indigenous comics. On another, it has led to an influx of European and Japanese comics on to the shelves, usually, but not always, in translation, which have carved their own niche as a genre. However, as we shall see, sales have rarely been as impressive (relatively) as in their region of origin, and, with a few notable exceptions, the history of international influence in this respect has been one of critical praise and public indifference.

European comics were the first to make an impression. Of course, 'Europe' is a big place, and we are really talking about several traditions. In France, for example, comics were christened 'BDs' or 'bandes dessinées', a term for 'drawn strips'; Spanish comics, or 'tebeos' take their name from TBO, one of the founding picture papers; the Italians call them 'fumetti', literally 'little smokes', after their visualization of speech balloons. What is important about these various terminologies is that none of them are loaded in the same way that 'comics' is in Britain and America.'

Historically speaking, the biggest and most important comics character was Belgian, and had his origins in the 1920s, though his success in the anglophone markets dates from the 1950s. We are talking, of course, about Tintin: a creation whose recognition factor worldwide today ranks with Disney's top characters, and whose adventures continue to far outsell those of any other European title.

Tintin was created in 1929 by Georges Rémi, who signed his work 'Hergé', and began life in a pull-out newspaper supplement designed for children. The character was essentially a boy scout, dressed in plus fours, who gets into scrapes in exotic locations – Africa, the Far East, South America and even the moon. There was certainly humour in the stories, mostly revolving around his friend Captain Haddock, the fearless seafarer, and Snowy, his trusty white dog. In essence, however, they were adventures, ostensibly 'innocent' but often with right-wing sub-texts; there was some controversy during and just after the war over whether Hergé was a Nazi sympathiser.[2]

On a creative level, what was remarkable about the Tintin strips was their quality. The narratives were carefully researched, usually by a team of creators who would often travel to the location to make accurate sketches. The chosen style for the final artwork came to be known as 'clear line', owing to its precision and lack of shadow (the opposite in many ways of the sensationalist American approach). This attention to detail was accentuated when individual stories were collected into albums (in the form of what would become known as 'graphic novels' in Britain and America), and found their way on to bookshelves. These were typically around 48 pages long, in full colour, and in hardback. In this form, they were collectable, and had a value as 'objects', as well as being entertaining. Moreover, these books found a market among adults as well as children: they were advertised as suitable for anyone between seven and seventy.

These *Tintin* albums started to go on sale in Britain from 1958, reprinted by a mainstream book publisher, Methuen. As such, they were not sold from newsagents like ordinary comics, but automatically became shelved in bookshops and public libraries. It was in this form that they became best known, although there were

attempts to serialize strips in conventional comics (notably in *The Eagle*). Unlike in Europe, Tintin was always assumed to be for a juvenile audience, and was not marketed to adults (at least, not in this period).[3] A similar pattern of sales was later established in America (the first album was published by The Golden Press in 1959), though relatively speaking Tintin never really took off here.

Tintin's commercial success grew exponentially with time. As licensing deals flourished all over the world, so too did cross-media exploitation, with the production of films, animated TV shows and all manner of merchandising. Today, albums still sell in the order of three million per year, and appear in thirty-six different languages. Hergé, who died in 1990, is now recognized as having had an impact on European comics analagous to that of Jack Kirby on the American industry, and as being one of the most important creators in the history of the medium. After him, European creators would either be categorized as followers of, or deviators from, the 'clear line' school.

The economics of comics production in Europe were thus established in this early period. The enormous impact of Tintin established a template that other titles would follow: specifically, to 'pre-publish' in a regular, newsstand magazine, and then to republish individual

This page: Tintin, whom President De Gaulle once referred to as his only international rival. Above: Detail from *Tintin: Prisoners of the Sun* (Methuen, 1962). Below: Page from *Tintin: Explorers on the Moon* (Methuen, 1959). Both art/script: Hergé. Note the precise 'clear-line' rendering, which became the standard art style throughout Europe.

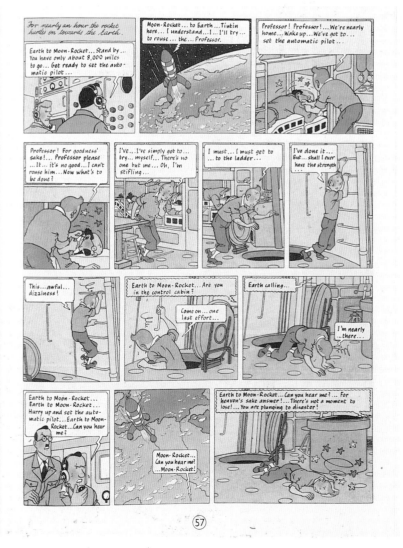

stories in album form later. This way, creators received two royalties. Thus, from the start, the assembly-line 'work for hire' method favoured by most British and American publishers was eschewed in favour of a system that, in theory at least, guaranteed a better quality product.

This process was bolstered in some countries by the fact that comics were a 'protected' industry. In France, for example, a law was passed in 1949 that effectively banned American comics from entering the country. American newspaper strips like 'Flash Gordon' and 'The Phantom' had been syndicated in the 1930s, and superhero comics had arrived with the GIs in the 1940s, but French Communist Party protests about 'cultural imperialism' and the need for more patriotic French heroes forced the legal safeguard, and led to a situation where French comics were allowed to develop in their own idiosyncratic way.[4]

Indeed, the most successful comic, in terms of influence, after Tintin came from France, and again capitalized on the album system. 'Asterix the Gaul' was the creation of the artist Albert Uderzo and the writer René Goscinny; the latter of whom had worked in America with Harvey Kurtzman, and had been much influenced by *Mad*. Concerning the adventures of a diminutive ancient Gaul with an impressive moustache, and his friends Obelix the muscle man and Getafix the Druid, and in particular their run-ins with the Romans in 50 BC, the strip was much more humorous than Tintin, with an altogether more liberal political slant (despite being very sexist). The artwork was more 'cartoony' as well, though still within the clear-line tradition.

Asterix's success was modelled on the Tintin marketing formula: strips were prepublished in a magazine (*Pilote*, from 1959) before being collected into albums, which were then translated into different languages, and sold internationally from bookshops. In Britain, Hodder and Stoughton were responsible for publishing these from 1969 (though there had been a short-lived attempt to serialize a story in *Ranger* from 1965–6); again, America caught on to the albums slightly later, though they never made a particular impact.[5]

France was also the country at the centre of the next wave of international comics successes. The indigenous industry had gone from strength to strength in the 1960s, but now America became a major influence for the first time since the 1949 law. The underground, with its content of sex, drugs and rock 'n' roll, and its hippie vision of psychedelic peace, started to become known, and to find echoes in Europe as anti-Vietnam War sentiment grew. Robert Crumb especially became a countercultural hero, and when France erupted in near revolution in 1968, the underground comics were as much a staple of the participants' reading matter as the radical press.[6]

This radical spark led to a boom in 'BDs pour adultes' in the 1970s. Initially, this took the form of anthology magazines – the main ones being *Métal Hurlant, Fluide Glacial, Circus, (A Suivre)* and *L'Echo des savanes* – all of which featured adult story lines, gags and images (especially in terms of depictions of sex). Though these were based in France, they tended to feature creators from all over Europe, especially from Italy. They were followed by the inevitable albums, which instead of acquiring the reputation of an 'underground' movement as had happened in America, instead went straight into mainstream bookshops. This assured their wide distribution, and at the height of the craze for adult comics, it was common for individual albums to sell in the region of 60,000.

This boom was accompanied by a solidifying of 'comics culture'. Albums came to be sold on the basis of creators' reputations, and thus an 'auteur' system developed whereby creators became as esteemed as film directors or novelists. Criticism of comics became every bit as intellectualized as that of film, with critical magazines appearing in every European country (especially in France, where the 'Cahiers de la bande dessinée' were intended to do the same job as the famous 'Cahiers du cinéma' in raising standards). Finally, establishment institutions became involved, with universities setting up courses on comics, and governments funding huge comics museums and study centres, such as the 8 million-pounds 'CNBDI' in France. When President Mitterand declared himself to be an avid fan of comics in 1986, nobody was in the least taken aback.

It should be noted that though this adult comics explosion is often perceived by British and American commentators as representing a peak of creative invention, like almost every other sudden expansion we have explored in different parts of the world, a large proportion of the material was not worth the paper it was printed on. For instance, in terms of content many of the comics included a great deal of sexism: these were essentially titles by men for men. In this respect, they followed the history of the undergrounds quite closely.[7]

This boom in mature comics eventually made it across the English Channel and then across the Atlantic Ocean. Individual strips were serialized in British and American anthology comics, while albums were reprinted and sold from the emerging network of fan-shops. Naturally, only the best or most 'sellable' work was selected for translation, which is another reason for skewed perceptions among critics. The albums appeared spasmodically in the 1970s, and then in the 1980s went through a boom as they became intertwined with the whole graphic novel phenomenon. For British and American publishers they represented an easy way to feed the new demand for longer length stories in book form. Publishers which

Right: Pages from *The Incal* (Marvel Comics, 1988). Art: Jean 'Moebius' Giraud. Script: Moebius and Alexandro Jodorowsky. A colourful science fiction thriller with New Age pretensions, from the combined talents of the *grand fromage* of French adult comics and the Chilean film director (*El Topo*). After Hergé, Moebius was the creator who most influenced the history of European comics: here, his take on the clear-line tradition is shown to good effect.

were particularly associated with European albums included Titan Books, Marvel/Epic, NBM, Catalan, and Heavy Metal Publishing.[8]

In terms of the overall influence on the British and American markets, science fiction was the genre that initially made the most headway, due to its affinity with the English language comics tradition. The groundbreaking science fiction anthology *Métal Hurlant* was extremely unusual among European titles in that it was imported in its original, untranslated form, and sold to comics fans who were typically content to enjoy the artwork by itself. The experimental nature of much of the art, plus its sexual content, was something that had not been seen in the context of science fiction comics before (bar one or two obscure undergrounds), and the quality of the paper stock, and of the production values generally, was also fresh. Consequently, as we have seen in Chapter 6, the comic was very influential, and not only spawned an American version of itself, *Heavy Metal*, but also became a huge influence on a wave of other adult science fiction anthologies. This was especially the case in Britain, where titles included *Pssst!*, *Graphixus* and *Brainstorm Fantasy Comix* (see p 139).

Science fiction albums as such were commonly collected and translated from the pages of *Métal Hurlant*, but could also have their origins in other European magazines. The science fiction *auteur* 'par excellence' was the Frenchman Jean Giraud, who worked as 'Moebius', and who after Hergé, was the creator with the biggest influence on British and American comics. His albums were numerous and diverse, and ranged from the druggy and spontaneous *Arzach* and *The Airtight Garage*, to the zen-like *Incal* saga. His story

Above and right: Pages from 'Approaching Centauri', *Heavy Metal* **(Heavy Metal Publishing, 1977). Art: Moebius. Script: Philippe Druillet. A terrifying SF yarn, with a level of violence and visual sophistication that was unusual to British and American eyes. The magazine** *Heavy Metal* **was instrumental in introducing readers to the 1970s French comics renaissance.**

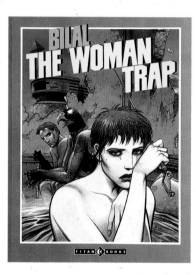

lines may not have been always coherent, but his artwork was never less than stunning, developing from a Crumb-inspired intensity in his early career to a more fluid clear-line approach later on. It was perhaps unsurprising that British and American publishers would try to poach him for themselves: he produced a variety of superhero comics for Marvel in the 1980s, including a run on the *Silver Surfer*.

Other creators who made their name in science fiction included: Enki Bilal, a Yugoslavian living in Paris, whose *Gods in Chaos* and *The Woman Trap* are set in a decadent future and populated by Egyptian gods (the latter vividly pictures a decaying London beset by tribal wars); Philippe Druillet, a Frenchman, whose *Lone Sloane* stories, about an adventurer's travels through time and space and across the fantastical world 'Delirius', had been a centrepiece of *Métal Hurlant*; Matthias Schultheiss, a German, whose *Bell's Theorem* was a dark technological thriller; and Don Lawrence, an Englishman (who had previously worked for children's comics such as *Look and Learn*), whose *Storm* volumes, about a muscular sword-wielding hero and his battles with sundry fantastic monsters, appeared first in Europe, and were then re-translated back into English.

If science fiction blazed a trail, other genres were soon to follow. Historical drama was a major draw in Europe, and had its share of English translations: the best comics demonstrated an historian's eye for detail in the artwork, combined with believable plotting; the worst tended to feature lashings of sex and violence in a phoney period setting. Every kind of historical era was covered, though different creators tended to specialize. For example, the Belgian Hermann was noted for his Medieval stories, *The Towers of Bois Maury*, which combined dark, photo-referenced art with mystery narrative themes, and included some stunning whole-page set-pieces. The Italian Hugo Pratt was more at home at the turn of the

Spanish Civil war ignite again as two factions consisting of elderly radicals pursue each other across contemporary Europe. Jacques Tardi also contributed to the genre with two *Nestor Burma* adventures, adaptations of private eye novels by Leo Malet, and *Adele and the Beast*, an album spoofing early twentieth-century thriller fiction, and starring a plucky heroine. Mention should also be made of the remarkable series *Sinner*, by two South American exiles working in Europe, Jose Munoz and Carlos Sampayo. The story involves the grim biography of a down-on-his-luck sleuth, as he witnesses modern Manhattan go to hell around him.

Sex albums were marketed as 'Eurotica', and found a small but devoted following. The most popular creators were both Italians: Milo Manara for his exquisitely rendered albums *Butterscotch*, about the adventures of an invisible sex maniac, and *Click!*, about a scientist who invents a machine that unchains women's libidos; and Guido Crepax for his more serious, and equally strikingly drawn, adaptations of *Emmanuelle* and *The Story of O*. Mention should also be made of the Frenchman Georges Pichard, whose 1977 album *Candide at Sea* featured a voluptuous heroine 'who just can't seem to keep her clothes on' (where have we heard that one before?), and who later became notorious for his *Illustrated Kama Sutra*.[9]

Last but not least, the European avant-garde also found a place in British and America comics shops. Two graphic novels by Italian Lorenzo Mattotti, both painted in an abstract style, exemplified the best of and worst of the genre. In the superb *Fires*, mysterious fire spirits take over an island, and disturb the minds of the sailors

Above: Detail from *Peter Pank* (Knockabout, 1990). Art/script: Max. A bizarre punk reworking of the JM Barrie story, from Spain. Above right: Page from *An Author in Search of Six Characters* (Catalan, 1989). Art/script: Milo Manara. An erotic twist on Pirandello, set in Africa. Below: Cover and pages from *Fires* (Penguin, 1991). Art/script: Lorenzo Mattotti. A fully-painted expressionistic fantasy about a seaman's encounter with fire spirits. Mattotti's jagged shapes in vivid reds have become a trademark.

34

Right: Cover to *Ranxerox 2: Happy Birthday Lubna* (Catalan, 1987). Art: Gaetano Liberatore. The outrageous Italian tale of an ultra-violent robot and his affair with a pubescent delinquent, which would no doubt have caused quite a stir in Britain and America had it been more widely distributed. Below: Panel and pages from *Pixy* (Fantagraphics, 1993). Art/script: Max Andersson. The creator is stylistically a sort of Danish Chester Brown, though the random surreal carnage of *Pixy* is purely his own.

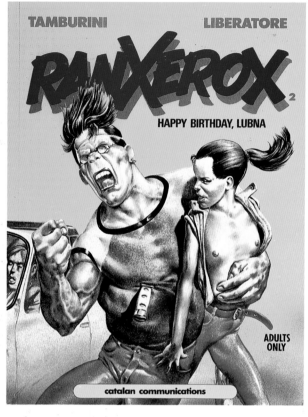

aboard a passing warship. In the infinitely more pretentious *Murmur*, scripted by Jerry Kramsky, a man with a burned face, lost in a strange land, finds salvation in nature. Humorous avant-garde titles included work that was analogous to the anglophone underground and alternative scenes. Early examples were the brace of albums starring the character Ranxerox (*Ranxerox in New York* and *Happy Birthday Lubna*), by Gaetano Libertore and Stefano Tamburini, about the incredibly violent (and amusingly amoral) adventures of a punk Frankenstein. A notable later addition was *Pixy*, by the Dane Max Andersson, which offered up a smorgasbord of bizarre images, where money eats people, buildings have personalities, and foetuses roam the streets armed with bazookas.

These were just some of the many European titles translated for a British and American readership over the last twenty years. The fact that in commercial terms none came anywhere close to rivalling the popularity of *Tintin* or *Asterix*, and that, indeed, most ended up in remainder bins, is not necessarily a comment on their quality. Like so many other graphic novels, they were not marketed properly, and fell foul of the mini-slump that followed the 'comics grow up' hype of the late 1980s. If indigenously-originated material of this kind had problems getting established, then it can be no surprise that the European output has fared even less well.

Ultimately, the influence of European comics was more subtle. For publishers, they pointed the way to new formats, and there can be little doubt that the graphic

Above: Detail from *Dragon Ball 2* (1995). Art: Akira Toriyama. A comedy adventure, and currently one of the best-selling comics in Japan. Above right: Page from *Tetsuwan Atom* (1951). Art/script: Osamu Tezuka. The best-loved Japanese SF comic starred a little robot with superpowers and human feelings. Unlike American superheroes, he fought not for freedom but for peace. (He is best known in the West as 'Astro Boy', after the 1960s TV cartoons inspired by the comic.) The artist, Tezuka, was responsible for virtually creating the comics industry in Japan after the Second World War.

novel was in part inspired by European albums. For the producers of fanzines, the European model showed that criticism need not be fawning and industry-led. The European system was an inspiration to British and American creators in a number of ways. It showed that working in comics need not be an anonymous and unglamorous occupation; it also proved that the idea of earning royalties was not so unthinkable. Above all, the maturity of European storytelling, and the flexibility of European art styles, influenced indigenous creators to expand the limits of their craft.

Japanese comics (or 'manga') were much slower to catch on in Britain and America. Whereas European comics were the product of a culture that was readily understandable, and of a comics tradition that was similarly not far removed, Japanese comics were much more alien in both respects. When they did finally start

to make an impact, in the 1980s, their influence was limited to a particular (cult) audience, and though the comics often achieved high sales by being sold through the network of fan shops, they remained a subculture within a subculture.[10]

In Japan, the manga industry started off by being orientated towards juveniles.[11] In the 1950s, manga could be rented from pay-libraries for a few yen, and this made them a staple of post-war children's reading. Boys' comics ('shonen') included subject matter such as historical adventure, samurai stories, and sport, while girls' titles ('shoji') focused more on Mills and Boon style romance or puppy-love stories. One creator who managed to appeal to both sexes, and in the process became central to this initial boom, was Osamu Tezuka, whose Disney-influenced comics, such as the enormously popular *New Treasure Island*, set the stylistic template for the majority of manga over the next two decades.

As the 1950s progressed, one kids' genre became especially important, namely, science fiction, and more specifically manga involving robot stories. Again, Tezuka was pivotal. His strip 'Ambassador Atom', which ran in *Shonen Magazine* between 1959 to 1968, reworked the Pinocchio story, and was about a little twenty-first century robot who can never become fully human. An animated TV series based on the manga followed, entitled *Astro Boy*, in 1963 (also masterminded by Tezuka), and started the robot craze in earnest. Hundreds of copyists followed, often accompanied by TV series: a boom that has continued to the present. According to historian Helen McCarthy, it reflected, and continues to reflect, real-life concerns: 'The first nation to make extensive use of the industrial robot is still the world's largest user of robot technology, and Japanese popular entertainment mirrors the general enthusiasm for the concept of the 'tin man'... [manga] have helped to

Above: Pages from _Dragon Ball 2_ (1995). Art/script: Akira Toriyama. This example, in its original form, demonstrates some of the problems involved with any translation. The text reads right to left, and therefore has to be 'flopped', while the onomatopeia, so integral to the action in Japanese artwork, needs to be carefully replaced.

encourage and maintain Japan's positive attitude to technology, and by making it both popular and acceptable have thus contributed considerably to the nation's progress and prosperity'.[12]

From the 1960s to the present day, the comics industry has built on these foundations, and quickly expanded to cover all sections of the population. This history has been well covered elsewhere (see note 10), but we can summarize by saying that those readers who had been introduced to manga as children continued to consume different kinds of manga as they grew up. Thus the kind of stigma attached to comics in many Western nations was circumvented. Science fiction continued to be very popular, but was joined by an incredible diversity of other adult genres: from splatter horror to mah-jong; surreal comedy to wok cookery; and martial arts to art appreciation. You could now learn to fix your car, study for accountancy exams, scrutinize political manifestos, and even improve your sex life from the pages of a manga.

Economically speaking, this growth had profound repercussions. By the start of the modern period, the Japanese economy was coming out of recession, and a manga-purchasing culture rapidly took over from the old pay-library system. Suddenly, big money was being made, and manga creators started to be taken seriously as celebrities. By the 1970s, they constituted many of the richest people in the country, with fan followings comparable to the hippest pop stars. Sales, it seemed, could not stop rising: by the mid-1990s it was estimated that between thirty and forty per cent of all Japanese publishing was devoted to manga, with sales in the region of a staggering two billion per year.

This explosion also necessitated new publishing methods. To maximize profits, publishers produced manga in a number of forms. Stories appeared first as serials in large digest magazines, with perhaps a few

dozen pages appearing per issue. These weekly and monthly publications were printed on low grade paper, were square bound, and often ran to over a thousand pages. With vast circulations, often with sales of individual titles in the millions, these manga could be priced very cheaply. If a particular story proved to be successful, it was reprinted in a higher quality version, possibly even in a hard cover, on better paper and without adverts. These volumes were usually around 200 pages long, and were designed to be kept on bookshelves rather than to be thrown away – the Japanese version of a graphic novel.

It was only a matter of time before such incredible sales figures for manga in Japan would lead foreign companies to buy sub-licenses and attempt to reproduce those successes in their own markets. By the 1980s, those markets were ready for such a move: American comics aimed at an older age range were becoming the new mainstream in the fan shops, and the development of 'direct sales' meant that minority-interest titles could prosper. Realistically, manga would be 'minority interest', at least to begin with: publishers might hope in the long run to imitate the mainstream success that they achieved in their home country, but at first, it was sensible to be cautious.

For one thing, there were factors to be considered beyond the obvious expense of translation. For instance, before manga could be sold into the home market, a number of technical problems had to be dealt with. In particular, the pages of artwork had to be reversed (or 'flopped' in publishing jargon), so that they read left-to-right, instead of right-to-left, as they would in Japan. Additionally, the original artwork needed to be touched-up, with Japanese sound effects replaced with more appropriate English onomatopaeia.

There were other Japanese storytelling conventions that were likely to be difficult for Western audiences, and which could not so easily be disguised. For example, comics symbolism could be very different. 'Sleep', for example, was not symbolized with a string of 'zeds', but with a bubble emanating from the character's nose. Similarly, facial characteristics were very different: for example, the heroes of many manga were drawn with over-large, Western-style eyes, in order to aid reader identification: the villains, by contrast, were usually rendered in more realistic fashion, in order to objectify them, to emphasize their 'otherness'.[13]

Finally, the pacing of Japanese stories could sometimes be very deliberate, and even slow. This was a huge contrast to the slam-bang tradition of American and British comics. The generation of mood was an essential aspect of lengthy manga, and there were many more 'silent' panels than in Western comics (in terms of format, there simply was not the same pressure on any one instalment to show a lot 'happening'): possibly, this attitude to pacing can be traced to the tradition of labyrinthine works of art in Japan. In the words of one historian, 'In Japan more than anywhere else, comics is an art of intervals.'[14]

Unsurprisingly, then, Western publishers had to be

very careful about the kinds of manga they tried to introduce into the domestic market. Partly for this reason, the first smattering of titles in the 1980s were chosen for their 'cultural acceptability': their artwork was not overly difficult, and the stories, though quintessentially Japanese, were not too alien. Three are worthy of particular note. *Gen of Hiroshima* by Keiji Nakazawa (Edu-comics, 1980), was probably the most famous because of its subject matter, and told the story of the author's family's experiences of everyday life during the Second World War, and of the ghastly consequences of the The Bomb; it was put out by an underground publisher in order to publicize the anti-nuclear movement. A thoughtful, vivid, and probing work, it was already considered a classic in Japan. *Lone Wolf and Cub* by Kazuo Koike and Goseki Kojima (First, 1987) was a samurai epic about a shamed warrior's life as an assassin, baby son in tow: realistically drawn, and very exciting, it included near-silent sword fights that lasted many pages. Finally, *Goodbye* by Yoshihiro Tatsumi (Catalan, 1987) was a collection of slice-of-life stories set in postwar Japanese cities – downbeat, subtle, and extremely moving.

These early titles were relatively successful: they received great critical acclaim in the comics fanzines, and attained some commercial success. This was especially true of *Lone Wolf*. Their main importance, however, was that they opened the doors: hereafter, manga would no longer be virgin territory for publishers. As a result, certain companies started to take much more notice of product from Japan, and to specialize in translations: in the early days, the most prominent included First Comics (publishers of *Lone Wolf*), a sub-licensee in Chicago, and Viz Communications, an American-based subsidiary of a Japanese publisher.

At this point, the story became rather more complicated. For it was clear that, despite these one-off hits, if manga

were really going to take off in any significant commercial fashion, they needed some extra impetus. The obvious answer was to link them somehow with the related business of Japanese animated films, or 'anime', as they were known, and to start integrated marketing campaigns. Thus, as anime became more popular among Western audiences in the 1980s and 1990s, so publishers producing manga worked ever more closely with the film and video companies, to such an extent that they became reliant upon each other, and their futures became largely intertwined. The specialist comics shops would soon take the extraordinary step of erecting shelves for manga and for videos next to each other.

To understand why anime became so influential, it is necessary to backtrack for a moment. In Japan, animation had first become popular in the form of television serials in the 1960s, and later had developed into a broader industry taking in full-length feature films. Although initially directed towards a juvenile audience, anime gradually became more sophisticated, to the point where they were a tiered product, for children, for teenagers and for adults. Thus, a night out at the cinema for the Japanese could mean going to see an anime. This was a situation that was barely conceivable in the West, where cinema-going meant live-action films, and where animation was considered 'kids' stuff' in just the same way that comics were.[15]

The links between anime and manga were very strong from the start, and some of the most popular animators were also manga creators (Tezuka being the first, and best-known example). As anime were more expensive

271

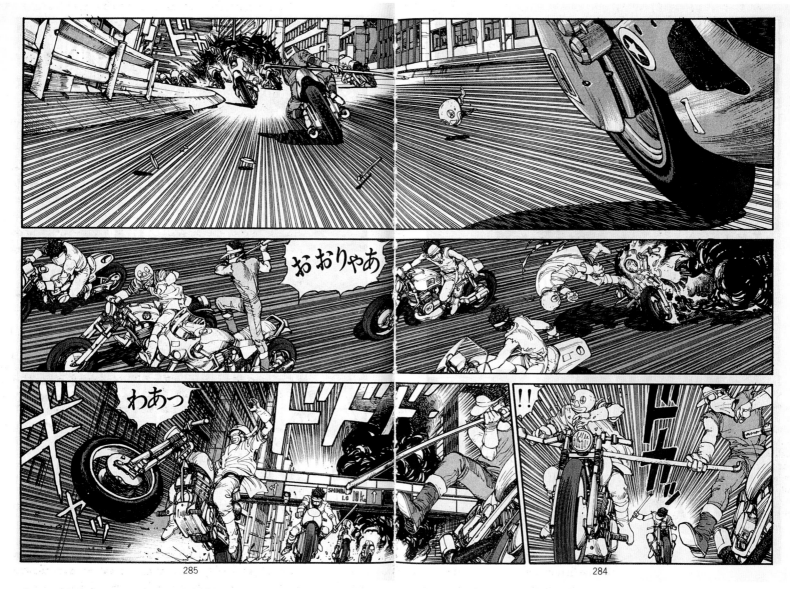

This page: The biggest Japanese comic in the West: *Akira*. **A cyberpunk story about bike gangs in post-apocalyptic Tokyo. All examples art/script: Katsuhiro Otomo. Above and below: Page and panel from the original manga (1988), demonstrating Otomo's stunning use of speed-lines. Below right: Still from the movie (1990) adapted from the comic, also directed by Otomo, which broke art house records across Britain and the United States.**

to produce, it was common for stories to originate in manga. The ladder was such that on the back of the popularity of a serialized manga story, it was possible to produce a graphic-novel collection and then a television series; full-length cinema feature films were also not uncommon. The quality of the animation itself could be exceptional: as for subject matter, this could be as broad as anything found in manga, including the same level of sex and violence. Once again, the popularity of the form in Japan was a spur for Western entrepreneurs to introduce it to their home markets.

In the West, television anime were first screened on British and American networks in the 1960s. Tezuka's series *Astro Boy* was a particular success: with skilful dubbing, it was hard to tell that it was not American.[16] It was followed by many others down to the present day, including most famously *Marine Boy* and *Transformers*. Actual animated features started to be shown in art cinemas in America and parts of Europe, particularly Italy and France, in the 1970s. But it was in the 1980s that things really started to get moving, with the rise of home video.

The title that ignited the anime boom, and in so doing gave an enormous boost to the manga business,

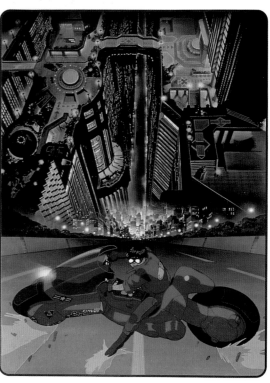

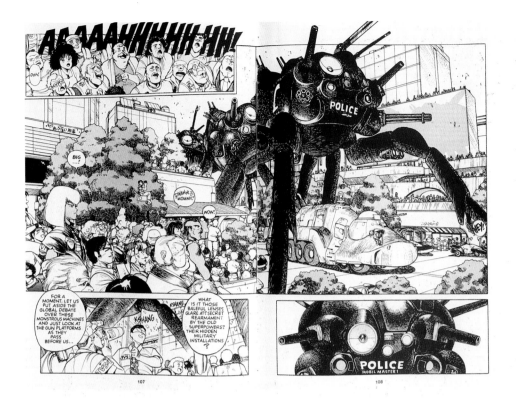

AAAAAAHHHHHHHHH!

107

108

was *Akira* (1987). This epic science fiction tale, by Katsuhiro Otomo (arguably Japan's second biggest ever anime/manga star after Tezuka), first came to wide public attention when the full-length movie broke attendance records in art cinemas across Britain and America in 1990. The story, set in post-apocalypse Tokyo in the year 2019, concerned a motorbike gang and their, often bloody, involvement with a mysterious force ('more powerful than a thousand nuclear bombs'), the result of secret government experiments with psi-power, code-named 'Akira'. The links with old-fashioned Japanese science fiction were clear, but this was an altogether more complex and spontaneous piece. Otomo himself explained: '*Akira* is rooted in the old-style robot shows like *Tetsujin 28* that I watched when I was younger. When I actually drew it, I was able to supply my own characters, and spin my own story. You'd think an author would be able to control what he writes, but I don't have much choice about it!'[17]

This essentially unfocused approach meant that the narrative itself left much to be desired (to call it shambolic would be kind). But as an example of state-of-the-art animation, it was stunning: Otomo used more than double the number of cells customary in conventional animation, and the resulting high definition, and sharpness in light and shadow, was impressive indeed. When *Akira* was released on video in 1991, it went straight to number one in the sales charts.

Why *Akira* should have taken off in the way it did certainly had much to do with its inherent quality. But it also tapped into the vogue for 'cyberpunk' among comics and science fiction fans, which had long made reference to an 'Asiatized future' and to Japan's status as a technological superpower.[18] It was also a novelty in so far as the film included scenes of graphic violence (especially some Sam Peckinpah-style shoot-outs), which was unusual in animation, and led to a certain notoriety.

In fact, the comic version of *Akira* had been available for several years, published by Marvel since 1988 under a 'Mature Readers' label. But in the wake of the movie and video's success, sales rocketed, and the trade paperback collections were major sellers. The comics had a special appeal: again, they were very high quality, with the use of speedlines and detailed backgrounds being especially effective. But the story was also slightly different: Otomo's original manga did not follow the storyline in the movie, and, at the time of writing, still has several instalments to go before it reaches its conclusion. Above all, being a science fiction story with visceral elements, it fitted more easily into the average *X-Men* fan's expectations of what a comic should be than any previous release from Japan.

At a stroke, *Akira* made anime and manga 'hip'. The result was a boom that took just about everybody by surprise. Inevitably, the comics and videos that followed were overwhelmingly in the *Akira* mould: loud, sassy, aimed at a fifteen to twenty-five audience, and science fictional. In the late 1980s and 1990s, anime became a significant branch of the home-video business, with new labels starting up to specialize in the area; at the same time, the manga industry expanded exponentially, with more translations appearing than ever before. Now bigger publishers like Dark Horse became involved in earnest.

Increasingly, anime and manga were sold next to each other in comics stores, and a new wave of fanzines emerged catering to the new market. Titles like *Animerica* carried dual-market adverts and garnered cult readerships. There were even comics made up of animation stills ('animekomikkusu' as they were known in Japan) – perhaps the ultimate expression of the incestuous nature of the subculture.

The post-*Akira* science fiction comics threw up new creative stars. To name just a few: Masumune Shirow, perhaps the most prolific, whose hits included *Dominion*, *Appleseed* and *Black Magic* (all Eclipse), and whose most accomplished work, *The Ghost in the Shell*, was a dynamic cyberpunk tale about a group of elite cyborgs; Yoshiki Takaya, whose popular *The Guyver* was a spectacularly

violent story involving alien-designed 'Guyver units' versus demonic-looking 'Zoanoids'; Go Nagai, a master storyteller, whose *Mazinger Z* (First, 1990) graphic novel was a 'giant robot' odyssey; and Hayao Miyazaki, whose *Nausicaa of the Valley of the Wind* (Viz, 1993) was a sophisticated ecological fable (with artwork very reminiscent of the 1970s work of Moebius), about a princess whose people are caught between two warring factions, one of which is planning to use a 'fire demon' to destroy 'the Toxic Forest'.

Other genres prospered as well. Thrillers included *Golgo 13* (Viz, 1993) by Takao Saito, about a contemporary assassin who travels the world in search of his prey, and *Crying Freeman* (Manga, 1995) by Kazuo Koike and Ryoichi Ikegami, another story about an assassin, this time one who weeps with shame after every 'hit', but who nevertheless rises to become the head of the Chinese mafia. Katsuhiro Otomo added to the genre with *Domu*, an offbeat, almost Hitchcockian, suspenser about a series of suspicious deaths in an apartment block, which turn out to be caused by a covetous old man who uses his psychic powers to force his victims to commit suicide.

Humour, too, made an impact. This is surprising, bearing in mind the notorious difficulties in making comedy 'travel' between nations. Especially important here was a female creator, Rumiko Takahashi, referred to by fans as 'the manga princess', and one of the richest women in Japan. Her bizarre titles included *Lum: Urusei Yatsura* (Viz, 1994) about a young boy who falls in love

Top: Pages from *The Guyver: Bio-Booster Armor* (Viz, 1995). Art/script: Yoshiki Takaya. A gleefully mindless slug-fest featuring an armour-plated superhero versus devilish 'Zoanoid' monsters. Above and right: Cover and pages from *Nausicaa of the Valley of the Wind* (Viz, 1993). Art/script: Hayao Miyazaki. A much more subtle SF tale, with an ecological theme.

Top: Pages from *Crying Freeman: Portrait of a Killer* (Manga Books, 1995). Art: Ryoichi Ikegami. Script: Kazuo Koike. A violent thriller about a hitman who is so sensitive about his trade that he sheds tears after each assassination. Top right: Pages from *Lum: Urusei Yatsura* (Viz, 1994). Art/script: Rumiko Takahashi. A surreal teen comedy with a cast including friendly aliens. Above: Pages from *Gon* (Mandarin, 1990). Art/script: Masashi Tanaka. The story of a midget dinosaur who never became extinct, and his domination by brute strength of the contemporary animal kingdom. Right: Panel from *Ranma 1/2 Volume 1* (Boxtree, 1994). Art/script: Rumiko Takahashi.

with the, very cute, leader of an alien invasion; and *Ranma* (Viz, 1993) about a boy who changes sex every time he gets wet (described on the jacket-blurb as 'a fast and furious tale of martial arts, schoolgirl crushes and gender-bending'). One other title is worthy of note: the remarkable *Gon* (Mandarin, 1990) a superbly drawn series of short stories about a foot-high dinosaur who has survived until the present, but who cannot quite come to terms with the contemporary animal kingdom. Though it was a slapstick premise, there were unusually violent overtones.

Less easily classifiable material, often in an 'underground' style, was also translated, and found a readership among comics fans interested in the 'alternative' titles (see chapter 8). Hideshi Hino's punky and incredibly gory horror tales *Panorama of Hell* and *Hell Baby* (both Blast Books, 1994 and 1995) were particularly impressive, as were the 'realist fiction' strips published within the pages of *Raw* (for example, 'Red Flowers' and 'Oba's Electroplate factory', by Yoshiharu Tsuge).

Finally, even one or two educational comics made it into translation. Foremost among them was *Japan Inc* (University of California Press, 1989) by Ishinomori Shotaro, which attempted to teach economics (in this case the trade war between Japan and America) by personalizing the issues. Company men debate interest rates and the collapse of Chrysler, while office secretaries sigh and fall in love with them. Preposterous stuff, but amazingly, the comic achieves its didactic aim.

This flurry of activity was accompanied by the attempts of mainstream book publishers to cash in on the manga craze, and to penetrate the high-street bookshop market in the wake of the boom in graphic novels. Penguin were quick to jump on the bandwagon, and marketed the two-volume *Barefoot Gen* (1989), an expanded version of *Gen*

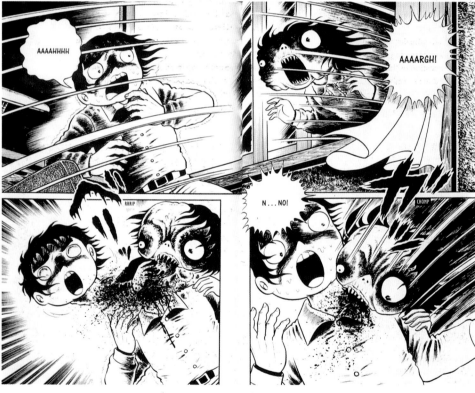

Above: Pages from *Hell Baby* (Blast Books, 1995). Art/script: Hideshi Hino. Horror Japanese style, about a mutant, vampiric toddler. Interpreted by some critics as a metaphor for the country's experience of post-Atomic birth defects.

of Hiroshima, as a follow-up to *Maus*. They received widespread attention in the review pages of newspapers, but sales were mediocre. Other companies, such as Boxtree, Mandarin and Bloomsbury went for more commercial material, and were marginally more successful.

Perhaps the main indication that manga had arrived was that Japanese rendering and storytelling styles began to influence Western creators, sometimes significantly. Frank Miller had long been interested in manga, and had provided covers for *Lone Wolf and Cub*, as well as producing a series for DC Comics about a samurai (*Ronin*, 1993). Now his art technique became more directly influenced, and by the time of his black-and-white epic *Sin City* in 1993, the Japanese-style speedlines and dynamic page layouts were clearly in evidence. Other creators were equally affected, but were not so willing to admit it: many of the Image superhero titles from the 1990s, for example, bear the stamp of manga.[19]

However, there was a more negative response to the boom. The sexual and violent content of some manga and anime might have been expected to cause a small stir, but nobody was prepared for the vitriolic nature of the media backlash when it came. The anti-manga piece 'Japanese Cruelty Comics Move In' in the *Daily Telegraph*, and the anti-anime rant 'Cartoon Cult With an Increasing Appetite for Sex and Violence' in *The Independent* were fairly typical.[20] They sensationalized odd scenes from various stories, and cheerfully played on old stereotypes of Japanese people as sadists (so familiar from children's war comics). What they did not report was that in Japan, crime figures were actually very low, and that here was a strong case for seeing the manga and anime as a 'safety valve'.

Nor did they make the obvious point that the more extreme sex and violence titles were only a fraction of those available, and by extension an infinitesimally small fraction of those available in Japan. This kind of subject matter was only evident at all because it was what the dominant fifteen to twenty-five year-old market in Britain and America wanted: more 'difficult' genres, such as sport, hardly got translated at all (not surprisingly, there is very little call for 600-page manga on mah-jong).

How the British and American manga industries will respond to this continuing negative press is hard to say. A broadening of subject matter would no doubt be a start, but this seems unlikely. The bulk of publishing is still tied to science fiction, and to 'youth culture' in general – a situation that is not helped by the symbiotic relationship with anime. For a time, the link between manga and anime was a bonus: they supported each other and secured valuable media awareness. But, now they appear to be entwined too closely, and cannot move on. It remains a hermetic environment, feeding off itself rather than reaching out to the outside world. Perhaps the fact that there has not been a success comparable to that of *Akira* in the years since is a sign that the fashion is dying out.

1. Histories of comics in individual countries do exist, but unfortunately they are almost all in European languages and have not been translated (for a bibliography, see Roger Sabin, *Adult Comics*, London, Routledge, 1993). Probably the best source in English, though by now very dated, is Maurice Horn, *The World Encyclopaedia of Comics* (New York, Chelsea House, 1976). Otherwise, articles in fanzines can be very informative.

2. The best sources on Hergé are Benoit Peeters, *Tintin and the World of Hergé* (Boston, Little Brown and Co, 1992) and Harry Thompson, *Hergé and his Creation* (London, Hodder and Stoughton, 1996).

3. In the 1980s, Tintin became somewhat trendy, and memorabilia shops opened in Britain and America catering to adult fans.

4. An indication of how important this American influence was to the French tradition can be gleaned from the amount of space given over to American strips in French published histories of their industry. See, for example, Pierre Couperie et al, *A History of the Comic Strip*, 1968 (re-published in New York by Crown), which started life as the catalogue to an exhibition at the Louvre in 1967.

5. It is worth noting that creators' rights in France were further improved by the actions of a group of artists on *Pilote*, who went on strike in 1966 for better pay and conditions.

6. There was an indigenous French satirical tradition based around the magazine *Hara Kiri* (founded 1964), which contained considerable comics content. It too played a role in the disturbances of 1968.

7. This was one major exception to the rule, *Al Nana* (1976), a feminist quarterly produced predominantly by women.

8. The best, and most comprehensive, listing of European comics in translation can be found in a British fanzine called *Panel House* (1995).

9. The Euro-porn albums were pre-figured to some extent by *Barbarella* by Jean-Claude Forest, which appeared in France in 1962, and was subsequently serialized in the US in *Evergreen Review*. The strip, however, remained little known, and the character only entered public consciousness with the release of the movie in 1968, directed by Roger Vadim and starring Jane Fonda.

10. For an excellent history of manga up until 1983, see Frederick Schodt, *Manga! Manga!* (New York, Kodansha International, 1983). On the publishing and marketing side of the story, as it related to Britain, there is a very useful university thesis: *Japan Inside: The Anime and Manga Publishing Industry* by Jonathan Clements (University of Stirling, M Phil, 1995).

11. The origins of manga are debatable. Some historians trace them to Medieval religious scrolls; others to the early nineteenth-century woodblocks by the artist Hokusai, responsible for coining the term 'manga'; others still to the late nineteenth-century boom in satirical cartooning. The 'industry' per se only developed in the 1920s, and was primarily orientated towards children.

12. Helen McCarthy, *Anime!* (London, Titan Books, 1993), p 14.

13. The depiction of 'big eyes' in Japanese comics is controversial for a number of reasons. Firstly, there is some dispute as to the origins of the device: most historians argue that it was adopted in imitation of Western cartooning styles at the turn of the century, when comic strips from Britain and America were becoming widely known (Western physiognomy was considered to be very attractive at the time, and the eyes were intended to reflect 'an ideal of beauty'). Some, however, insist that it was borrowed from Disney animated films, and thus should really be dated as a trend from the 1930s: certainly, Tezuka was a big Disney fan, and was fond of using 'Mickey Mouse eyes' in his work.

Secondly, there is controversy over whether reader identification is actually aided by the device. Scott McCloud makes a case for this in his *Understanding Comics*, but provides little evidence: the question of 'identification' is a notoriously difficult one, but it is certainly true that readers identify with characters 'as people', which is to say with recognizable personality traits, more than with any particular form of stylized rendering .

Thirdly, the effect of 'big eyes' on certain characters is to make them seem younger then they are meant to be, and this can be problematic when it comes to the depiction of women. For example, it can make them look like girls, which can be very disorientating for Western readers when it comes to scenes involving sex. Much feminist criticism of manga and anime has centred on this fundamental problem.

14. Scott McCloud, *Understanding Comics* (London, Tundra, 1993) p 81–2.

15. For a short, but useful, history of anime, see McCarthy, *Anime!*

16. *Astro Boy* also appeared as a number of comic books, the most notable of which was published by Gold Key in 1965.

17. Katsuhiro Otomo, interviewed by Jonathan Clements, 'Mangaka', *Comic World*, issue 36 (Feb 1995), p 28.

18. *Akira*'s relationship to cyberpunk is contentious. 'Cyberpunk' refers to a high-tech, Asiatized, urban future dominated by technology and, in particular, by computers. All definitions cite William Gibson's 1984 novel *Neuromancer* as the defining source, but many refer to the 1982 movie *Bladerunner* as a major influence. Although *Akira* does not focus on computers, it does share many of the preoccupations of cyberpunk, and many of Otomo's citiscapes resemble those of *Bladerunner*: it is disputed, however, that he was directly influenced by that film, and *Akira* certainly pre-dates *Neuromancer*.

19. Certain publishers also began to produce what became known among fans as 'pseudomanga' – comics based on original manga, but drawn by Western artists. The most famous example was *Dirty Pair* (Eclipse, 1989) by Toren Smith and Adam Warren. The idea behind this was that the more 'alien' elements of Japanese storytelling (for example, pacing) could be ironed out.

20. Sally Malcolm-Smith, 'Japan's Cruelty Comics Move In' (*Sunday Telegraph*, April 11, 1993); David Lister, 'Cartoon Cult with an Increasing Appetite for Sex and Violence' (*The Independent*, October 15, 1993).

Right: Pages from *Mr Arashi's Amazing Freak Show* (Blast Books, 1992). Art/script: Suehiro Maruo. A classically Japanese tale of a little lost orphan ensnared in a travelling freak show. By turns repulsive and surreal, it compels us to become voyeurs.

Conclusion

Above: Panel from 'Sunshine State', *World War 3 Illustrated*, (self-published, 1995). A witness in the trial of cartoonist Mike Diana, discovers that the defendant has been found guilty and jailed. A scandal that refutes the postmodernist notion of the 'breaking down of cultural barriers'.

We live in changing times. But just how 'changing' remains open to question. It is fashionable, in the mid-1990s, to see modern culture as being in the process of transformation by huge, almost apocalyptic, forces which will leave it unrecognizable in a very short space of time. We can see this in two interlinked areas in particular: the hopes and fears surrounding the 'digital revolution', and the current fondness for postmodernist theory.

Both themes are extremely relevant to comics. The digital revolution, for example, is said to herald the end of print. The argument runs roughly as follows: books, newspapers and comics will all disappear as computers take over, and people get their information and entertainment from the Internet. With the Net growing at an exponential rate (10 million new users in last year alone), and more and more companies using it to publish their wares, this progression is seemingly inevitable. In the forthcoming digital age, to coin a pun, the days of the comic are numbered.

Postmodernist visions of the future are more optimistic. For example, in our introduction, it was suggested that comics have never been accepted into the realm of 'real art', and that this was due to a number of interwoven prejudices against popular culture. But recently, a number of postmodernist philosophers and writers have suggested that this division between art and popular culture has been breaking down. We live in an era, it is said, where the media dominates cultural products, and where, therefore, surfaces and style have become more important than content. Under these circumstances, there are no longer any agreed and inviolable criteria which can serve to differentiate art from popular culture. Comics, therefore, are not dying out, but entering a new era of acceptance.

But before we get carried away, events need to be seen in perspective. Taking the digital revolution first, it's necessary to question who the revolution is for. Certainly, it won't benefit the majority of the world's population, who cannot afford telephones, let alone expensive computers. Taking this as a starting point, it is easy to challenge the idea that the Net and comics share the same properties. They do not. One is cheap and one isn't; one is mobile, one isn't. (Although it's possible, we don't think in terms of taking a computer on the bus.) Of course, computers have the advantage for certain kinds of storytelling: they can be interactive, for instance. But at the present state of

technology, the experience of reading from a computer screen compared to that of reading from a comics page is no contest. They are, in other words, two completely different media, and therefore the rise of one does not by any means automatically presage the decline of the other.

As for postmodernism, it is a seductive argument, and it would be very tempting to apply it to the history of comics. After all, we have seen how in the 1980s and 1990s, comics have become more 'respectable'. *Maus* won a Pulitzer Prize, and graphic novels were reviewed in the literary pages of the quality newspapers. Even the existence of an art book such as this, devoted to such 'trash', could be taken as a sign of a change in the cultural climate.

But let's be clear. On the rare occasions that comics have popped their heads over the wall of media indifference, there have usually been reasons other than an acceptance of the medium as a whole. *Maus*, for example, was a one-off, while the mainstream reviews of graphic novels were largely inspired by their novelty value. Certainly, in some countries, such as Japan, comics are accepted as art. But, as we have seen, this has been due to a distinct set of historical circumstances. So far as Britain and America are concerned, a few decent reviews in the press do not a revolution make.

So where does that leave us? Marginalized for sure, but such a marginal position is an attractive one for many creators and consumers. The comic's exclusion from the art establishment enables it to eschew the dampening appraisal of art criticism. Moreover, its association with street culture gives it a certain edge, which many contemporary artists have vainly attempted to transfer to the gallery. Whereas fine art can only send shocks through the art world, comics – available to a far broader audience – are still regarded as dangerous enough to be clamped down on intermittently.

Comics seem to be going through a golden age right now. When I see recent books like Joe Sacco's *Palestine* and Chester Brown's *I Never Liked You*, I am filled with admiration for the medium. Sacco and Brown's generation of creators were inspired by the underground generation before them, and I'd be willing to bet that sometime soon they'll inspire a future band of comics stars with their own take on what 'a comic' can mean. As ever, the medium remains worthy of any message.

Further reading

Adams, J P *Milton Caniff: Rembrandt of the Comic Strip*, New York, David McKay, 1946.

Bails, J and J Ware *The Who's Who of American Comic Books*, Detroit, Simpson, 1973.

Barker, M *A Haunt of Fears: The Strange History of the British Horror Comics Campaign*, London, Pluto Press, 1984.

– *Comics: Ideology, Power and the Critics*, Manchester, Manchester University Press, 1989.

– *Action: the Story of a Violent Comic*, London, Titan Books, 1990.

Barker, M and R Sabin *The Lasting of the Mohicans*, Jackson, University of Mississippi Press, 1996.

Barrier, M *Carl Barks and the Art of the Comic Book*, New York, M Lilien, 1981.

Barrier, M and M Williams *A Smithsonian Book of Comic Book Comics*, Washington DC, Smithsonian Institute Press/Harry N Abrams Inc, 1981.

Baxendale, L *A Very Funny Business*, London, Duckworth, 1978.

– *On Comedy*, Stroud, Reaper Books, 1989.

Becker, S *Comic Art in America*, New York, Simon and Schuster, 1949.

Benton, M *The Comic Book in America*, Dallas, Taylor Publishing, 1989.

– *Horror Comics*, Dallas, Taylor Publishing, 1991.

– *Superhero Comics of the Silver Age*, Dallas, Taylor Publishing, 1991.

– *Superhero Comics of the Golden Age* Dallas, Taylor Publishing, 1992.

– *Science Fiction Comics*, Dallas, Taylor Publishing, 1992.

– *Crime and Detective Comics*, Dallas, Taylor Publishing, 1993.

– *Masters of Imagination: Comic Book Artists Hall of Fame*, Dallas, Taylor Publishing, 1994.

Berger, A A *L'il Abner: A Study in American Satire*, New York, Twayne Publishers, 1970.

– *The Comic-Stripped American*, New York, Walker and Co, 1973.

– *Pop Culture*, New York, Pflaum/Standard, 1973.

Bloom, C *Dark Knights*, London, Pluto, 1993.

Canemaker, J *Winsor McCay*, Berkeley, University of California Press, 1987.

Carlin, J and S Wagstaff (eds) *The Comic Art Show: Cartoons in Painting and Popular Culture*, New York, Fantagraphics Books, 1983.

Carpenter, K (ed) *Penny Dreadfuls and Comics*, London, Victoria and Albert Museum, 1983.

Clark, A and D Ashford *The Comic Art of Roy Wilson*, London, Midas, 1983.

– *The Comic Art of Reg Parlett*, London, Golden Fun, 1986.

Clark, A and L Clark *Comics: An Illustrated History*, London, Greenwood, 1991.

Clarke, P and M Higgs *Nostalgia about Comics*, Birmingham, Pegasus Printing, 1991.

Couperie, P, M Horn, P Destefanis, E Francois, C Moliterni and G Gassiot-Talabot *A History of the Comic Strip*, New York, Crown, 1968.

Crawford, H H *Encyclopedia of Comic Books*, New York, Simpson, 1978.

Crompton, A *The Man Who Drew Tomorrow: Frank Hampson*, Bournemouth, Who Dares Publishing, 1985.

Cutler, D, F Plowright, A Snowdon, S Whitaker and H Yusef *Two Decades of Comics: A Review*, London, Slings and Arrows, 1981.

Daniels, L *Comix: A History of Comic Books in America*, New York, Bonanza Books, 1971.

– *Fear: A History of Horror in the Mass Media*, London, Paladin, 1977.

– *Marvel: Five Fabulous Decades of the World's Greatest Comics*, London, Virgin, 1991.

– *DC Comics: Sixty Years of the World's Favorite Comic Book Heroes*, London, Virgin, 1995.

Davidson, S *The Penguin Book of Political Comics*, rev edn, Harmondsworth, Penguin, (1976) 1982.

De Laet, D and Varende, Y *Beyond the Seventh Art*, Brussels, Ministry of Foreign Affairs, 1979.

Dorfman, A *The Emperor's Old Clothes*, London, Pluto Press, 1983.

Dorfman, A and A Mattelart *How to Read Donald Duck*, rev edn, New York, International General, (1975) 1991; with introduction by David Kunzle.

Drotner, K *English Children and Their Magazines*, New Haven, Yale University Press, 1988.

Eco, U *The Role of the Reader*, London, Hutchinson, 1981.

Eisner, W *Comics and Sequential Art*, Florida, Poorhouse Press, 1985.

– *Graphic Storytelling*, Florida, Poorhouse Press, 1995.

Estren, M *A History of Underground Comics*, rev edn, San Francisco, Straight Arrow, (1974) 1987.

Feiffer, J *The Great Comic Book Heroes*, New York, Dial Press, 1965.

Fleischer, M L *The Encylopaedia of Comic Book Heroes: Batman*, vol 1, New York, Macmillan, 1976.

Freeman, G *The Undergrowth of Literature*, London, Thomas Nelson and Sons, 1967.

Fulce, J *Seduction of the Innocent Revisited*, New York, Huntingdon House Publishers, 1990.

Garrick, P R *Masters of Comic Book Art*, New York, Images Graphiques, 1978.

Gifford, D *Discovering Comics*, London, Shire, 1971.

– *Happy Days: A Century of Comics*, London, Jupiter, 1975.

– *Victorian Comics*, London, Allen and Unwin, 1976.

– *The International Book of Comics*, London, W H Smith, 1984.

– *The Encyclopaedia of Comic Characters*, London, Longman, 1987.

Gilbert, J *Cycle of Outrage: America's Reaction to the Juvenile Delinquent in the 1950s*, New York, Oxford University Press, 1986.

Glubok, S *The Art of the Comic Strip*, New York, Macmillan, 1979.

Goddin, P *Hergé and Tintin, Reporters*, New York, Sundancer, 1988.

Goulart, R *The Great History of Comic Books*, Chicago, Contemporary Books, 1986.

– *The Adventuous Decade*, New Rochelle, Arlington House, 1975.

– *The Great Comic Book Artists*, vols 1 and 2, New York, Publications International, 1982.

– *The Encylopedia of American Comics*, New York, Publications International, 1988.

– *Over 50 years of American Comic Books*, New York, Publications International, 1991.

Groth, G and R Fiore (eds) *The New Comics*, New York, Berkley Books, 1988.

Hardy, C and G F Stern (eds) *Ethnic Images in the Comics*, Philadelphia, Balch Institute, 1986.

Harris, P (ed) *The DC Thomson Bumper Fun Book*, Edinburgh, Paul Harris Publishing, 1977.

Harrison, H *The Art of Jack Davis*, New York, Stabur, 1987.

Herderg, W and D Pascal (eds) *The Art of the Comic Strip*, Zurich, Graphis, 1972.

Hildick, E W *A Close Look at Comics and Magazines*, London, Faber and Faber, 1966.

Horn, M *Seventy Five Years of the Comics*, Boston, Boston Book and Art, 1971.

– (ed) *The World Encyclopaedia of Comics*, 6 vols, New York, Chelsea House, 1976.

– *Comics of the American West*, New York, Winchester Press, 1977.

– *Women in the Comics*, New York, Chelsea House, 1980.

– *Sex in the Comics*, New York, Chelsea House, 1985.

Inge, M Thomas *The American Comic Book*, Columbus, Ohio State University, 1985.

– *Handbook of American Popular Literature*, New York, Greenwood Press, 1988.

– *Comics as Culture*, Jackson, University Press of Mississippi, 1990.

Jacobs, F *The Mad World of William Gaines*, New York, Lyle Stuart Inc, 1972.

Kane, R *Batman and Me*, Forestville, Eclipse Books, 1989.

Kelly, W *Ten Ever-Loving Blue-Eyed Years with Pogo*, New York, Simon & Schuster, 1988.

Kerekes, D *Critical Vision*, Cheshire, Headpress, 1995.

Kunzle, D *History of the Comic Strip: The Early Comic Strip*, vol 1, Berkeley, University of California Press, 1973.

– *History of the Comic Strip: The Nineteenth Century*, vol 2, Berkeley, University of California Press, 1988.

Kurtzman, H *My Life as A Cartoonist*, New York, Simon & Schuster, 1988.

– *From Aargh! to Zap!*, New York, Prentice Hall, 1991.

Legman, G *Love and Death*, New York, Breaking Point, 1949.

Louvre, A and J Walsh (eds) *Tell Me Lies About Vietnam*, Oxford, Oxford University Press, 1986.

Lowenthal, L *Literature, Popular Culture and Society*, Englewood Cliffs, Prentice Hall, 1961.

Lupoff, D and D Thompson *All in Colour for a Dime*, New York, Arlington House, 1970.

McClelland, G *Rick Griffin*, Limpsfield, Dragon's World, 1980.

McCloud, S *Understanding Comics*, London, Harper Collins, 1994.

McDonnell, J *et al*, *Krazy Kat: The Comic Art of George Herriman*, New York, Abrams, 1986.

Marschall, R (ed) *The Fantastic Vision of Winsor McCay*, Westlake, Fantagraphics, 1988.

– *America's Greatest Comic Strip Artists*, New York, Cross River Press, 1989.

Mitchell, W J T *Iconology: Image, Text, Ideology*, Chicago, University of Chicago Press, 1987.

Murray, C S *Shots From the Hip*, London, Penguin, 1991.

Murrell, W A *History of American Graphic Humour*, 2 vols, New York, Cooper Square, 1933 and 1938.

O'Sullivan, J *The Art of the Comic Strip*, College Park, University of Maryland, 1971.

– *The Great American Comic Strip*, Boston, Bulfinch Press, 1990.

Pearson, R and W Urrichio (eds) *The Many Lives of the Batman*, London, BFI Publishing/Routledge, 1991.

Peeters, B *Tintin and the World of Hergé*, Boston, Little, Brown and Co, 1992.

Perry, G and A Aldridge *The Penguin Book of Comics*, rev edn, Harmondsworth, Penguin, (1967) 1971.

Reidelbach, M *Completely MAD*, New York, Little, Brown and Co, 1991.

Reitberger, R and W Fuchs *Comics: Anatomy of a Mass Medium*, London, Studio Vista, 1972.

Reynolds, R *Superheroes: A Modern Mythology*, London, Batsford, 1992.

Richler, M *The Great Comic Book Heroes and Other Essays*, Toronto, McLelland and Stewart, 1978.

Robbins, T *A Century of Women Cartoonists*, Princeton, Kitchen Sink, 1992.

Robbins T and C Yronwode *Women and the Comics*, Forestville, Eclipse, 1985.

Robinson, J *The Comics: An Illustrated History of Comic Strip Art*, New York, G P Puttnam's Sons, 1974.

Rosenkranz, P and H Van Baren *Artsy Fartsy Funnies*, Laren, Netherlands, Paranoia, 1974.

Rovin, J *The Encyclopaedia of Superheroes*, New York, Facts on File Publications, 1995.

– *Panel by Panel*, Sydney, Cassell, 1979.

Sassiene *The Comic Book*, London, Ebury Press, 1994.

Savage, W *Comic Books and America 1945–1954*, Oklahoma, University of Oklahoma Press, 1990.

Schodt, F *Manga! Manga! The World of Japanese Comics*, New York, Kodansha International, 1983.

Schoell W *Comic Book Heroes of the Screen*, London, Plexus Publishing, 1988.

Seldes, G *The Seven Lively Arts*, New York, Sagamore Press, 1957.

Sheridan, M *The Comics and their Creators*, Boston, Hale, Cushman and Flint, 1942.

Steranko, J *The Steranko History of Comics*, 2 vols, Pennsylvania, Supergraphics, 1970 and 1972.

Thomas, J L (ed) *Cartoons and Comics in the Classroom*, Littleton, Libraries Unlimited, 1983.

Thompson D and D Lupoff (eds) *The Comic-Book Book*, New York, Arlington House, 1973.

Thompson, H *Hergé and His Creation*, London, Hodder and Stoughton, 1991.

Threaker, D *An Introduction to Canadian Comic Books*, Ontario, Aurora, 1986.

Tsuzuki, K and A Birnbaum (eds) *Manga – Comic Strip Books from Japan*, London, Saunders and Williams, 1991.

Tucker, N (ed) *Suitable for Children?* London, Chatto and Windus, 1976.

Vaz, M C *Tales of the Dark Knight*, London, Futura Publications, 1989.

Wagstaff, S (ed) *Comic Iconoclasm*, London, Institute of Contemporary Arts, 1987.

Waugh, C *The Comics*, New York, Macmillan, 1947.

Wertham, F *Seduction of the Innocent*, New York, Rinehart, 1954 and London, Museum Press, 1955.

White, D M and H Abel (eds) *The Funnies: An American Idiom*, New York, Simon & Schuster, 1963.

Willette, A *Top Cartoonists Tell How They Create ...* Fort Lauderdale, Simmons Press, 1964.

Witek, J *Comic Books as History: the Narrative Art of Jack Jackson, Art Spiegelman, and Harvey Pekar*, Jackson, University Press of Mississippi, 1989.

Wooley, C *Wooley's History of the Comic Book 1899–1936*, Lake Buena Vista, Charles Wooley, 1986.

Yronwode, C *The Art of Will Eisner*, rev edn, Princeton, Kitchen Sink, (1982) 1989.

Index